TWIN STATES, DIFFERENT PATHS

Twin States, Different Paths

The Politics of New Hampshire and Vermont

BRIAN L. PORTO

UNIVERSITY OF MASSACHUSETTS PRESS
Amherst and Boston

Printed in the United States of America

ISBN 978-1-62534-961-3 (paper); 962-0 (hardcover)

Designed by Deste Relyea
Set in Minion Pro and Rationalist
Printed and bound by Books International, Inc.

Cover design by adam b. bohannon
Cover photo by Sherrie A. Greeley, courtesy of the photographer.

Library of Congress Cataloging-in-Publication Data
Names: Porto, Brian L. author
Title: Twin states, different paths : the politics of New Hampshire and Vermont / Brian L. Porto.
Description: Amherst : University of Massachusetts Press, [2026] | Includes bibliographical references and index.
Identifiers: LCCN 2026004818 (print) | LCCN 2026004819 (ebook) | ISBN 9781625349613 paperback | ISBN 9781625349620 hardcover | ISBN 9781685752811 ebook | ISBN 9781685752828 epub
Subjects: LCSH: New Hampshire—Politics and government | Political culture—New Hampshire—History | Vermont—Politics and government | Political culture—Vermont—History
Classification: LCC JK2916 .P67 2026 (print) | LCC JK2916 (ebook) | DDC 306.209742—dc23/eng/20260518
LC record available at https://lccn.loc.gov/2026004818
LC ebook record available at https://lccn.loc.gov/2026004819

British Library Cataloguing-in-Publication Data
A catalog record for this book is available from the British Library.

The authorized representative in the EU for product safety and compliance is Mare Nostrum Group.
Email: gpsr@mare-nostrum.co.uk
Physical address: Mare-Nostrum Group B.V.,
Doelen 72, 4831 GR Breda, The Netherlands

For Jere Daniell, Samuel Hand, Frank Bryan,
and all the scholars of New Hampshire and Vermont
history and politics whose work has informed this book.

You cut the trail and marked it well.

CONTENTS

PREFACE

Sometimes, one's best-laid plans come to fruition. That is true for this book, which was part of my retirement plan for three decades, during which I taught political science, practiced law, and then taught law, retiring in 2022. Throughout those years, I researched and wrote about other subjects while maintaining an ever-expanding file of newspaper clippings, book lists, and reports by public and private entities about the respective political personalities of New Hampshire and Vermont. Eventually, retirement brought the freedom to pursue this project, which derives from professional training in political science and law and a deep attachment to both states. I have worked in each of them as a lawyer and a state employee, and have spent countless recreational time in both, experiencing matchless natural beauty while hiking, cross-country skiing, snowshoeing, or kayaking.

Another inspiration for this project was stimulating conversation with friends and colleagues over the years about the similarities and (especially) the differences between the two states regarding regulation, taxation, and the funding of public services. Comparing them on these metrics is a popular conversation topic at dinner parties on both sides of the Connecticut River. Often, dinner guests suggest a single cause for the political contrast between New Hampshire and Vermont. Some emphasize geological differences that have produced divergent economic opportunities, others note the effects of a seacoast in New Hampshire, which Vermont lacks, and still others note the longstanding migration of tax-weary professionals from Massachusetts to New Hampshire.

Such conversations were food for thought as I studied the economic and political histories of the two states and the process of historical scholarship. My research taught me that societal outcomes rarely derive from one cause—instead they usually result from a confluence of factors. That is certainly true for the political cultures of New Hampshire and Vermont: in each state, political culture developed from a geological heritage and the natural resources and economic opportunities born of that heritage. These forces made New Hampshire more industrial and Vermont more agrarian. But each state also shaped its own future, attracting both visitors and migrants by advertising either its modern amenities and low costs (NH) or its pastoral peace and quiet (VT). Today, most residents of both states were born elsewhere, so the respective public images projected to prospective migrants influence and even reinforce political culture.

Accordingly, the book concludes that the raw materials of political culture in New Hampshire and Vermont are geology, geography, and advertising and place reputation, each of which the succeeding chapters will define and explain. This book recounts historical events that shaped political culture in these states, highlights contemporary manifestations of the respective cultures, and, eventually, explains how those cultures have affected policy responses to current housing shortages and school funding deficiencies in both states. In so doing, it aspires to lend a bit of academic rigor to a favorite topic of dinner-party conversation.

ACKNOWLEDGMENTS

My journey through the thickets of New Hampshire and Vermont politics would have been less enjoyable and productive without the help I received along the way. David Schultz sharpened the focus of the book's prospectus. Michael Birkner, Stuart Wallace, and Frank Meyers shared their expertise in New Hampshire history, resulting in a more precise and readable Chapter Two. Paul Searls did the same for Chapter Three's discussion of Vermont history.

Equally valuable help was forthcoming on the policy issues discussed in later chapters. Jason Rasmussen offered useful insights into the differences between New Hampshire and Vermont regarding land-use regulation. Phil Sletten kindly answered my questions about taxation and education funding in New Hampshire. Wayne Gersen and Michael Harris shared with me their expertise about education funding in both states and its connection to political culture. Lola Duffort steered me to her reporting about Vermont's 2025 education transformation bill, and Jake Feldman explained the existing tax system for funding Vermont's schools. I am deeply indebted to all these professionals for their wise counsel.

Kay Schlueter contributed her considerable computer skills to this project, making the manuscript submission deadline far less daunting than it would otherwise have been. Melissa Kalinen, the interlibrary loan librarian at Vermont Law and Graduate School's Cornell Library, and Melissa Ayres, who holds the same position at the Windsor (VT) Public Library, obtained a wide array of research materials for me, always promptly and professionally. At the University of Massachusetts Press, Editor-in-Chief Matt Becker believed in the book and was immensely helpful in guiding it toward publication.

My greatest debt of gratitude, though, is to my wife, Sherrie Greeley, whose good humor, emotional support, and keen proofreader's eye all proved invaluable to me. Any remaining errors or omissions, substantive or stylistic, are solely my responsibility.

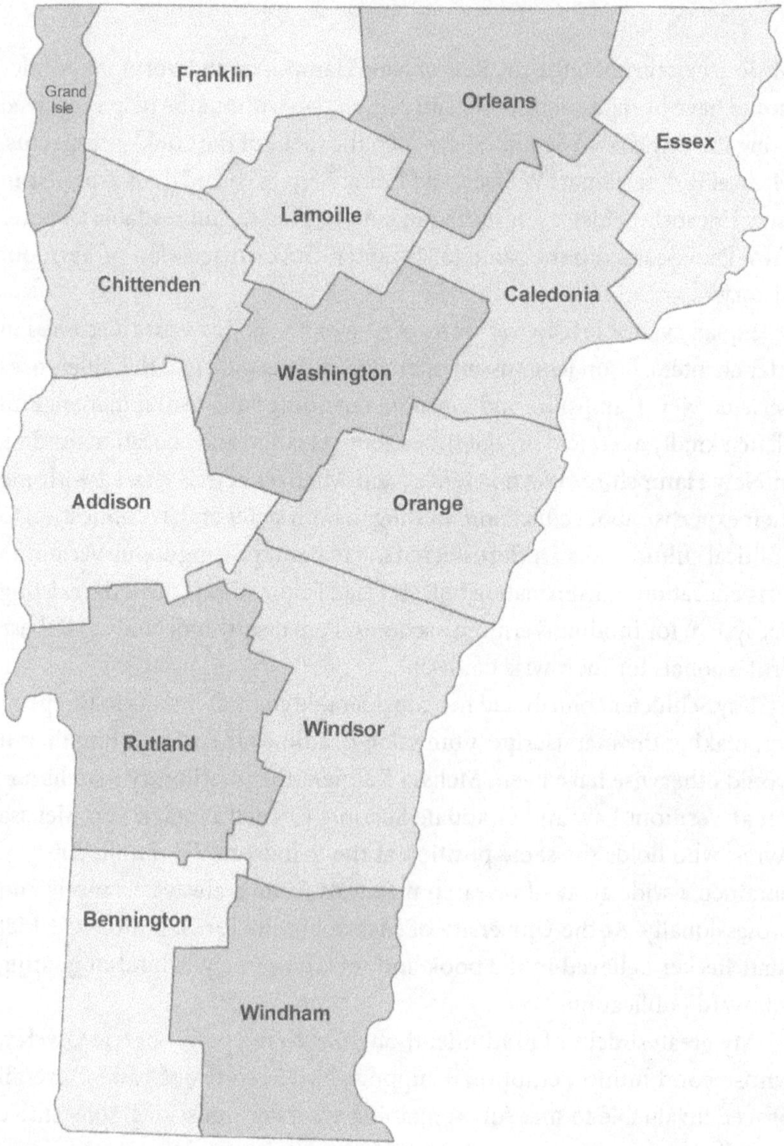

Vermont and Its Counties

New Hampshire and Its Counties

TWIN STATES, DIFFERENT PATHS

CHAPTER ONE

Fraternal, Not Identical

An Introduction to Politics in the Twin States

A Tale of Two Political Cultures

THE NARRATOR IN ROBERT Frost's poem "The Road Not Taken" faces two alternative paths while walking in the woods and must choose between them, knowing that regardless of the path chosen, he is unlikely to see the other one again. Like Frost's two roads that "diverged in a yellow wood," New Hampshire and Vermont appear at first blush to be similar, as befits their joint nickname, the Twin States. But, again like the two diverging paths in the poem, the two states are quite distinct, representing contrasting philosophies of government that are effectively encapsulated in their respective mottoes, New Hampshire's "Live Free or Die" and Vermont's "Freedom and Unity." The first emphasizes ensuring individual freedom as government's foremost aim, whereas the latter acknowledges the importance of freedom, but also assigns equivalent significance to cooperation and participation in community life.

To be sure, the two states share some noteworthy similarities, including physical similarities, as Frost himself recognized in his poem "New Hampshire," where he wrote,

> And they lie like wedges,
> Thick end to thin end and thin end to thick end[1]

They are also similar in size, ranking forty-fifth and forty-sixth among the fifty states in total land area, with Vermont having just 267 additional square miles. They are similar demographically, too; Vermont is the second whitest state, while New Hampshire ranks fourth. Vermont is the second oldest state, with New Hampshire ranking fourth in that category too.[2] Furthermore, as the late Vermont author and preservationist Ralph Nading Hill observed, "Vermont is thought of as rural and New Hampshire as industrial, yet Vermont has considerable industry, and New Hampshire has hundreds of square miles of rural countryside."[3]

The similarities between the two states extend to their people, who tend to be understated and unpretentious. If the appropriate epigram for the Lone Star State is that "everything is bigger in Texas," the proper equivalent for the Granite State (NH) and the Green Mountain State (VT) is that "less is more and small is beautiful." According to New Hampshire author Barbara Radcliffe Rogers, in her state, "a family's net worth often bears no relation to the size of their home or the make of their car."[4] Similarly, Vermonters "want things on a small scale," "desire face-to-face interaction," and "have an aversion to arrogance and self-importance."[5]

Still, the most interesting feature of New Hampshire and Vermont to a political observer is their differences, especially in political philosophy. Deborah ("Arnie") Arnesen, a radio talk show host and former Democratic state legislator and gubernatorial and congressional candidate in New Hampshire, says that her state "has a tax-free, self-serving, if-you-make-it-you-can-keep-it economic philosophy."[6] That philosophy reflects a political culture, according to former Vermont governor and national Democratic Party chair, Howard Dean, that is "centered around local governments doing things for their own people," instead of the more state-government-centric culture that operates in Vermont.[7]

Before discussing political culture, it is worth noting that one can see the effects of this concept at work in New Hampshire and Vermont sometimes just by looking out one's car window, as a Canadian visitor did on a trip south from Montreal in 1970. Turning east and south from St. Albans, Vermont, she recounts "driving through green, rolling hills then climbing into the uplands," describing the scenery as follows:

> Beautiful, beautiful: farmland and rounded, purple peaks, green fields, and blazing leaves. Villages that looked straight out of Currier and Ives etchings. Church steeples, white fences, silence except for the wind whenever we stopped the car to take a picture.[8]

Continuing south, the author and her husband eventually crossed the Connecticut River, entering New Hampshire where, she noted, "the difference between the states, so similar in many ways, became apparent." She recalled many years later that "one of the first things that caught our eyes was a big billboard announcing that New Hampshire had no sales tax."[9] Therein lies a prime example of the Twin States' divergent political cultures: New Hampshire's emphasis on individual freedom is reflected in a large billboard touting low or no taxes, while Vermont's more community-oriented focus shows off its stunning countryside and lack of billboards. A shorter explanation states: "In New Hampshire, they fight taxes; in Vermont, Wal-Marts [*sic*]."[10]

Political culture, which reflects political attitudes and influences public policy decisions, has long fascinated political scientists, who have used it to characterize politics in different countries, states, and localities. Political culture includes a range of components, such as citizens' attitudes about the proper role of government in society, citizens' willingness to participate in political activity, the degree of respect they have for public officials, the degree to which they wish to change society, whether they identify with and are loyal to a political party, and the degree to which they identify with and take pride in a political entity such as their country or state. Two pioneers in the study of political culture have written: "How people feel about their political systems is an important component of political culture."[11]

The American states exhibit three different types of political culture: moralistic, individualistic, and traditionalistic. Moralistic political culture—as the name suggests—considers politics as an activity centered on the public good. In this view, a government's merit is measured by the degree to which it promotes the public good, and its officeholders are judged according to their honesty, selflessness, and commitment to the citizens they serve.[12] The individualistic political culture views a political entity, including a state, as a marketplace, with government's role limited to those functions the citizens demand, focused primarily on the economic realm. In this view, government should encourage private rather than government-led solutions to problems and should ensure widespread economic opportunity through minimal regulation. This political culture also features a tendency by citizens to see politics as corrupt and by officeholders to limit the scope of government by not creating new programs or expanding existing ones.[13] Finally, the traditionalistic political culture, which does not exist in New Hampshire or Vermont, reflects a paternalistic or hierarchical view of society that authorizes those who are on the top rungs of the socioeconomic ladder to dominate government. Family ties and social position tend to perpetuate governance by an established elite. Traditional political culture survived in parts of the South—especially the Deep South—into the late twentieth century, and may survive there still. However it is not a focus of this book because it never took root in New Hampshire or Vermont.[14]

Professor Daniel Elazar, who was the foremost student of political culture in the American states, characterized Vermont as a moralistic political culture and New Hampshire as a hybrid moralistic/individualistic political culture.[15] In keeping with its moralistic politics, which seeks to serve the public good, Vermont has been bold and innovative in policymaking, adopting an extensive welfare system, a progressive tax structure, and high consumer protection standards. For its part, New Hampshire retains part of the moralistic political culture—notably, high levels of citizen participation in public affairs and a low tolerance for corruption—while also exhibiting the individualistic element of skepticism toward government.[16]

Under these circumstances, nobody should be surprised that New Hampshire doggedly resists enacting a state income or sales tax, whereas Vermont long ago enacted both, and that members of the Free State Project, who loathe taxation and regulation, chose New Hampshire as their rural refuge from perceived government overreach. This book aims to show not only the policy consequences, but also the historical roots of the Twin States' divergent political personalities. Toward that end, it is necessary to identify several important influences—human and otherwise—on the development of political culture in New Hampshire and Vermont. To do so is to apply some rigor to a subject that politically observant residents of the two states discuss regularly, but usually at a casual level of analysis that is prone to single-cause explanations for political cultures born of multiple influences. The discussion now turns to those influences.

Influences on Political Culture

Geology was instrumental in shaping the political cultures of New Hampshire and Vermont. From the earliest days of both states, Vermont's land has been well-suited to agriculture, but New Hampshire's has not. Long ago, geology caused New Hampshire to industrialize earlier and to a greater extent than Vermont. "Geology" refers to the physical structure and substance of the earth. It is the first link in the causal chain that underlies the respective political cultures of New Hampshire and Vermont. Geology helps to explain why, in the mid-nineteenth century, when both states lost residents to westward migration induced by the lure of more fertile land, the discovery of gold in California, and the restless adventurism of youth,

Vermont suffered a greater net population loss than New Hampshire. Immigrants seeking work in New Hampshire's growing mills and factories more than compensated for the loss caused by westward migration.

New Hampshire's nickname—the Granite State—reflects its subsoil base. Granite is hard and resists erosion, but it makes few soluble minerals available to plants. Limestone, on the other hand, is soft, weathers easily, and includes a high concentration of soluble calcium.[17] Although Vermont features considerable amounts of granite too, most of its surface is the soft, worn-down limestone common to the Appalachian Mountain chain. Forest now covers nearly 80 percent of Vermont. As the ice sheet moved southward a million years ago, covering even the highest peaks, it carried away less soil from Vermont than New Hampshire, and when it eventually melted, it deposited less stone in Vermont. For those reasons, and because of the way in which the mountains were formed, Vermonters have been able to earn a living from agriculture in the valleys. Furthermore, agriculture was more suitable than industry not only because the land favored agriculture, but also because geography so widely scattered Vermonters as to discourage industrial development. In Vermont, writes political scientist Frank Bryan, "valleys and hills, twisting ridges, dark gulches, and bright slopes create a mosaic of opportunity for little clusters of settlement. They also preclude big ones."[18] In New Hampshire, by contrast, agriculture was difficult because, in the words of Ralph Nading Hill, "the White Mountains are high and jagged and . . . . their blanket of boulders and stones is so heavy that the land in many places has never been reclaimed."[19]

Geography has also influenced the political cultures of New Hampshire and Vermont. "Geography" means the ways in which people adapt and relate to the physical features of the earth. It is another link in the causal chain that produced the respective political cultures of the Twin States. In 1800, the best source of mechanical power besides horses and oxen was waterfalls, much to New Hampshire's advantage, because the ten best hydropower sites in the Twin States were in New Hampshire. Indeed, farmer and author Chuck Wooster describes the entire state as "a river valley" because two-thirds of it are "drained by the Merrimack River," which runs south then northeast for 117 miles from central New Hampshire until it empties into the Gulf of Maine at Newburyport, Massachusetts.[20] In the mid-nineteenth century, large hydropower sites were key to the manufacture of wool and its increasingly important rival—cotton. New Hampshire's hydropower helped run thirty-two major cotton mills, as opposed to just six in Vermont.

Indeed, by 1850, almost as many people were employed in the factories of Manchester, New Hampshire, on the banks of the Merrimack, as worked in all of Vermont's factories combined. By 1900, because of industrialization, New Hampshire had become one of the most urban states in the country, as measured by the percentage of people living in towns and cities with more than 2,500 residents, whereas Vermont remained one of the most rural.[21]

An even more important geographic influence on political culture in the Twin States, though, was New Hampshire's possession of, and Vermont's lack of, a seacoast. At first blush, New Hampshire's seacoast merely explains why the state's mills enjoyed an economic advantage over their Vermont counterparts. The goods made in the former could be shipped from an in-state seaport at Portsmouth, whereas goods shipped from the latter required a costly and inefficient overland journey to reach a port.

But political consequences also flowed from this geographic disparity between the two states. They were already quite distinct from one another in the late 1770s, when they drafted their respective constitutions. New Hampshire had been settled for 150 years, had a diverse economy, distinct geographical regions, and a settlement pattern that ranged from wealthy merchants living in opulent houses on the seacoast to hardscrabble subsistence farmers struggling to support themselves in the interior. As a result, in 1784, when New Hampshire amended its constitution, it sought to overcome class distinctions and regional resentments by incorporating the town—the entity with which most residents identified—as the basic unit of legislative representation and by limiting the power of state government as much as possible. True to its historic distrust of concentrated political power, New Hampshire to this day has a legislature comprised of 424 members, pays them just $200 every two years, and has an independently elected five-member Executive Council with authority to check the governor's power by approving or disapproving state contracts and gubernatorial appointees.[22]

To be sure, New Hampshire's state government grew and became more active during the 1910–12 term of progressive Republican Robert Bass, as the state added a public service commission, a tax commission, and a workers' compensation program. More than a decade later, another progressive Republican governor, John G. (Gil) Winant, who served three terms, signed bills aimed at improving highways, increasing funding for the state university, augmenting state aid to cities, regulating banks, and assisting towns with hospital construction.[23] But despite some successes, progressive reformers faced strong opposition from conservative Republicans, who usually dominated the party. Consequently, Governor Winant's proposals for a forty-eight-hour work week, a teachers' retirement system, a pension law, and both personal and corporate income taxes failed.[24]

Unlike New Hampshire, Vermont had been settled for less than two decades when it drafted its first constitution, and its economy—based entirely on farming—lacked the diversity and the accompanying class distinctions already evident in New Hampshire at the time of the American Revolution. Without a seacoast or a merchant class, Vermont exhibited what historian Charles Morrissey termed a "fierce equality [that] has characterized Vermonters in their relations with each other for two centuries."[25] The emphasis on equality is evident in Vermont's 1777 constitution, which was the first one adopted in this country that outlawed slavery and guaranteed universal suffrage for men by abolishing property qualifications for voting.

Vermont's agrarian economy and egalitarian ethos influenced the expansion of the state's government during the late nineteenth and early twentieth centuries. During that period, the state government revamped public education, began regulating businesses and public utilities, and expanded public services because Vermont's many small farming towns could not afford to fund these services for themselves. To pay for expanded state services, the legislature ended its reliance on statewide property taxes in 1931, substituting a personal income tax to ease the tax burden on farmers, who were often land-rich but cash-poor. Thus, Vermont's state government responded to the resource limitations of an agrarian economy with noteworthy flexibility, expanding public services to meet pressing public needs. As a result, the progressivism that characterizes Vermont politics today—defined here as a willingness to use the government to improve social and economic conditions for ordinary people—has roots in the state's expansion of services for its citizens and creation of a revenue stream to fund those services during the late nineteenth and early twentieth centuries. Today's Vermont progressivism, unlike its predecessor, is housed in the Democratic Party and takes new forms, such as advocacy for environmental protection, reproductive rights, and affordable childcare. However both versions of progressivism derive from the state's agrarian roots and egalitarian ethos.

As early as the 1920s, Vermont's agrarian economy also helped the state to market itself as a clean, pastoral place that harkened back to a less hurried America. Aiding this effort were the establishment of two progressive colleges during the Depression Era—Bennington in 1931 and Goddard in 1938. Another aid was the popularity of Helen and Scott Nearing's 1954 book, *Living the Good Life*, which told the story of their 1932 migration from city life to a farm in Vermont.[26] Dorothy Canfield Fisher—one of the many artists, writers, and intellectuals to settle in Vermont in the early twentieth century—wrote that "the Vermont tradition" was "based on the idea that group life should leave each person as free as possible to arrange his own life."[27] This tradition features "the unquestioned right of anyone to practice variations—if harmless to others—from the way of life generally accepted by the majority of his neighbors."[28] Over time, according to a social science study of the "place reputations" of New Hampshire and Vermont, as more creative people and aspiring ruralists moved to Vermont, they "helped to expand and entrench" its reputation as "a place offering a unique array of noneconomic benefits: from hippie enclaves to 'artsy' towns and organic farms."[29] As a result, three transformations occurred in Vermont in the twentieth century: a shift to the left politically; a growing reputation as a haven for artists, writers, and intellectuals; and a more varied landscape including not just isolated hill farms but also vacation homes, recreational amenities, and college towns.

In contrast, New Hampshire's real estate and tourist industries did not market their state as a retreat for those who sought to paint or write in peace. For example, a 1930s-era pamphlet inviting visitors and prospective migrants to the Monadnock Region in southwestern New Hampshire emphasized the area's proximity to Boston, modern conveniences such as electricity, and low property taxes for buyers of both homes and businesses. And two travel articles, one about New Hampshire and the other about Vermont, both of which appeared in *The New York Times* in 1955, used contrasting imagery to describe the two states. The New Hampshire article touted the state's horse racing track and its fifty-six golf courses, whereas the Vermont article—written by the same author—highlighted the revival of small-town fairs and the sense of community they conveyed. In short, the materials promoting New Hampshire were designed to appeal more to business owners and retirees than to artists, writers, or professors.

Today, New Hampshire has a place reputation that is quite distinct from Vermont's. Cultural migration continues to influence that reputation, as a 2020 demographic study by University of New Hampshire researchers shows. The study found that among recent migrants to the state, the reasons for migrating varied greatly by income. Although the wish to be closer to family members was the greatest motivator across all income categories, the influence of "employment" and "taxes" on decisions to move to New Hampshire increased with each income bracket surveyed. For low- and middle-income earners, employment influenced the decisions of fewer than 30 percent of the migrants, whereas it influenced the decisions of nearly 40 percent of the high-income earners. Similarly, taxes influenced the decisions of fewer than 10 percent of the low-income earners, 18 percent of the middle-income earners, and 30 percent of the high-income earners.[30] Among recent migrants over age fifty, 20 percent ranked taxes as a reason for moving to New Hampshire.[31] These data suggest that a sizeable portion of migrants to New Hampshire, especially those with high incomes, are attracted to the state's reputation for low taxes.

That is certainly true for supporters of the Free State Project, a libertarian group whose 2003 poll ranked New Hampshire as the most libertarian-friendly state. They recommended it as a place where its members should move. A spokesman for the group said at the time that New Hampshire won the poll because it "boasts the lowest state and local tax burden in the continental U.S., the 'leanest' state government in the country . . . a citizen legislature, a healthy job market, and perhaps most important, support for our movement."[32]

Thus, geology and geography, reinforced by voluntary migration, have shaped the economies, social structures, and politics of New Hampshire and Vermont, giving each state a distinct atmosphere, what one observer called "an upscale counterculture" in Vermont and a "blue-collar" feel in New Hampshire.[33] Nobody who is familiar with the two states will be surprised to learn that per capita, Vermont has twice as many stores that sell Birkenstock sandals as New Hampshire has, along with more vegetarian restaurants and dealers in hemp products. New Hampshire has more Harley-Davidson dealerships and Dairy Queen restaurants.[34] Indeed, Vermont has no Dairy Queens, apparently preferring that its ice cream be served with a scoop of progressive politics from Ben and Jerry.

No single cause is responsible for creating the political culture of either New Hampshire or Vermont; New Hampshire's political culture is not solely the result of an exodus of tax-weary corporate executives from Massachusetts, nor is Vermont's political culture only the result of migration "back to the land" by aspiring organic farmers. Instead, the political culture of each state is an artifact of geology, geography, marketing, the economic benefits and burdens they produce, and the peculiar mix of individuals who have chosen to move there or stay there. Having now examined the raw materials of political culture, it is time to introduce the major policy consequences of the Twin States' divergent political cultures.

Policy Consequences of Political Culture

Political cultures have public policy consequences. Evidence shows that states with moralistic political cultures tend to produce more policy innovation because they seek to serve the public good by devising new, imaginative means of solving pressing public problems. Often, the policy responses are "liberal" or "progressive" in the sense that they feature the expansion of government services and expenditures, such as publicly funded prekindergarten, daycare centers, or job training programs for unemployed adults. But that need not be so; a state with a moralistic political culture could be politically conservative. In that case, the populace could be genuinely concerned with promoting the public good, yet hesitant to use government for that purpose, preferring instead that charitable organizations and individual donors lead the way in responding to human needs.[35] In states with more individualistic political cultures, however, government tends to be less assertive, hence less innovative, in addressing public problems because limited government and maximum individual freedom are key features of an individualistic political culture. Therefore, one reasonably expects more dramatic and assertive governmental responses to public problems in Vermont, which has a moralistic political culture, than in New Hampshire, whose political culture is a hybrid of moralism and individualism.

Later chapters will address in greater detail policy responses by New Hampshire and Vermont to specific public issues, especially land-use regulation and public school finance. Still, readers are entitled here to a preview of those discussions and a brief mention of other issues to which the Twin States have responded differently, but consistently with their respective political cultures. One example of an issue that triggered different responses from New Hampshire and Vermont is the COVID-19 pandemic. To be sure, New Hampshire joined Vermont and forty-one other states in issuing stay-at-home orders in March and April, 2020, when the virus emerged in the United States and no vaccine existed. Still, New Hampshire governor, Chris

Sununu, a Republican, was the last governor in New England, and one of the last in the nation, to issue a mandate that prohibited people from going out in public without wearing a mask. New Hampshire's other responses to COVID-19 were to (1) ask residents to restrict their travel; (2) practice social distancing; and (3) quarantine voluntarily if someone with whom they had been in close contact notified them of a positive test result.[36]

Vermont also had a Republican governor in the spring of 2020—Phil Scott—but the state imposed four requirements that New Hampshire did not, including increased restrictions on gatherings between households, indoor dining at restaurants, and in-person religious services, along with closing bars. As of mid-December 2020, Vermont no longer had a stay-at-home order in place, but it maintained some restrictions, such as on indoor dining in restaurants. Several New Hampshire physicians and healthcare executives who favored Vermont's greater restrictions acknowledged that New Hampshire's political culture prevented such restrictions. One healthcare professional expressed the hope that New Hampshire would not become the "Live Free *and* Die" state during the pandemic because of its aversion to regulation.[37]

Another public health issue affected by the divergent political cultures of New Hampshire and Vermont is the regulation of firearms. New Hampshire's libertarian ethos is front and center in recent legislative developments with respect to gun safety. In 2017, Governor Sununu signed a law that made New Hampshire a "constitutional carry" state by eliminating the gun owner's need to apply for a permit to carry a concealed firearm. In 2019, with new Democratic majorities in both houses of the state legislature, three gun-safety bills were passed, which (1) required background checks for all firearms purchases, including those made at gun shows; (2) barred people from carrying guns on school property; and (3) established a three-day waiting period before one could purchase a firearm. But Governor Sununu vetoed all three bills, saying they ran counter to the state's "culture of responsible gun ownership and individual freedom."[38] In 2020 he vetoed a "red flag" law that had passed with Democratic majorities and that would have authorized courts to temporarily confiscate firearms from people deemed threats to themselves or others.

In November 2020, the Democrats lost their legislative majorities, and they have hesitated to offer gun-safety proposals ever since. The only exception to that hesitancy was a bill considered early in 2022 that would have tightened the rules concerning background checks for gun purchases and would have applied them to all commercial sales in New Hampshire, not just those made by licensed retailers. But the bill failed by a vote of 179–144 on the house floor.

As of early 2025, the research and policy arm of the Everytown for Gun Safety organization ranked New Hampshire thirty-eighth among the states regarding the relative strength of its gun regulations. That ranking is based on, among other things, the state's lack of a state background check law, a waiting period before finalizing a firearm purchase, a red flag law, and laws prohibiting high-capacity magazines or setting a minimum age to purchase a firearm. The group acknowledges, however, that New Hampshire requires domestic abusers to relinquish their firearms when restraining orders are placed on them and bars them from possessing firearms while under such orders. It also prohibits anyone who has been convicted of a hate crime from possessing a firearm. And it permits its colleges and universities to decide for themselves whether to prohibit firearms on campus.[39] Thus, New Hampshire's hybrid moralistic/individualistic political culture is reflected in its gun regulations, which separate domestic abusers and persons convicted of hate crimes from their firearms and let colleges prohibit firearms on campus, but otherwise favor the freedom to obtain, keep, and bear arms.

In the same report, Vermont ranks seventeenth among the states regarding the relative strength of its gun laws. Predictably, Vermont's moralistic political culture, with its emphasis on serving the public good rather than maximizing individual freedom, is reflected in more restrictive gun laws in the Green Mountain State. In 2018, after police discovered and foiled a teenager's plan to carry out a mass shooting at a Vermont high school, Governor Phil Scott supported a package of gun-safety measures that made major changes to the state's gun laws. The new laws (1) required the assistance of a licensed gun dealer to sell, trade, or otherwise transfer firearms between two persons not licensed to do so; (2) prohibited the sale of firearms to persons under age twenty-one, unless the buyer is a police officer or a member of the armed forces or national guard; (3) barred the manufacture, possession, or transfer in Vermont of large-capacity magazines (more than ten rounds of ammunition for a long gun and more than fifteen rounds for a handgun); (4) outlawed the possession of "bump stocks" (a.k.a. "bump-fire stocks"), which can effectively transform a semiautomatic into a fully automatic firearm); and (5) authorized the issuance of an "extreme risk protection order" (a.k.a. red flag law) permitting police officers to seize firearms from individuals deemed to be an imminent risk to themselves or others.[40]

In June 2023, the Vermont legislature augmented its gun laws with Act 45, the purpose of which was to reduce both suicides and community violence. That goal reflected the grim realities that of the more than 700 Vermont residents who died of gunshot wounds between 2011 and 2020, 88 percent committed suicide and that suicides by Vermont men and boys are 50 percent higher than the national average. This law (1) imposed criminal penalties for negligently storing firearms when the person who has custody of them knows or should know that a child or prohibited person can gain access to them; (2) increased the penalties if death or serious bodily injury resulted; (3) broadened the existing red flag provision by adding family or household members to the list of persons (previously a state's attorney or the Office of the Attorney General) authorized to ask a court to issue an extreme risk protection order; and (4) established a 72-hour waiting period before a licensed dealer could transfer a firearm to a buyer.[41]

Governor Scott allowed the bill to become law without his signature. His reluctance to sign resulted from the waiting period, which he feared might be unconstitutional in light of the United States Supreme Court's decision in *New York State Rifle and Pistol Association v. Bruen*, in which the Court wrote that to justify a firearm regulation, "the government must demonstrate that the regulation is consistent with the Nation's historical tradition of firearm regulation."[42] This language suggests that unless Vermont can show a waiting period is a long-standing form of firearm regulation, a court will likely find it in violation of the Second Amendment. Still, Scott was content to await the outcome of expected litigation, so he permitted the bill to take effect without his signature. Thus, although Vermont joins New Hampshire in separating from their guns individuals who are under domestic abuse restraining orders and in allowing colleges to prohibit guns on campus, Vermont's laws go well beyond those restrictions to limit access by potentially dangerous individuals, as befits a moralistic political culture.

State policies concerning COVID-19 and the regulation of firearms illustrate the consequences of divergent political cultures. Nevertheless, this book will feature land-use regulation and public school finance in demonstrating the policy consequences of political culture. Several reasons explain that choice. Regarding land-use regulation, the Twin States—despite their many differences—face virtually identical problems. Both states must revamp long-standing zoning regulations that favor single-family homes if they are ever to build the affordable workforce housing necessary to attract more working-age individuals, especially migrants who are needed to replace retirees and keep the state economies vibrant. If they fail to meet that need in the coming years, both states face the prospect of becoming economic backwaters. Thus, the connection between the current housing crisis and future economic sustainability makes political culture worthy of attention because it will undoubtedly influence the policies the two states devise to address the crisis.

Public school finance deserves to be highlighted here in part because it is closely related to land-use regulation. No two issues affect American families more than finding an affordable house in a desirable community and a suitable public school system to educate their children. And few factors influence the appeal of a community for families more than the quality of its schools. But when property taxes are the primary mechanism for funding public schools, the quality of a school system is often tied to the property wealth of the community where it is located. In property-wealthy communities, single-family zoning rules tend to make housing unaffordable for many families, who then find themselves relegated to living in less desirable communities with poorly funded schools.

New Hampshire and Vermont have both faced court orders to fund their schools more equitably, relying less on property taxes, yet they have responded in dramatically different ways to this continuing problem, as befits their contrasting political cultures. Therein lies another reason to feature public school finance in this book: it illustrates the power of political culture to influence policy choices. Finally, public school finance warrants close attention because nothing is more important to the future economic viability of a state—making it attractive to current residents and newcomers alike—than a well-educated population able to compete for jobs in an ever-changing economy.

Thus, although later chapters will highlight other policy decisions that reflect the respective political cultures of New Hampshire and Vermont, the primary examples of the connection between culture and policy in these two states will be the discussions of land-use regulation and public school finance in Chapters Six and Seven, respectively. Those chapters will show how New Hampshire's devotion to small government and Vermont's preference for a more assertive state government are evident in their distinct responses to the problems posed by a shortage of affordable housing and by the need to fund public education adequately and equitably.

The Plan of the Book

Chapter Two will present a short political history of New Hampshire, tracing the development of its political culture from colonial times to the present day. New Hampshire's founders were entrepreneurs who sought to establish "plantations"; unlike other states it did not have a single strong-willed leader or a religious sect that wished to shape its development with a unifying vision or theology. Accordingly, decentralized authority was characteristic of New Hampshire from its earliest days as four small settlements huddled along the seacoast in the mid-seventeenth century. The preference for small government and local autonomy has continued to influence the state's politics from the Revolutionary era, through the partisan shift from the Federalists to the Jeffersonian Republicans during the early national period (1828–52), the subsequent dominance of the Republican Party for more than a century, beginning in 1860, and the modern era of population growth and increased competition between Democrats and Republicans. That same preference has also withstood New Hampshire's transition from a prosperous maritime economy to a struggling economy of small farms and small manufacturing ventures to an industrial economy of large mills run by hydropower to a present-day economy of high technology and large healthcare providers. The chapter will conclude by noting the challenges that twenty-first-century problems pose for New Hampshire's political culture.

Similarly, Chapter Three will offer a short political history of Vermont. In contrast to New Hampshire, Vermont lacks a seacoast, was largely unsettled until the 1760s, and, thanks to more fertile soil, was principally agrarian thereafter, fostering a more egalitarian society than existed in New Hampshire. Vermont's agrarian economy gradually shifted from subsistence to commercial farming and, within the latter, from wool production to dairy farming. Vermonters' political loyalties, like those of their neighbors in New Hampshire, also shifted over time, from the Federalists to the Jeffersonian Republicans to the Jacksonian Democrats to the Republicans just prior to the Civil War and for a century thereafter. After the Civil War, Vermonters migrated in large numbers, either to cities or to cheaper, more fertile land in the Midwest or West, making people Vermont's most valuable export. That exodus helped to spur the expanded role for state government noted earlier because Vermont's small, rural towns were often unable to fund for themselves public services, such as road and bridge maintenance. Today, state government remains more active in Vermont than in New Hampshire;

the former's billboard law and regulations regarding large-scale land development and firearms are prominent examples. These initiatives all reflect the state's moralistic political culture.

In Chapter Four the scene shifts to the effects of New Hampshire's libertarian ethos on contemporary policy decisions. The discussion will highlight the clearest example of individualism in New Hampshire's political culture: a reluctance to spend public dollars. The Granite State allocates a smaller share of its resources to public investments, such as education, parks, and infrastructure, than higher-spending states such as Vermont. The sustainability of this political culture is open to question, though, considering the major changes that have occurred in recent years to the state's demographic and political profiles. Both migration and generational change have produced closer party competition in the past generation. Democratic control of the state legislature, once virtually unheard of, is no longer unusual, as legislative majorities have shifted from one party to the other in successive elections. Still, changing partisan patterns have thus far not altered New Hampshire's devotion to small government; indeed, no Democratic governor has proposed an income or sales tax. Therefore, New Hampshire will face the challenges presented by a lack of affordable housing and the need to fund public schools fairly and adequately with a small-government ethos that may prevent bold and effective action. This chapter will conclude, then, that New Hampshire's economic future will depend in large measure on how its political culture responds to these two challenges.

Similarly, Chapter Five will examine contemporary Vermont politics through the lens of the state's political culture, which values both individual freedom and community welfare. To protect freedom, Vermonters opposed the Alien and Sedition Acts in the late 1790s, have long defended the right to keep and bear arms, and have supported civil unions and later, same-sex marriage. To preserve community welfare, they have guided land development, regulated firearms, and subsidized childcare generously. Some of these policy choices were controversial when adopted, and others remain so. The enactment of a centralized school funding mechanism in 1997 and a civil unions law in 2000 spawned a backlash—the "Take Back Vermont" movement—that reflected anger toward migrants who brought their cultural and political progressivism with them to Vermont in recent decades. In the wake of this backlash, Democratic governor, Howard Dean, survived electoral close calls in 1998 and 2000, but eighteen legislators whose votes for or against civil unions alienated their constituents were swept from office in 2000. Today, Vermonters routinely replace a retiring Democratic governor with a Republican and vice versa and have done so since 1969. Democrats have dominated the legislature, though, for most of the past thirty years. Both parties must reckon with a demographic freight train hurtling toward them: fewer workers and more elderly people. It is unclear whether Vermont can find enough workers to power its economy, house them affordably, and care properly for its elderly residents. Vermonters will need every bit of their traditional boldness and civility to meet these challenges.

Chapter Six will compare the responses of New Hampshire and Vermont to land-use regulation as it relates to the affordable housing crisis. The discussion begins by tracing the changes in land-use patterns that occurred in New Hampshire from colonial times through the mid-twentieth century, when automobiles supplanted railroads, causing populations to disperse, as residents increasingly lived some distance from their work. Zoning and suburbanization followed, with zoning causing the segregation of land uses, for example, keeping the chemical plant away from the elementary school. But zoning also separated residents based on race and socioeconomic status. Such exclusionary zoning continues, favoring single-family homes by making the construction of multifamily or rental housing difficult in many communities and perpetuating both housing segregation and differences in educational quality between school districts. Curing the effects of exclusionary zoning in New Hampshire is difficult because zoning is largely a local responsibility, which the political culture reinforces. The state government has tried to nudge communities to build more affordable housing, but home prices remain high, and the vacancy rates for rental units are extraordinarily low. The political culture and the local nature of zoning make reform a major challenge for New Hampshire.

In Vermont, land-use law has sought for two generations to preserve the traditional settlement pattern of a village center, featuring commercial establishments and private homes, surrounded by farm fields and forests. Since the late 1960s, development spurred by completion of the interstate highway system has threatened the traditional arrangement. But such development also prompted greater attention to environmental protection and growth management. The plan announced by the International Paper Company in 1968 to build vacation homes in southern Vermont prompted Act 250, a comprehensive land-use law enacted in 1970. It authorized regional commissions to evaluate large development projects according to ten criteria pertaining to each project's environmental, social, and fiscal consequences. Later statutes sought to encourage development in town centers and the building of multifamily homes and accessory apartments attached or adjacent to single-family homes. In June 2023, Vermont enacted Act 47, which ended the long-standing preference for single-family zoning. Still, Vermont remains far short of the number of housing units it will need to solve its affordability crisis. To solve that crisis, while also avoiding sprawl, will be especially difficult.

The impact of political culture on this issue is muted, though, because zoning is a municipal choice, not a constitutionally mandated state responsibility like education. The chapter will conclude that the Twin States have responded similarly to this crisis—with more nudges than mandates—but that Vermont's greater inclination for statewide regulation, as reflected in Act 250 and Act 47, may make it better able than New Hampshire to accommodate growth without encouraging sprawl.

Chapter Seven will compare the Twin States' policy responses to the issue of funding public schools. The funding of public schools is a long-standing dilemma in New Hampshire. The system continues to rely disproportionately on local property taxes, so school districts with lower-than-average property values struggle to raise the funds to educate every child adequately. Consequently, this issue has been the subject of litigation for more than thirty years. The state supreme court held in the 1990s that the state's constitution required New Hampshire to (1) fund an adequate education for its schoolchildren and (2) use a formula that is "equal in valuation and uniform in rate," which the property-tax-based system was not. Despite varying attempts since then to find a suitable funding formula, litigation continues, along with New Hampshire's perennial school funding debate. In July 2025, the state supreme court held, as it has done since the 1990s, that the existing school funding mechanism shortchanged property-poor districts, thereby violating the state constitution's requirement of "adequacy." But, as the court has also done since the 1990s, it declined to order state officials to immediately increase school funding. Instead, it preferred to "urge the legislative and executive branches to act expeditiously to ensure that all the children in public schools in New Hampshire receive a state-funded constitutionally adequate education."[43] Similar admonitions by the court in previous cases have not spurred dramatic changes in state funding of public schools in New Hampshire, and nothing suggests that the most recent decision will produce a different result. Policymaking will likely remain paralyzed because New Hampshire's tax-averse political culture makes school funding endlessly controversial.

In Vermont, two landmark events, beginning in 1998–99, produced a major change in the mechanism for funding the state's public schools. First, the state supreme court held that the system then in existence, which relied largely on local property taxes, violated the state constitution for failing to provide equal educational opportunity. Second, the legislature enacted Act 60, which added the proceeds of a statewide property tax to other monies in the state's General Fund, thereby boosting the state's share of the funding for public schools considerably. Act 60 also required wealthy towns to contribute to a "sharing pool" if their property taxes raised more money than the law allowed. Nonresident owners of businesses and second homes complained that the sharing pool forced them to pay higher school taxes in towns where they could not vote. The legislature modified Act 60 in 2003 by creating for the objecting owners a separate property tax with a statewide rate not tied to local spending decisions in which they lacked a vote.

More recently, the legislature (in Act 127, passed in 2022) has modified the funding system to direct additional money to schools that are small, have many students from low-income families, and have English language learners. Unfortunately, partly because of poor communication between state officials and school districts, the change prompted increased spending by school districts and the prospect of soaring property tax bills by 2024. Responding to a public outcry against the anticipated higher taxes, Governor Phil Scott saw a chance, during the 2025 legislative session, to transform the ways in which public education is organized, operated, and funded in Vermont. The result is Act 73, which is slated to take effect on July 1, 2028, assuming the governor and legislators can agree on the number and size of the new, larger school districts the legislation envisions. It is a work in progress, and for the next few years at least, its aim to make Vermont's schools less expensive, more efficient, and more equitable will remain a focus of educators and elected officials in Vermont.

This chapter will show that political culture has a more profound effect on school finance than on land-use regulation in New Hampshire and Vermont. Both states' constitutions make education a state responsibility, and when responsibility rests with state officials, political culture is likely to affect policy decisions. New Hampshire's localism and distaste for broad-based taxes force continued reliance on local property taxes as a principal funding source. Vermont's more state-centric political culture has spawned a state-run system that has improved financial and educational equity but must still become more efficient and less expensive.

Chapter Eight will conclude the book by underscoring Chapter One's assertion that New Hampshire and Vermont are fraternal, not identical, twins. To compare the two states, the chapter will use as examples Styles Bridges of New Hampshire and George Aiken of Vermont, who served together in the United States Senate for twenty years. Both men were born in the 1890s, raised in rural northern New England, held professional positions in the Farm Bureau, and entered politics in the 1930s. But although both were Republicans who customarily voted with their party, Bridges was a reliable conservative, whereas Aiken earned a reputation as a maverick in intraparty disputes, such as by voting to censure Senator Joseph McCarthy in 1954 and by supporting Senator Margaret Chase Smith over the more conservative Senator Barry Goldwater for president in 1964.

Just as Senators Bridges and Aiken had much in common, yet distinct ideological orientations, so do New Hampshire and Vermont have many similarities, yet some noteworthy political differences too. Even when both states were solidly Republican, New Hampshire was more wedded to local control, small government, and minimal taxation than Vermont. More recently, New Hampshire has become less Republican, but localism and a reputation for low taxes still attract some migrants to relocate there. And differences in political culture can produce different policy choices on important issues. Sometimes, those differences are subtle, as with land-use regulation, where local volunteer boards and private land developers and builders are major players. At other times, those differences are dramatic, as with public school finance, where state government has a constitutional mandate to educate children. Thus, the metaphor of fraternal twins is apt for New Hampshire and Vermont. They share many physical and attitudinal traits, but their divergent political cultures produce markedly different policy outcomes on some issues, which can affect the lives of their citizens profoundly.

Historical context must precede discussions of contemporary politics and policies, though. Accordingly, Chapter Two will present a short political history of New Hampshire.

CHAPTER TWO

From Seacoast Aristocracy to Jacksonian Democracy to Temporary Republican Hegemony

A Short Political History of New Hampshire

The Colonial and Early National Periods

SINGLE CAUSES RARELY EXPLAIN complex events. Therefore, a good historical discussion begins with a particular phenomenon—such as New Hampshire's political culture—and seeks to identify the processes that produced it.[1] The task at hand is to trace the origins of New Hampshire's political culture backward until we uncover the bedrock attitudes, values, and events that helped to form that culture and continue to influence it today. Happily, notes historian John Lewis Gaddis, "past processes have generated surviving structures—documents, images, memories—that allow us to reconstruct in our minds, and then on our word processors, what happened."[2] This chapter aims to reconstruct the development of New Hampshire's political culture.

Decentralized authority has characterized New Hampshire since colonial times. New Hampshire was distinct from other colonies in that it was not founded by a "strong-willed proprietor" who would shape its formation, nor was it born of religious convictions or guided by the orderly prescriptions of a written compact.[3] Instead, as early as 1614, Captain John Smith visited the nearby Isles of Shoals and then promoted the idea of settlement on the New England coast.[4] Beginning in 1622, entrepreneurs Ferdinando Gorges and John Mason, acting for the British Crown, dispatched settlers to the colony to establish "plantations" (farms) there. The entrepreneurs were not interested in governing, so the early plantations and towns huddled together in the present-day Seacoast Region, trying to fend off anarchy and annexation.[5]

Mason founded the Laconia Company, which sent settlers to New Hampshire to build a plantation and engage in the fur trade with the Native peoples. He named the colony "New Hampshire" after his family seat in Hampshire, England. That name meant almost nothing to the settlers, though, who did not identify with the colony per se, but rather, with its individual towns, which numbered four by 1640: Strawberry Banke (Portsmouth), Exeter, Hampton, and Hilton's Point (Dover). The colony might have collapsed when the Laconia Company later failed sometime before 1634, stranding sixty-six men and twenty-two women there. But immigration from England and even greater migration north from the Massachusetts Bay Colony saved it. The Massachusetts migrants shared a desire for economic opportunity and dissatisfaction with the strict rules of the Puritan regime in Massachusetts. As a result, by 1640, almost half the nearly one thousand English residents who lived in New Hampshire had come there from Massachusetts.[6] New Hampshire and Massachusetts were a single entity from 1640 until 1679, when the British Crown separated them.[7] A decade later, though, as a new king took power in England, the two entities joined forces once again. By the end of the seventeenth century, New Hampshire had an elected assembly, an appointed council, and a lieutenant governor, who served under the governor of a combined Massachusetts and New Hampshire.[8]

Gradually, New Hampshire's founders and early settlers began to take advantage of the natural amenities of the Piscataqua River region where they lived: fur, fish, and, later, timber. The settlers could not have profited from the trade in furs—notably, beaver pelts—without the cooperation of the Native population, though. The original inhabitants of New Hampshire were related, in both blood and cultural traditions, to the neighboring tribes in Vermont, southern Quebec, western Maine, and northern Massachusetts. They all belonged to a larger group known as the western Abenaki—the Dawn Land People.[9] The largest Abenaki subgroup in New Hampshire was the Pennacooks.[10]

The Native inhabitants and the English settlers were bound to have conflict because their values and ways of living were dramatically different. To many settlers, the Natives' apparent poverty was shocking because the surrounding landscape held abundant resources. Such "poverty" was misleading, though, because the Native people were seminomadic: they did not acquire and retain permanent possessions. In the summer, they lived on fish and berries. In mid-September, they moved inland, to smaller creeks, where they caught eels. And from October to March, their villages broke into small family-based bands that hunted and consumed beaver, caribou, moose, deer, and bear meat along with corn and beans stored from the previous fall's harvest.[11] Accordingly, they did not establish permanent homes to fill with signs of permanence, ownership, and material success. In their view, an item was "owned" if it was useful; if it ceased to be useful or if someone else needed it more, one could easily give it away. Therefore, the Natives did not perceive that they owned the land, but instead, only the items located on the land during certain times of the year.[12] Thus, the European view of land and personal property as commodities subject to trade in a market was foreign to the Indigenous inhabitants of colonial New Hampshire.[13]

Moreover, the settlers interpreted the Natives' hunting and gathering as a justification for expropriating their land. In the settlers' view, the Natives squandered the resources available to them, so only the fields that the women cultivated should be off-limits to Englishmen.[14] Because of this mindset, New Hampshire and other parts of New England saw, during the seventeenth and eighteenth centuries, the replacement of the Natives' village system of shifting agriculture and hunter-gatherer activities by a pattern of agriculture that raised crops and domesticated animals, subject to fixed boundaries and within reach of commercial markets. The settlers' agricultural practices conflicted with the Natives' subsistence traditions. The dams the settlers built in the smaller streams and rivers to power grist and lumber mills disrupted the habits of the salmon the Native people relied on for food. The settlers harvested trees for lumber, driving wild game deeper into the wilderness, which made hunting more difficult, and the domestic animals they had brought from England roamed at will, regularly spoiling crops the Native women raised.[15] The animals' ever-growing herds and need for grazing land prompted the settlers to take increasing amounts of Native land for pasturage.[16]

Trade provided Native people with good metal cutting tools and guns, but it made them depend on those goods too. And owning guns, knives, and blankets enhanced one's social status within the tribe, disrupting long-standing social patterns among tribal members. Access to the settlers' liquor was also problematic because the Natives saw drunkenness as possession by an evil spirit, absolving them of personal responsibility for bad behavior.[17]

These problems increased as the population of English settlers in New Hampshire grew during the seventeenth century; in the 1630s they began arriving in large enough numbers to establish permanent communities along the coast, and by the end of that decade their number exceeded that of the Native people. By the 1680s the tribes of southern New Hampshire recognized that even if they accommodated the English settlers, the cultural survival of Native people there was not guaranteed. The settlers built permanent homes ever closer to where the Native people hunted, fished, and planted crops.[18] That is why Passaconaway and Kancamagus left their homes in the upper Merrimack River Valley in the mid-1680s to join the eastern Abenaki in Maine; disease, warfare, and defections had decimated their people.[19]

Mortality rates from European diseases were routinely eighty or ninety percent in Native villages, and it was not unusual for the population of an entire village to be eliminated. By the end of the seventeenth century, tuberculosis had become common, and influenza in combination with pneumonia occurred regularly in epidemic proportions, as did measles, typhus, dysentery, and syphilis. Consequently, between 1600 and 1675, the Native population in New England declined from well over 70,000 to fewer than 12,000; in New Hampshire and Vermont, the western Abenaki declined from a population estimated at ten thousand to fewer than five hundred. Thus, death by disease became another justification for English settlers to commandeer Native lands, as many New England towns built their first settlements on the sites of abandoned Native villages.[20]

Warfare was the other major cause of population decline among the Native people. They waged war frequently with the settlers during the seventeenth and eighteenth centuries, writes historian Jill Lepore, "in response to incursions on their cultural, political, and economic autonomy."[21] Meanwhile, the settlers fought to gain land and eliminate a race they thought was inferior for its worship of spirits, lack of a written language, and practice of polygamy. In any event, off and on for a hundred years, English settlers and Abenaki tribesmen fought each other, sometimes with the Natives supporting the French in battle against the English. These conflicts included King Philip's War (1675–76), King William's War (1689–98), Queen Anne's War (1703–13), and the Seven Years' War, better known as the French and Indian War (1754–63).[22] They all brought horrific violence by both sides: surprise raids and destruction of Native villages by the settlers and bloody reprisals by the tribes, featuring burned settlements and captured women and children to use for ransom or to replenish depopulated tribal communities. In the long run, though, according to historian Jere Daniell, the Native people "suffered most" because, even when assisting a European ally, "[t]hey did most of the fighting, lost population, saw the permanent destruction of many villages, and when peace finally came had little to show for their efforts."[23]

Peace came in 1763, but instead of helping the remaining Natives, it unleashed into the interior of New Hampshire, including the lands along the Connecticut River, an unprecedented flood of new settlers. Indeed, this migration was largely attributable to the settlers' recognition that the Indigenous population had been so decimated so that it no longer posed a threat. By 1765, the government of New Hampshire had granted charters to more than two dozen townships on the eastern side of the Connecticut River Valley and many more on the west side.[24]

At this point in the story of New Hampshire's development, it is useful to set the frontier warfare aside to examine the colony's economic and political development during the century preceding 1763, when the French and Indian War ended. By 1763, New Hampshire had housed settlers for more than a hundred years and had been a distinct colony for more than eighty of those years. The early settlers had learned to exploit the natural amenities in the Piscataqua region along the coast: fur, fish, and later, timber.[25] The popularity of beaver hats in England prompted settlers to establish a commercial partnership with Native tribes whereby the tribesmen expanded their customary hunting for beaver pelts, which they then traded with the settlers for knives, pots, guns, and other manufactured goods, enabling the settlers to meet the English demand for fur. This arrangement was a rude introduction to capitalism for the Natives, who for the first time were encouraged to kill more beavers than necessary to meet tribal needs, only to discover, by 1700, that English tastes in headwear had changed and the supply of beaver had shrunk dramatically. Besides, by that date, deaths attributable to war and disease had drastically reduced the number of Native hunters available to supply beaver pelts.[26]

The early settlers had also benefitted from a lively trade in timber, especially white pine trees, which became masts for British warships. The largest ones on record measured seven feet, eight inches across, and some particularly tall ones stood as high as 250 feet. More often, though, they grew to be a yard across and 100 feet high.[27] Taken together, then, the forests and waterfalls in the Piscataqua region not only spurred coastal settlement, but also quickly birthed a timber industry that produced masts, lumber, barrel staves, containers for preserving and shipping food, household tools, and naval stores—notably tar, pitch, and turpentine.[28] The bountiful coastal setting spurred other early settlers to go to sea to either catch or trade in fish. Some of New Hampshire's commercial fish supply went to Spain and Portugal in return for salt and wines, but most of it was a form of "remittances" to English merchants, who in turn supplied cloth, clothing, cordage for a ship's rigging, metalware, and other manufactured goods.[29]

New Hampshire's timber industry represented an early attempt by Britain to regulate economic activity in North America. White pine trees were so important to the British Navy that beginning in 1685, a "surveyor of pines and timbers" operated in New England. Later termed the surveyor general, this official was appointed to supervise the hacking of a crowfoot-shaped "Broad Arrow" on trees reserved for the Navy and then to protect the marked trees from private timber cutters. In 1721, an Act of Parliament prohibited the unlicensed cutting of any white pine tree, regardless of size, not growing within a designated township. The hated regulation brought constant violations, physical abuse of the agents responsible for enforcing it, numerous lawsuits over titles to private property, the creation of "paper townships" designed to evade the law, and political conflict between the colonial government and the timber cutters. This "woodland rebellion," writes historian Charles Clark, "was a precursor to the conflicts that eventually produced the American Revolution."[30]

Like those later conflicts, this one threatened the settlers' profitable commercial activities, particularly the ocean trade they had developed absent regulations from England. Some ships sailed to the West Indies with lumber, barrel staves, and "trash fish," returning with cargoes of rum and molasses. Barbados was the most profitable Caribbean market, as Barbadians needed clapboards, shingles, and oak barrels in return for their rum, molasses, and sugar. Other ships sailed for southern Europe, carrying better grades of fish, and brought salt, wine, and brandy back to New Hampshire.[31]

Meanwhile, away from the coast, New Hampshire communities measured their economic development by the extent of their shift away from extractive industries, such as fishing and lumbering, and toward agriculture. As the seventeenth century yielded to the eighteenth, the fishing industry moved away from the coastal villages of New Hampshire to richer fishing grounds in Newfoundland and Nova Scotia. Similarly, years of indiscriminate logging had diminished coastal forests, forcing the lumber industry inland. Coastal merchants now ran the industry from afar. Besides, many English settlers believed that farming fostered the Puritan virtues that had inspired the settlers to emigrate to New Hampshire: hard work, the importance of property and community, a close family life, and the chance to develop mechanical and entrepreneurial skills.[32]

By the time a frontier settlement had become an established town, the principal occupation of almost every householder was farming, which demanded skill, resourcefulness, and an extra portion of patience. To clear even the smallest pasture for cultivation, one had to cut and burn trees or "girdle" them by cutting a ring around the tree, leaving it to die and be burned another year. Once some land was cleared, the farmer would follow a spring rain by planting seeds in holes or crevices because plowing was impossible until the land was relatively free of stones, which had to be dug out by hand and piled along the edge of the field, a process that usually required three years to clear even a rough pasture.[33] Thus, the stone walls that surround New Hampshire pastures today, inspiring hikers, artists, and photographers, are the artifacts of a long-ago farm family's dogged struggle against a hostile landscape.

The Puritan ethic valued community as well as hard work, though, so farm families organized themselves as residents of towns. The town had been the preferred form of local government in New Hampshire since the mid-1650s, following the Massachusetts model. The town concept provided a process by which community leaders were chosen and their respective responsibilities were defined. Annual elections enabled the removal from office of any moderator, selectman, fence viewer, constable, or other official who proved to be incompetent or corrupt in carrying out his responsibilities.[34] Reflecting that success, towns proliferated in New Hampshire in the eighteenth century, as 60 percent of the state's 234 municipalities (221 towns and 13 cities) were settled between 1715 and 1765.[35]

If farming facilitated municipal organization, it also depended on family units, preferably large ones, to manage the multiple tasks associated with farm life. Although many of the original immigrants to New Hampshire were single, by the mid seventeenth century (1640–80), more residents lived inside than outside of family units. The adoption of a town form of government, the availability of land, and the promise of economic opportunity spurred people to seek a permanent location in which to raise a family. The settlers produced a new generation of children whose numbers gradually reduced the large gender imbalance that had favored men, thereby promoting the formation of additional families.[36]

Beyond one's family and town, all English settlers were subject to the authority of the colonial government. The model for each New England state called for a royal governor—or his lieutenant governor stand-in—to exercise the ultimate executive authority, the limits of which were specified both by the chief executive's commission and by instructions from the Board of Trade, which managed the North American colonies for the Crown. A royally appointed council, which possessed a mixture of legislative, executive, and judicial responsibilities, assisted the chief executive. The third component of colonial government was a body of representatives elected from within the various towns in the colony, which was known as either the assembly or the house of representatives. Within this structure, the royal governor of New Hampshire had great authority. He could suspend members of the council and appoint temporary replacements, decide when elections should occur, convene or dismiss the assembly at will, and veto proposed legislation. He also controlled the colony's militia and, jointly with the council, appointed members of the judiciary. [37]

The governor's authority increased somewhat after 1740, when England's Privy Council—of which the Board of Trade was a part—delineated a clear boundary between New Hampshire and Massachusetts, adding several hundred square miles to New Hampshire. Before 1740, nobody had known for certain where the border between the two colonies lay. The Privy Council's decision established that the boundary line would run three miles north of and parallel to the Merrimack River until the river reached its southernmost point, then would proceed westward.

Another Privy Council decision in 1741 made Benning Wentworth the independent governor of New Hampshire, now separate from Massachusetts. Within two years of Wentworth taking office, a survey of New Hampshire's eastern and southern borders was complete, and Massachusetts authorities reluctantly accepted the results.[38] Benning Wentworth was part of a seacoast aristocracy of prosperous merchant families, centered around Portsmouth, who exercised considerable economic and political power in New Hampshire. Having made fortunes in the shipping industry, these families often rejected the Puritan values of their less affluent neighbors, as reflected in the opulent houses they occupied, which sometimes included enslaved people and indentured apprentices. "To a degree unparalleled north of Virginia," Charles Clark writes, "the gentry of Portsmouth lavished great concern on the preservation and improvement of social status as well as family wealth and power."[39]

Key to Benning Wentworth's aspirations for greater wealth and power was his cavalier assumption that land on both sides of the Connecticut River lay within his jurisdiction. He believed he was authorized to grant townships well to the west of the Connecticut River in what is now Vermont and did so to the tune of 129 townships between 1749 and 1764,[40] even though New York claimed title to the same land.[41] His belief may not have been fanciful, however, because some land agents had confused the Connecticut River with Lake Champlain, which may have caused Wentworth to conclude that New Hampshire extended west of the river to Lake Champlain and Lake George.[42] In any event, Benning and his family members who served in the colonial government rewarded virtually every male member of their extended family with land grants.[43] In 1761 alone, the Wentworth regime, through its New Hampshire Grants, facilitated the chartering of sixty towns on the disputed west side of the Connecticut River and eighteen on the east side.[44] Most of the grants went to speculators—with five hundred acres of each grant reserved to the governor himself—whereupon the speculators sold individual lots to aspiring settlers, leaving to chance the precise form the township would take.[45]

Benning's nephew John was the last member of the Wentworth dynasty to govern New Hampshire; he was just twenty-nine years old when he succeeded his uncle. A warm and gregarious man, the younger Wentworth was open and honest and kept New Hampshire residents loyal to the provincial government during most of his term as governor. He chartered Dartmouth College in 1769 to train clergy, encouraged the settlement of New Hampshire's interior to produce an agricultural surplus for export, and established a system of county courts so people in the northern and western parts of the colony did not have to travel to Portsmouth to transact legal business.

By the 1770s, though, he began to lose political control amidst the growing revolutionary spirit in New Hampshire, which increasingly shifted power to the assembly. In the spring legislative elections of 1774, he requested that delegates be chosen only from the minority of towns where his friends and supporters lived. That request backfired, causing the election of more revolutionaries than had belonged to the previous assembly. Thereafter, he watched helplessly as extralegal meetings supporting independence for the colonies, which he could neither prevent nor influence, occurred in 1775. Ultimately, on June 12, 1775, Wentworth and his family fled to Nova Scotia, where he later became royal governor, never to return to New Hampshire.[46] New Hampshire had effectively ceased to be a British colony.

After John Wentworth's departure, leaders of the colonial assembly took responsibility for creating a new institution comprised of town delegates, which they called the Provincial Congress. That body obtained permission from the Continental Congress to draw up a state constitution.[47] In January 1776, the Provincial Congress declared itself the new House of Representatives of New Hampshire and adopted a written constitution, the first of the former colonies to do so. Thus, by the time the federal Continental Congress had met in Philadelphia to declare independence from Great Britain, New Hampshire had established its own state government.[48] The new constitution confirmed the Seacoast town of Exeter, to which the Assembly had relocated after Wentworth's exit, as the seat of government, and left that government in control for the duration of the Revolutionary War and some time thereafter. This arrangement angered the western towns, which felt underrepresented, as well as Portsmouth, whose citizens fumed at no longer being the seat of government.[49]

Indeed, the new constitution was problematic. The convention that approved the constitution turned itself into the legislature that the constitution established, enjoying almost unlimited powers. The constitution was not subject to ratification by the people. Furthermore, it limited the people's role in government to an annual vote for a representative and a councilor, and it lacked a bill of rights.[50] Still, its adoption coincided with a noteworthy democratization of state government, as men who had not exercised political muscle when the Wentworth oligarchy controlled the assembly and the council now assumed office and wielded power. Indeed, members of the oligarchy largely withdrew from politics during this time.[51]

Because of deficiencies in the 1776 constitution, it is not surprising that in June 1778 a constitutional convention was called to draft a new document. The convention proposed several constitutions that the delegates rejected before they and the voters finally approved one in 1784. Casting off monarchy and oligarchy, it limited executive power—in the form of a popularly elected president (later governor), forbade anyone from holding more than one office at a time, separated the respective branches of government, and established checks and balances between them. It also established a bicameral legislature, including a senate comprised of county-based delegates and a house of representatives, with one member from each town that had at least 150 voters.[52] At the insistence of the western towns, the incorporated town was fixed as the basis for legislative representation. Residents of those towns likely remembered that before the Revolution, they were largely unrepresented in the legislature. In 1773, for example, only 46 of New Hampshire's 147 towns were represented, and 40 percent of the colony's taxes were collected in towns without representation. Thus, the 1784 document sought to resolve a long struggle to link the eastern and western New Hampshire towns under one banner. Despite New Hampshire's small size, the various regions had previously resisted being melded into a cohesive political unit. The new constitution also reflected New Hampshire residents' traditional attachment to their respective towns and to grassroots democracy.[53]

Although the American Revolution upended political traditions in New Hampshire, the war itself had relatively little direct effect on the new state because no fighting occurred within its borders.[54] Indeed, New Hampshire was the only state the British Army did not invade during the war.[55] And the percentage of men who left New Hampshire for extended periods of time during the war was much smaller than the comparable figures during the various colonial wars noted earlier. After 1776, that percentage never exceeded one tenth of those who were eligible for military service. Moreover, the state's population continued to increase during the war and immediately thereafter, reaching 95,000 by the mid-1780s.[56]

Still, a New Hampshire man, General John Stark, was a hero of the Battle of Bennington in 1777. In July of that year, authorities in Vermont, which was then an independent republic, sought New Hampshire's help in defeating British commander General John Burgoyne, as he marched down the Champlain Valley, seeking to cut New England off from the rest of the colonies. New Hampshire's Assembly persuaded General Stark—who coined the phrase "Live Free or Die"—to come out of retirement and lead the New Hampshire troops. The Americans' victory at the Battle of Bennington foiled Burgoyne's strategy and gave them confidence that by fighting guerilla style in the woods, they could neutralize the British soldiers' superior numbers and firepower.[57] By 1778, after the capture of Burgoyne's army following battles at Stillwater and Saratoga in New York State, the Americans' fear of a British invasion from Canada diminished, and the locus of the war moved southward. In that same year, some New Hampshire troops fought at the Battle of Monmouth in New Jersey. Finally, in 1781, New Hampshire troops fought at the Battle of Yorktown in Virginia, where they captured General Cornwallis's army, effectively ending the fighting and ensuring American independence.[58]

Two years later, a peace treaty ended the American Revolution, but not the disputes regarding titles to land west of the Connecticut River, where about one hundred towns chartered under the New Hampshire Grants were located. Contrary to Benning Wentworth's wishes, the British Crown had determined in 1764 that the river should form the boundary between New York and New Hampshire; hence, the towns west of the river belonged to New York. Ultimately, these towns joined Vermont when it became an independent republic subject to a constitution in 1777. To complicate matters, though, thirty-six towns located on the east bank of the river that were unhappy with their lack of representation under New Hampshire's 1776 constitution, temporarily joined Vermont in June 1778.[59] But this first of two "Eastern Unions" between Vermont and certain New Hampshire towns ended when Ethan Allen persuaded members of the Vermont Assembly that Congress would not grant Vermont statehood as long as the Eastern Union existed. The Assembly dissolved the cross-border union on October 21, 1778.

The Eastern Union resurfaced in 1781–82, however, as the Vermont Assembly voted to annex thirty-four Connecticut River Valley towns, along with fifteen Hudson Valley, New York, towns, creating a "Greater Vermont" that doubled the physical size of the Green Mountain State, greatly increased its population, and "extended its jurisdiction west to the Hudson River and north through the Champlain Valley to Canada.[60] The matter languished until 1782, when the Vermont Assembly, at the urging of George Washington, renounced any jurisdiction over towns east of the Connecticut River or west of Lake Champlain. Thus, the river became the boundary between New Hampshire and Vermont, which it still is today.[61]

Other important changes also followed the war. On June 21, 1788, New Hampshire ratified the United States Constitution by a 57–47 vote. New Hampshire's tally was the ninth and decisive vote for ratification.[62] In the 1790s the character of American and New Hampshire politics began to change with the emergence of two political parties—the Federalists and the

Jeffersonian Republicans. The Federalists, who included George Washington, achieved early dominance in New Hampshire, enjoying their greatest success in March 1799, when Governor John Taylor Gilman was elected to his sixth successive one-year term with 86 percent of the vote and the Jeffersonians in the state legislature were virtually wiped out.[63] The Federalists dominated areas of the state involved in commerce, such as the Seacoast and the Connecticut River Valley, which favored a strong national government that could foster economic development and protect the rights of creditors. In contrast, the Jeffersonians appealed to farmers in the Merrimack Valley, who were relatively isolated, largely self-sufficient, and without opportunities to develop markets for their surplus produce. Forced to pay cash for necessities obtained from coastal merchants at high prices, they distrusted banks and ardently supported paper money.[64]

The Jeffersonian philosophy of government coincided with the values of many New Hampshire farmers because both favored frugal government, distrusted banks, and resisted federal government expenditures for the internal improvements of the day, such as roads, bridges, and canals. In short, Jeffersonian principles reflected many of the principles in the New Hampshire Constitution: small government with checks on executive power, broad representation of the people in government, and rotation in office.[65] After 1800, the Federalists' early dominance of New Hampshire politics gave way, first to a competitive two-party system and later, dominance by the Jeffersonian Republicans. Thomas Jefferson won a close presidential election in 1800, followed by a landslide in 1804, losing the electoral votes of only Connecticut and Delaware.[66] In 1808, Concord replaced Exeter as New Hampshire's capital, reflecting the Jeffersonians' growing political clout relative to that of the old Seacoast aristocracy. Between 1809 and 1816, the two parties competed evenly, with each one winning four of the eight annual elections, as foreign policy issues related to the War of 1812 dominated the debate. After the war's end in 1814, though, the Federalists floundered, both nationally and in New Hampshire. By 1818, no state senator in New Hampshire was a Federalist, and after 1820, the party made no organized effort at the polls.[67] Its force was spent.

The nineteenth century brought big economic changes to New Hampshire, which challenged the prevailing belief that the state should be an agrarian republic in the Jeffersonian tradition. These economic changes reflected the reality that market forces and thin, rocky soil were making agriculture unprofitable in New Hampshire and necessitating a search for alternatives. Even Governor Isaac Hill, a passionate Jeffersonian, recognized the problem, informing the legislature as early as 1836 that parts of New Hampshire, particularly the Merrimack River Valley, no longer produced enough food to feed their people and had begun to rely on other locations for food supplies.[68] By the 1850s, a New England farmer spent forty to fifty cents to produce a bushel of corn, whereas an Illinois farmer spent only twelve to fifteen cents to do so. Predictably, then, New Hampshire began to see an exodus of young people from the farms—in the second decade of the nineteenth century sixty-one towns lost population.[69] Often, the young men went west in search of more and better land, whereas their sisters pursued steady wages in the budding textile industry in Manchester and Nashua.[70]

Nevertheless, Andrew Jackson's Democratic Party, which had succeeded the Jeffersonians and controlled New Hampshire politics by 1832, continued to row against the current, especially the party's radical wing, known as the "Locofocos." They sought to shrink the industrial segment of the state's economy until that economy rested entirely on farming, even though, by 1840, New Hampshire ranked ninth out of thirty states in the percentage of its capital that was invested in manufacturing. The Locofocos resisted allowing railroads, then in their infancy, to take land by eminent domain, thereby delaying railroad construction to the point that only fifty-seven miles of track were laid in New Hampshire during a five-year period in the 1840s. They also blocked industrial growth, failing to charter one new mill or manufacturing company between 1840 and 1842. They even made individual stockholders responsible for the debts of corporations in which these individuals held stock, which for a time made New Hampshire a most undesirable site for a new corporation. Almost as quickly as this trend emerged, though, it abated, as the Puritan ethic that favored progress overcame the rural bias against corporations and industrial development.[71]

Like the Jeffersonians before them, the Democrats promoted democracy, opposed privilege, and extoled the values that had prompted the American Revolution. They were skeptical of federal funding for internal improvements and hostile to a protective tariff against imported goods, primarily because protection for American manufactured goods resulted in farmers and artisans paying higher prices for them.[72] Accordingly, New Hampshire Democrats welcomed President Jackson's veto of a bill to charter a Second Bank of the United States in July 1832; they saw the political battle that had ensued over the charter as a "contest between the Bank and the People."[73]

Jackson had first won the presidency in 1828, despite losing New Hampshire to John Quincy Adams of Massachusetts. In 1832, though, he won reelection while winning New Hampshire by a vote of 26,269 to 19,627 over Henry Clay of Kentucky. Between 1832 and 1855, New Hampshire was a one-party Democratic state, often called "the South Carolina of the North" because it mirrored that state in its dogged allegiance to the Democrats.[74] They survived the rise of an opposition party—the Whigs—in 1838, internal divisions over state matters, and, until 1855, an insurgency of party members who were antislavery. Indeed, in 1852, a New Hampshire Democrat—Franklin Pierce—even won the White House, capturing twenty-seven of thirty-one states in the general election. Pierce defeated Whig candidate Winfield Scott despite having been the surprise Democratic nominee, selected on the forty-ninth ballot. Beginning in 1855, though, the slavery issue tore the Democratic Party apart, relegating it to minority status in New Hampshire politics.[75]

During the Democrats' heyday, their candidates fared best in the poorer towns as well as in the more productive farming communities of the White Mountains, but they were competitive with the Whigs almost everywhere in the state. As late as the late 1840s and early 1850s, only in 39 of 210 towns did Democratic candidates regularly receive less than 45 percent of the votes cast, whereas in 117 towns, they usually won more than 55 percent. The Whigs, on the other hand, were most successful in the towns of the Connecticut River Valley, the lower Merrimack River Valley, and the Seacoast Region.[76] In the 1832 presidential election, the archetypal "Andrew Jackson town" in New Hampshire was—appropriately enough—Jackson (formerly named Adams), a small White Mountain community of 515 residents. It was poor because its farms were small and its soil was rocky; indeed, only fifteen New Hampshire towns had a smaller tax base. "The strongest Democratic towns in New Hampshire," historian Donald B. Cole wrote, "were Democratic principally because they were rural, poor, small, not Congregational, and out of the mainstream of New Hampshire life."[77] In 1832 Andrew Jackson received all eighty-five of Jackson's votes. In contrast, the archetypal "Henry Clay" town was Exeter, a community of more than 3,000 people in the Seacoast Region whose tax base was almost twice the size of Jackson's. It boasted stately homes, two Congregational churches, and a manufacturing company. Henry Clay won Exeter by a vote of 307–140 in 1832.[78]

In the 1840s and 1850s both the Democrats and the Whigs in New Hampshire suffered from bitter internal divisions attributable largely to slavery—whether it should be permitted to spread to the growing territories and, later, whether it should be abolished throughout the United States. Reflective of this partisan maelstrom was the public career of John Parker Hale, who was elected once to Congress from New Hampshire and three times to the Senate. During his lone House term, as a Democrat, he became a vehement opponent of slavery and its extension, along with the annexation of Texas in 1845. The New Hampshire Democrats, led by Franklin Pierce—who supported slavery as the price of maintaining the Union and saw abolitionists as selfish and divisive—declined to renominate Hale for a second term.[79] After his subsequent election to the Senate, Hale stood almost alone in that body for two years as a spokesman for the antislavery movement, having been the first senator elected by an antislavery coalition and the first one who had embraced the antislavery cause before his election.[80] The predominantly Democratic legislature rebuffed Hale's reelection bid in 1852, but he was reelected in 1855 to an unexpired term and again in 1858 to a full six-year term, as a Republican by a predominantly Republican legislature.[81] The state legislature denied him reelection in 1864, believing he had served long enough, so Hale was unable to celebrate emancipation or assist in restoring southern states to the Union, for by then he was serving as the American minister to Spain.[82]

By 1855 the Democrats were a minority party in New Hampshire, and the Whigs had disappeared. Both parties were casualties of the new Republican Party, a coalition of disaffected Democrats, northern Whigs, and former members of the antislavery Free Soil Party. By 1856, the Republicans had fashioned a coalition that mirrored the Whigs' appeal to the business and professional classes, opposed slavery to varying degrees, and resented Catholicism and the immigrants who practiced it.[83] In 1860, Republican Abraham Lincoln won New Hampshire on his way to the White House, amassing 57.3 percent of the Granite State's vote against three other candidates; in 1864, Lincoln's New Hampshire tally declined to 52.5 percent, but he won reelection nonetheless.[84] The Republicans dominated state politics in New Hampshire for the next hundred years.

The Civil War and Its Aftermath

The Civil War affected New Hampshire profoundly, even though none of the war's military confrontations occurred there. Several New Hampshire regiments were in the thick of the fighting: the Second fought in the Peninsula campaign in Virginia and at the Peach Orchard in Pennsylvania; the Third at the Wilderness in Virginia; the Sixth at Vicksburg in Mississippi; the Ninth at Antietam in Maryland; the Eleventh at Spotsylvania, Virginia; and the Twelfth at Chancellorsville, Virginia. But no New Hampshire regiment saw more action or took more casualties than the Fifth, which fought at Antietam in Maryland; at Chancellorsville, Fair Oaks, Fredericksburg, and Farmville in Virginia; and at Gettysburg in Pennsylvania. Of the Fifth's original 1,012 soldiers, nearly one in five died in battle, and fewer than one in ten remained with the regiment after two years of service.[85]

The war's consequences continued long after the fighting ended, though. Notably it prompted migration away from the small farms and the granite hills to cities and to more fertile land in the Midwest, where one could grow cash crops instead of settling for subsistence agriculture. In the 1870s, for example, more than 9,000 people worked in textile mills in Manchester out of a total population of 23,000. Even in small villages, such as Allenstown and Berlin, more than half the population held industrial jobs. Most rural communities lost population steadily.[86] Indeed, between 1880 and 1900, New Hampshire's urban population increased by 35.9 percent, whereas its rural population declined by 44.9 percent.[87] An example of the nineteenth-century farm exodus is the Town of Washington in southwestern New Hampshire. First settled in 1768, it was incorporated in 1776, the first town in the United States to be named for George Washington. Considerable growth during the next fifty years enabled the town to reach its peak population of 1,135 in 1830. Between 1830 and 1850, it lost population as the viability of farming declined, but it still had more than a thousand inhabitants in 1850. By 1880, though, the population had shrunk to 682.[88] And the number of farms in town dropped from more than one hundred in 1860 to sixty in 1920 and forty-nine in 1925.[89]

The post–Civil War era brought some modest gains for New Hampshire women, though. State legislation enacted in 1865 eliminated most of the restrictions that had prevented married women from owning property. New laws also granted married women the right to testify against their husbands in court and to make contracts in their own names. And in 1872 New Hampshire women won the right to serve on local school boards, although they could not vote in school board elections until 1878.[90] By 1900, a total of 170 women served on school boards statewide, and two women were among the five commissioners on the state Board of Charities and Correction.[91]

The growth of urban populations after the Civil War prompted the expansion of state government, even in such a bastion of local autonomy as New Hampshire. During the postwar years, the legislature established a state geologist, public printer, surveyor of hydrographic power, boards of agriculture and pharmacy, a bureau of labor statistics, and a fish commission. New regulations required licenses for physicians and pharmacists and restricted false advertising in sales of commercial fertilizer. And new fishing regulations aimed to replenish the state's declining fish population.[92]

The legislature also gave towns several powers it previously had conferred only by special legislation: eminent domain and the authority to build bridges, jails, sewers, cemeteries, and sidewalks and to establish village greens, parks, and fire reservoirs. In 1870, the lawmakers chartered a state normal school to train teachers, with free tuition for graduates willing to teach in the state for a specified time period, and they began to require state certification for teachers. The following year, the state agricultural college opened its doors, offering free tuition for indigent students. The always-cost-conscious Democrats had opposed both schools but did not try to close them after achieving legislative majorities in 1874.[93] More education legislation followed in 1885, as the legislature sought to consolidate tiny, inefficient rural school districts located within the same town into one district per town. The new law mandated that (1) each town would encompass one school district; (2) each town would take possession of all school buildings and property within its boundaries; (3) elected, three-person schoolboards, serving three-year terms, would govern the new districts; (4) the boards would provide as nearly equal resources as possible to all students within a district; and (5) after five years, any town could vote to return to the old system if it wished.[94]

But increased funding does not necessarily accompany increased authority, so New Hampshire schools—especially rural schools—often struggled to fund their new responsibilities. Property taxes were the dominant source of public money, and town governments collected them locally. Towns then contributed a fixed amount to the state government—ranging from $400,000 to $500,000 in 1900, along with a small percentage to their county government. The state redistributed most of this income (along with corporate tax income) to the towns, but rural towns invariably felt deprived in the delivery of public services because their property tax yields were inadequate, especially if their property lists included abandoned farms.[95]

Under these circumstances, the turn of the twentieth century saw multiple campaigns to enact a statewide, broad-based tax (e.g., an income or sales tax) to pay for public education. The State Teachers' Association, successive state school superintendents, and the Grange—a nationwide advocacy group for farmers and rural communities—often led the charge for change. Ultimately, though, these efforts failed.[96]

The only other societal change after the Civil War as significant as the exodus from New Hampshire's farms was the state's embrace of the railroads. The Republicans, who dominated New Hampshire politics after the war, promoted railroads instead of regulating them, by ignoring or repealing regulations the Democrats had implemented decades earlier. Small rail lines had existed in New Hampshire since 1836, but in the 1870s and 1880s, with most state politicians cheering it on, the industry consolidated at a furious pace, as many small operators became a few large ones. That process concluded in the 1890s, when the Boston & Maine Railroad (B&M), headquartered in Boston, absorbed the Concord Railroad—the last of the state's locally controlled rail lines.[97] The B&M consolidated its hold on New Hampshire politics by awarding either a small retainer or a free pass to almost every newspaper editor and lawyer in the state—including legislators—thereby silencing likely opponents and causing potential plaintiffs to face huge obstacles when contemplating a lawsuit against the B&M. Beyond that, B&M executive John Sanborn bestowed electoral endorsements on political candidates whose views were congenial to his company and made sure that members of the state's Railroad Commission championed its interests.[98] Under these circumstances, it is no wonder that, by 1900, the B&M controlled 1,136 miles of track in New Hampshire—all but twenty-two of the state's railroad miles—and that residents referred to it simply as "The Railroad."[99]

The increased importance of the railroad industry after the Civil War also facilitated the development of other nascent industries in New Hampshire, notably, the timber and tourist industries. The initial prompt for the timber industry was the decline of farming in the mid-nineteenth century; the hilly country that had been farmland gradually became timberland, as former pastures and farm fields returned, naturally, to forests. The state's 1867 sale of 172,000 acres of land in the White Mountains to local landowners and speculators for $25,000—to aid public schools—also boosted the timber industry.[100] Railroad tracks into the forests made the traditional log drives on rivers less efficient, and the advent of major wood-products firms such as the Berlin Mills Company and the International Paper Company meant that shipping logs elsewhere for processing was no longer necessary.[101] But the relative ease of hauling timber along logging roads to a railroad siding, following unsustainable clear-cutting—harvesting all growth from a particular forest lot simultaneously—created unsightly and ecologically unhealthy "death valleys" where primeval forests had once stood. When an area was stripped of timber, the temporary logging camps and the portable sawmills would move to another location and repeat the process.[102]

The timber companies, though, had not anticipated the resistance that emerged from the budding tourist industry. Tourists and outdoor enthusiasts were disgusted with the loggers' slipshod harvesting tactics, which left behind debris that precipitated floods and forest fires. Indeed, timber industry excesses spurred awareness of the need to protect woodlands from irresponsible forestry practices. As early as 1885, state legislators began to feel pressure from the emerging tourist industry to end such practices, which prompted the creation of a commission to investigate the condition of the state's forests. Over time, a coalition of parties interested in responsible forest management—nature lovers, innkeepers, and like-minded politicians—began to advocate for such management. As a result, in 1901 a group of state leaders formed the Society for the Protection of New Hampshire Forests, which continues to pursue that mission today. In 1911, Congress passed the Weeks Act, which enabled public ownership of close to 700,000 acres of land for conservation and recreation, to be called the White Mountain National Forest.[103]

Thus, ironies abound in the post–Civil War economic development of New Hampshire. The same railroads that facilitated irresponsible forestry practices also brought to northern New Hampshire the vacationers and outdoor enthusiasts who helped to end, or at least mitigate, those practices. Because of their efforts and those of succeeding generations, by the 1980s, nearly 90 percent of New Hampshire was once again woodland, and many former logging roads had become hiking trails in the National Forest.[104]

The Twentieth Century and Beyond

By 1910, the B&M had secured a hold on New Hampshire politics, enabling it to routinely elect favored candidates—usually Republicans—to the legislature, Executive Council, governorship, and Congress. In 1901, the railroad was even able to prevent the reelection by the legislature of United States Senator William E. Chandler, a progressive Republican who had long been a vocal critic of the railroad's political influence. At that time, before passage of the Seventeenth Amendment to the federal Constitution provided for the direct election of senators, state legislatures chose senators, and the B&M controlled enough legislators' votes to deny Senator Chandler a third term.[105]

But Chandler was not the only Republican to challenge the B&M's control of New Hampshire politics. In 1906 a group calling itself the Lincoln Republicans organized in support of the gubernatorial candidacy of Winston Churchill, a novelist from the small Connecticut Valley town of Cornish. Churchill, whose brand of Republicanism rejected the railroads' and party leaders' control of the party, failed to win the governorship in 1906. Four years later, though, fellow progressive Robert Bass used New Hampshire's new direct primary law—which had ended B&M-controlled party conventions for nominating candidates—to win that post.[106] Bass's sole term as governor brought changes such as the establishment of a public service commission to regulate public utilities, a tax commission, and a workers' compensation program for workers injured on the job. Bass also signed into law acts defining and prohibiting certain corrupt practices in government, barring political activity by corporations, requiring disclosure of political campaign contributions, mandating inspections of factories and strict controls on child labor, acquiring for the state the majestic Crawford Notch area in the White Mountains, and establishing the registration and taxation of automobiles, then still new to New Hampshire.[107] Bass was not reelected in 1912, though, because his support for third-party presidential candidate Theodore Roosevelt that year cost him votes among more moderate and conservative Republicans.[108]

Still, Robert Bass was not the last progressive Republican to be elected governor in New Hampshire. Indeed, Gil Winant, a former teacher at St. Paul's School in Concord, was elected three times: in 1924, 1930, and 1932. His first term saw enactment of a large highway-improvement law, a substantial appropriation for the University of New Hampshire, and an appropriation to hire legal counsel to oppose (successfully) B&M's proposal to abandon many of its tracks in New Hampshire—a sure sign of the automobile's ascendancy.[109] In his later administrations, Winant signed legislation that provided a minimum wage for women and minors, put an administrator appointed by the governor in charge of public assistance, increased state aid to cities, regulated banks and sales of stock, and appropriated funds to assist municipalities with hospital construction. His proposals for a forty-eight-hour workweek, personal and corporate income taxes, a teachers' retirement system and an old-age pension law, however, failed.[110] After three terms as governor, he embarked on an international career, including two stints at the International Labor Organization and another, during World War II, as the American ambassador to Great Britain.

Historian James Wright notes that despite their occasional victories, the progressives were unable to wrest control of the Republican Party of New Hampshire for the long term. He also identifies significant barriers the progressives faced in responding to new problems, including shared power, checks and balances, and rotation-in-office. Gubernatorial terms then, as now, are only two years, but early in the twentieth century (unlike today), New Hampshire governors often served only one term, limiting their achievements. They also shared power with the Executive Council, which was responsible for approving gubernatorial appointments and many expenditures, and whose members often served only one term.[111] Under these circumstances, the legislative accomplishments of Governors Bass and Winant are impressive.

More representative of twentieth-century Republican politicians in New Hampshire, though, was H. Styles Bridges, a progressive-turned-conservative who won the governorship in 1934 and served one term before his 1936 election to the United States Senate, where he served until his death in 1961. Bridges's sole term as governor coincided with the demise of the Amoskeag Manufacturing Company of Manchester, which had dominated life in that city for nearly a century. The governor was not responsible for the company's collapse, though; rather, its own inability to adapt to changing economic conditions forced that outcome.

In its heyday, the Amoskeag, as the company was known, was, in the words of one historical study, "a giant."[112] It opened in 1838, but its heyday occurred early in the twentieth century, when it was the world's largest textile plant, employing up to 17,000 workers and encompassing approximately thirty major mills, each of which was equivalent to a large textile mill elsewhere. Early in the company's history, it had employed young women eager to escape the drudgery of farm life, but by the mid-nineteenth century, it began to hire Irish immigrants, who paved the way for French Canadians, Germans, Swedes, Scots, Greeks, and Poles, who made Manchester a multiethnic city. In 1860, 27 percent of Manchester's residents were foreign-born;

by 1910 French Canadians alone comprised 35 percent of the Amoskeag's workforce and 38 percent of Manchester's population.[113]

The company was a one-stop social and financial services organization. Its benevolent paternalism established a playground; sponsored a visiting nurse's service, a shooting club, and a baseball team; put on musicals and Christmas parties; and published a semi-monthly magazine. It also offered house lots to employees after five years of employment and let them pay off half of the mortgage for a dollar; after another five years, the homeowner could pay off the balance for another dollar. The company even helped workers obtain bank loans for home construction.[114] And for women, it offered a welcome alternative to domestic work or taking in laundry because women could perform many of the same jobs in the textile industry that men did, for the same wages. The heavier mechanical jobs, machine repair, and jobs featuring chemical processes were restricted to men, but "in most cases, no clear-cut division between male and female work according to specific job skills had been established."[115] But the good times did not last; after World War I, antiquated machinery, inefficiency, and competition from lower-cost Southern mills all hurt the company's bottom line.

A 1922 cost-cutting measure—longer working hours and a 20 percent wage cut—produced the first long-term strike in the company's history, which lasted nine months and poisoned relations between labor and management. A second strike, in 1933, was violent, requiring intervention by members of the state's national guard.[116] Afterward, because it could not reduce wages further, the company sought to lower costs by speeding up the machinery, which made the workers' lives more difficult and dangerous, souring labor–management relations further. Finally, in 1936, a bankruptcy court ordered the liquidation of the company, which was a major blow amidst the ravages of the Depression.[117] About ten years later, New Hampshire's economy suffered another blow when its other textile giant, the Nashua Manufacturing Company, ceased production.[118]

Still, New Hampshire, like other states, benefitted economically from the military buildup necessitated by America's entry into World War II. During the war, New Hampshire factories accustomed to producing work boots began to produce paratroopers' boots; cotton looms made parachutes and cloth for uniforms; and hosiery mills made gloves. Meanwhile, the paper- and wood-products industry "produced everything from K-ration wrappers to map papers to labels and tapes of all kinds, and a granite company manufactured antitorpedo nets, which were suspended from booms to protect cargo ships from submarine attacks."[119]

Depression and war had nudged New Hampshire out of its staunch Republicanism somewhat; although the Granite State supported Republican Herbert Hoover in the 1932 presidential race and elected Republican Styles Bridges to the governorship once (1934) and the Senate twice (1936 and 1942) during this period, it also elected Democrat Fred Brown to the Senate in 1932 and supported Franklin Roosevelt for president in 1936, 1940, and 1944.[120] After the war, though, the state would elect mostly Republicans to statewide and federal offices for the rest of the twentieth century. A contributing factor in those results was the 1946 purchase of the *Manchester Union Leader*, New Hampshire's only statewide newspaper by William Loeb, a vitriolic archconservative whose front-page editorials lavished praise on his political friends and heaped scorn on his foes. Those editorials reflected what one observer called Loeb's "conspiratorial view of politics, in which the forces of good [were] constantly engaged in a struggle with the forces of evil."[121] In Loeb's mind, the forces of good were small government, low taxes, and a vehement anticommunism; the forces of evil were activist government, the taxes necessary to support it, and a reluctance to use American military force overseas. And a person was either with him or against him.

Loeb's candidate did not always win at the polls. For example, although he had consistently lambasted Thomas McIntyre, a Democratic candidate for Senator Bridges's seat after Bridges's death, McIntyre won the seat in a special election in 1962 and was elected to full Senate terms in 1966 and 1972.[122] Yet Loeb was largely responsible for the political career of Meldrim Thomson, the archconservative owner of a small publishing company whom the *Union Leader* introduced to the New Hampshire electorate and promoted endlessly, fueling Thomson's election as governor in 1972 and reelection in 1974 and 1976. Still, Loeb's greatest influence in New Hampshire politics was indirect. He kept opposition to broad-based taxes front and center, causing candidates to take "the pledge" to veto any proposed income or sales tax. He also likely discouraged potential candidates from running for fear of facing his wrath.[123] Beyond that, because he controlled New Hampshire's largest newspaper, which, by the early 1970s, enjoyed almost 40 percent of the circulation of all dailies published in the state, he commanded an outsized megaphone.[124] Finally, because most aspiring political candidates in New Hampshire feared that Loeb's influence was real, they hedged their bets by either not running for office or trying not to anger him. Thus, Loeb likely influenced more campaign strategies than election results during his tenure in New Hampshire.[125]

Meanwhile, as William Loeb sought to become a kingmaker in New Hampshire politics, the state's economy bumped along in the wake of the mill closures in Manchester and Nashua. The population grew slowly, but it grew older too; in 1952, for example, New Hampshire had a higher proportion of citizens over age sixty-five, relative to its overall population, than any other state.[126] Postwar economic conditions, particularly the loss of war-based government contracts for many mills and factories, made politicians cautious, reinforcing the state's inclination toward small government, frugal budgets, and minimal taxation. Opposition to the enactment of a sales or income tax deepened. But legislators were not averse to taxing their fellow citizens' vices and pastimes—notably, liquor, tobacco, and horse racing. At times, these three taxes produced about two-thirds of New Hampshire's tax revenue. In 1964, the state instituted the first legal sweepstakes lottery to be conducted in the United States in seventy-five years.[127] As postwar tourism developed, rooms and meals taxes were added to the mix.

Tourism was a ray of sunshine amidst the economic clouds. Early in the 1950s , Governor Hugh Gregg (1953–55) initiated a new advertising program that, combined with improved highways, lured tourists to New Hampshire.[128] The improved highways were part of the Eisenhower Interstate Highway System, which created I-89, I-93, and I-95, all of which made northern New Hampshire's forests and ski slopes more accessible than ever before from metropolitan areas to the south.

New Hampshire's leaders had known since the late nineteenth century that tourism would supplant agriculture in economic importance someday; hence, they had long encouraged the renting of rooms in farmhouses to summer boarders, such as teachers, librarians, writers, and others with extended summer vacations. Later, summer hotels emerged; usually, they were wooden structures with thirty or forty bedrooms upstairs and large public rooms downstairs. As early as the 1880s and 1890s, some people bought second homes for summer use, usually abandoned farms whose owners had left for the West or a city years before.[129] Poet Donald Hall has recounted the triumphs and tragedies of New Hampshire's agriculture-to-tourism transition in a poignant boyhood memoir, *String Too Short to Be Saved*.[130]

By the 1930s, although summer visitors remained the backbone of the tourist industry, a new market had emerged—winter visitors interested in skiing. The B&M Railroad operated the first ski train, bringing skiers to New Hampshire in 1931, and eight years later the Eastern Slope Ski School opened in North Conway. World War II put skiing on hold for several years, but it resumed after the war, restoring and expanding New Hampshire's winter tourism season. By the 1980s, tourism and recreation—including skiing—provided between 10 and 15 percent of New Hampshire's annual income.[131]

The tourist industry may owe a debt to New Hampshire's presidential primary election for helping to make the state's lakes, mountains, beaches, and other amenities more visible to the potential visitor than they would otherwise be.[132] The primary began in 1915; in 1920, it became the first presidential primary on the calendar every four years. Initially, though, voters were only able to select delegates to the political parties' national nominating conventions; they could not vote for presidential candidates directly. Consequently, the voters and the press could not easily determine who the "winner" was, which limited public interest in the event. But in 1949, Governor Sherman Adams signed a law allowing primary voters to express a candidate preference in addition to selecting delegates. Three years later, New Hampshire's revamped and more visible primary coincided with a decision by World War II hero General Dwight Eisenhower to allow his name to appear on the ballot as a Republican despite not yet having committed to running.[133] Since then the New Hampshire primary has achieved a prominent, even iconic, status in American politics.

The biggest economic boost for New Hampshire in the twentieth century, though, was the arrival of "high-tech" manufacturing in the state's southernmost counties, which abut Massachusetts. This business began in the Boston area after World War II but, as the 1970 Census showed, a substantial portion of it later moved to New Hampshire. The state's population grew from 606,921 in 1960 to 787,681 in 1970, a 21 percent increase. For the first time since the dawn of the Census in 1790, New Hampshire had grown more rapidly than the United States as a whole. Its lower cost of living, access to transportation routes, and proximity to several universities had made it a desirable location for high-tech manufacturing.[134]

This unprecedented growth had noteworthy political consequences, shifting the balance of two-party strength in the state toward the Democrats. In 1968, the Republicans had an edge of 60,000 registered voters over the

Democrats. By 1980, though, the gap had shrunk to 40,000 voters, as the Republicans were 40.1 percent, Democrats were 32.5 percent, and Independents were 27 percent of registered voters in New Hampshire.[135] Much of this partisan shift was the result of former Massachusetts residents relocating to New Hampshire.[136] Thus, the same population growth that fueled economic development in the state—which Republican officials generally welcomed—also boosted the electoral fortunes of Democratic candidates.

Democrats were especially successful in congressional races, likely because the tax issue was largely absent there, reducing the clout of William Loeb's *Manchester Union Leader*. For example, as early as the mid-1970s, the four-member New Hampshire congressional delegation featured three Democrats, including First District Congressman Norman D'Amours and Senators Thomas McIntyre and John Durkin.[137] On the state level, Democrat Hugh Gallen defeated incumbent Republican Meldrim Thomson for governor in 1978 after Thomson's favored energy project—the Seabrook Nuclear Power Station—proved so expensive to construct that the owner proposed a surcharge on electric rates to help pay for it.[138]

Still, the Republican Party was far from dead despite Hugh Gallen's election in 1978 and reelection in 1980. After Gallen's 1982 reelection loss to John Sununu, the governorship remained in Republican hands until 1996, when Jeanne Shaheen beat Ovide Lamontagne to become the first woman to win the governorship and the first Democrat to do so in fourteen years. Both the Gallen and Shaheen victories underscored the observation in 1986 by former New Hampshire Democratic Party chair Joe Grandmaison that "if [the Republican] candidate is too far to the right . . . then our candidate can pull in undeclared voters and liberal Republicans."[139] Moderation enabled Jeanne Shaheen to be reelected governor in 1998 and 2000. It also fueled four gubernatorial wins by fellow Democrat John Lynch between 2004 and 2010. Another moderate Democrat—Maggie Hassan—won the office in 2012 and 2014, before Chris Sununu (the son of Governor John Sununu) reclaimed it for the Republicans in 2016.[140] In 2006 Democrats also captured the state's two congressional seats and secured majorities in both houses of the state legislature for the first time since 1872. In 2018, the Democrats won control of both houses of the state legislature by flipping party control of five seats in the senate and gaining nearly sixty seats in the house. They also won a 3–2 majority in the Executive Council for the first time since 2008 by flipping party control of two seats.[141] Thus, rough parity now exists between the two parties; each can claim approximately 40 percent of the adult population.[142] In 2024, Republican Kelly Ayotte succeeded Chris Sununu as governor. At this writing, her party also controls the council and both legislative chambers.

Conclusion

Despite the historical changes noted here, New Hampshire continues to favor local solutions to problems, minimal taxation, and a small state government. Its political culture is reflected in vestiges of the colonial and Revolutionary eras, including a two-year gubernatorial term, an Executive Council, and a large legislature whose members earn just $100 per year for their service.[143] To be sure, noteworthy policy changes have occurred: same-sex marriages are now legal and the death penalty is illegal in New Hampshire.[144] But voters remain allergic to broad-based taxes, and twenty-first-century problems, such as housing and school funding, challenge the state institutionally and financially. Ultimately, Granite Staters will have to decide whether the type of government they have long favored is a match for the contemporary challenges they face.

CHAPTER THREE

From Independent Republic to Republican Stronghold to Progressive Bastion

A Short Political History of Vermont

The Colonial and Early National Periods

VERMONT'S POLITICAL CULTURE, LIKE New Hampshire's, is the product of multiple causes. This chapter will examine the attitudes, events, and influences that produced the political culture of contemporary Vermont. Once again, Professor Gaddis's observation that "past processes have generated surviving structures—documents, images, memories—that allow us to reconstruct . . . what happened" will guide the examination.[1]

During the colonial era, Vermont was "a land in between" New Hampshire and New York, both of which sought to absorb it.[2] The eager settlers who poured into this territory after the French and Indian War ended in 1763 entered a legal no-man's land: the New Hampshire Grants. Governor Benning Wentworth of New Hampshire had been issuing grants of land to establish towns on both sides of the Connecticut River since before the war began in 1754. He issued his first charter west of the river—for what is now Bennington, Vermont—in 1749, to be followed by fifteen more charters through 1753.

Land settlement was stalled during the war because the frontier was unsafe. Afterward, Wentworth resumed granting land even though titles were disputed, as New York contested his jurisdiction to issue land grants west of the Connecticut River. According to the "Yorkers," those lands belonged to New York. Despite New York's claims, Wentworth continued granting lands and chartering townships west of the river until early 1764, when the Board of Trade in London ordered him to cease because the Crown had determined that the lands west of the river were in New York.[3]

Most of the settlers and land speculators who obtained their grants from Governor Wentworth refused to surrender their claims or pay New York authorities for the land, opting instead for litigation and armed resistance.[4] Before recounting the litigation and the armed resistance in more detail, though, it is necessary to discuss the Abenaki people, whom the litigation and the armed resistance partially displaced in Vermont. They are part of Vermont's political origin story, and their lives debunk the long-standing myth that Vermont was uninhabited until the late eighteenth century.

Hindsight suggests that conflict between the European settlers and the Abenakis was almost inevitable. The latter valued cooperation and unselfishness, not individualism and acquisitiveness. Individuals were expected to be satisfied with life as it was instead of wishing it were otherwise. Humans were viewed as part of the natural order rather than superior to it; therefore, one should not try to alter the natural order, but rather, to fit into it. And egalitarianism was paramount, so whatever one had was shared freely with other members of one's kinship group. The more resources one possessed, the more one was expected to share them.[5]

The arrival of Europeans profoundly affected the Abenakis' way of life. Their traditional seminomadic lifestyle gradually broke down as they concentrated on trading furs for tools, cloth, and metal jewelry and grew dependent on Europeans or raids on other Native communities for food.[6] European diseases reduced Native populations throughout New England by 90 percent during the colonial era. Several epidemics preceded the founding of Fort Dummer (in southeastern Vermont) in 1724, and even more epidemics preceded the influx of migrants to Vermont from the Puritan colonies of southern New England after 1763. As a result, when the migrants began to flood into the Upper Connecticut and Missisquoi Valleys during the 1760s, they did not encounter Native people in the southern portions of those valleys, but only farther north, where the Abenakis occupied the most desirable land.[7]

Fearing the fast-approaching settlers, the Abenakis negotiated long-term leases of land and formally appealed to British authorities, especially those in Canada. British authorities in Canada were more sympathetic to the Abenakis' claims than were British authorities in New Hampshire and New York, with whom the Abenakis had battled for almost a century. Therefore, when the American Revolution broke out, the Abenakis withdrew to land north of Lake Champlain, out of the line of fire between the British and the Americans. Most tried to remain neutral, although some sided with the British, seeing England as a guarantor of their territorial rights, unlike the colonists, whom they viewed as invaders. The likely source of this view was the Quebec Act of 1774, which prohibited settlement of lands west and northwest of the Appalachian Mountains that the Americans coveted. The most accurate characterization of the Abenaki attitude toward the revolution, though, is ambivalence. Some supported the British, others even supported the Americans, but most sought to avoid the conflict altogether.[8]

In October 1780, Abenaki warriors joined British troops in a raid on the town of Royalton, where they burned buildings, scattered and slaughtered livestock, killed four settlers, destroyed crops and other food sources, and took thirty-two captives. Returning north, they burned the neighboring town of Randolph.[9] The Royalton raid, and similar actions along the New York frontier at Lake George and in the Mohawk Valley north of Albany, aimed to prevent a second American attempt at invading Canada (a previous try had failed) and to force the Americans to exhaust scarce resources in defending their northern frontier. The Abenakis' "tracking and woodcraft skills and familiarity with the wilderness" were immensely valuable to the British.[10]

While the Abenakis struggled to maintain their foothold on the northern frontier, the conflicting claims of New Hampshire and New York to the "land in between" them continued, prompting many settlers to support the American Revolution. They equated their wish to be free of New York's jurisdiction over the New Hampshire Grants to the colonies' wish to be free of Britain's jurisdiction over America. That feeling emerged and gradually intensified in the years following the Treaty of Paris in 1763, which ended the French and Indian War and made the northern frontier part of the British Empire. A question remained, though, as to which British colony—New York or New Hampshire—would control it. New York anchored its claim in the 1664 grant by King Charles II to his brother James, the Duke of York, who later became King James II and dubbed the granted lands "New York." Based on that grant, New York contended that all land west of the Connecticut River belonged to it. Still, the land descriptions and boundaries in the grant reflected a limited knowledge of the region's geography; hence, the grant's authority was in doubt a century later when New Hampshire and New York both claimed the territory between the Connecticut River in the east and Lake Champlain in the west.[11]

By 1764, when Governor Wentworth ceased making land grants, he had granted charters to 138 towns, encompassing nearly three million acres, or approximately one-third of the future Vermont, pocketing a fee with each grant.[12] In that same year, as settlers began to occupy the disputed territory, the King and his advisers tried to resolve disputed land claims by declaring the west bank of the Connecticut River to be the boundary between New Hampshire and New York. That action resolved nothing; on the contrary, by placing holders of titles conveyed by Governor Wentworth in New York, where their claims were invalid, rather than in New Hampshire, it instead spurred the litigation and armed resistance noted earlier.[13] Settler responses to the King's order derived from a difference in the law of land ownership between New York and the New England colonies from which the new settlers had come.

Under New Hampshire law, the settlers who purchased land according to a township charter granted by Governor Wentworth owned that land outright upon paying the purchase price. In legal parlance, the settler owned the land in fee simple absolute, which gave him unconditional authority to sell it or give it away during his lifetime. If the settler died without a will, the property went to his heirs. Under New York law, however, settlers could not enjoy fee simple ownership, but instead, only leases from large landowners who held "patents" from the King and collected annual "quitrents" from their leaseholders.[14] And those quitrents were considerably higher than the prices paid by settlers for land under New Hampshire law. Indeed, when pleading New York's case to the Board of Trade, Governor Cadwallader Colden had emphasized that New York would lose up to one thousand pounds annually if New Hampshire law governed the disputed territory.[15]

The impetus for settlement was overcrowding in Connecticut and Massachusetts, where large farming families found the prospect of acquiring enough land to divide amongst their children increasingly unlikely. In Connecticut, for example, between 1732 and the mid-1760s, the population had grown from 32,000 to 150,000, making it the most densely populated American colony.[16] Thus, land-hungry migrants headed north in the 1760s in two distinct waves. One wave included people from places generally east of Hartford, Connecticut, and from eastern Massachusetts. Another wave followed the Housatonic River north from western Connecticut to establish homesteads in western Vermont. The second wave included the Allen family.[17]

As a speculator who bought and sold land in the New Hampshire Grants in fee simple, Ethan Allen was determined that neither the land he owned nor the land he had sold would fall under New York law. He hated the thought of being a tenant of wealthy New Yorkers such as the Livingston or Schuyler families.[18] But as long as the New Hampshire Grants remained in dispute, he could neither obtain nor give to a buyer clear title to land there. Thus, he had a powerful financial incentive to prevent New York from controlling the "land in between." If New York law governed, the Onion River Land Company that Ethan had formed with his brothers would likely collapse.

Ethan Allen, however, never gave up without a fight. Born in Litchfield, Connecticut, in 1738, he grew up in Cornwall, in that state's northwest corner, where he was a voracious reader and, as a teenager, studied with Reverend Jonathan Lee to prepare for entry to Yale. But when his father died in 1755, Ethan, as the oldest of eight children, had to go to work to help his mother save the family farm and pay his father's debts.[19] He learned the craft of mining iron ore and manufacturing the huge cast iron pots that were a vital part of the potash industry. Potash, the first industrial product of the American colonies, is a chemical salt made by burning hardwood trees to ashes, soaking the ashes in water, and boiling the resulting lye solution down to a powder. It was used in the chemical industry, in gunpowder, and in bleach for dying textiles.[20] Later, Allen owned an open pit lead mine in Northampton, Massachusetts, with his two brothers-in-law. Still later, after banishment from both Salisbury, Connecticut, and Northampton for his irreverence, profanity, and tendency to settle disputes with his fists, Allen spent the winters of 1767–1770 hunting for skins to sell in the spring and feeding his restless spirit amidst the wild, wooded beauty of the New Hampshire Grants.[21]

By 1769, Allen had bought a farm in the small Bennington County town of Sunderland. Soon thereafter, seeking to protect land titles in the Grants from New York authorities, he organized a group of about two hundred men following decisions by the New York Supreme Court that refused to admit their land titles as evidence in litigation. According to the New York court, New Hampshire lacked authority to grant such titles within New York's territorial jurisdiction. Thus began the Green Mountain Boys, who leaped into the confusion and conflict caused by disputed claims to the New Hampshire Grants.[22]

In court, the settlers argued that the use of the words "to be" in the 1764 order that set the Connecticut River as New Hampshire's western boundary signaled a change in jurisdiction, effective from the date of the royal order forward; hence, all New Hampshire charters issued before that date superseded New York's later land grants. New York countered that the 1764 royal order had merely affirmed its ownership of the misnamed New Hampshire Grants.[23] Because the gap between the conflicting claims of jurisdiction could not be bridged, New York held ejectment trials in 1770 and 1771 designed to remove settlers who lived between the Connecticut River and Lake Champlain from its territory unless they paid the fees that New York law required. The settlers lost when the New York court rejected their claim that the Wentworth grants should prevail because they predated those of the New York patent holders.[24]

Ironically, the settlers' lawyer directed Ethan Allen to obtain from New Hampshire authorities copies of the original documents reflecting the land grants and showing Governor Wentworth's authority to make them. But Allen failed to do so, leaving the lawyer without any documentary evidence to support his clients' arguments. No evidence exists to indicate whether Ethan Allen met with New Hampshire authorities, requested specific documents, and was rebuffed or, alternatively, neglected this task entirely. In any event, the settlers lost trials in 1770 and 1771, after which the Green Mountain Boys decided to resist the court's ejectment orders by force.[25]

The creation of the Green Mountain Boys lacks a precise date; historians generally note that the group began after Ethan Allen returned to Bennington from the first round of ejectment trials in 1770, when a meeting of settlers vowed to transition from "the defensive tactics of riot and resistance to offensive insurgency."[26] Additional legal defeats in 1771 and New York's attempts to enforce court judgments inflamed settler passions, spawning armed resistance and threats of violence. Early in January 1771, the sheriff of Albany County tried to serve writs of possession on two Bennington-area settlers, remove them from their properties, and return those properties to the true owners under New York law. But when the sheriff and his posse arrived at John Breakenridge's farm, they encountered a large group of armed men led by Ethan Allen, who threatened to "blow [the sheriff's] brains out" if he tried to enforce the court order. The same scene was repeated at Josiah Fuller's farm.[27]

By the spring of 1771, guerilla warfare was common on the northern frontier. Bands of armed men routinely threatened settlers loyal to New York who remained in the New Hampshire Grants, vowing to destroy their fences, barns, and houses unless they left. Ethan Allen and his associates formed committees of safety in eleven communities in what is now southwestern Vermont, and the Green Mountain Boys unanimously elected him to the paid post of "colonel commandant."[28] Leading an extralegal militia for the New Hampshire Grants was Ethan Allen's first act of open rebellion against British colonial authorities. No militia could be formed legally without the approval of the royal governor of a province. As historian Willard Stearne Randall has observed, though, by late 1773, "the only justice being dispensed on the Grants . . . was the version being practiced by Allen and the Green Mountain Boys."[29]

Allen's frontier justice so angered Governor George Clinton of New York that in March 1774, he ordered the drafting of the Bloody Acts, which required Allen and several associates to surrender within seventy days, or risk being convicted without a trial and executed. Soon thereafter, in the southeastern corner of the Grants, an angry group of settlers opposed to New York's land claims attempted to seize the county courthouse at Westminster. A New York sheriff's posse responded by killing two settlers, wounding two more, and jailing ten. The next day, when the judges tried to convene the court, an even larger crowd freed the prisoners and forced the judges to adjourn. Later, militia from Massachusetts and New Hampshire streamed into town, captured the sheriff and his posse, and marched them off to jail in Northampton, Massachusetts. Ethan Allen, who was both a fighter and a propagandist, dubbed this event the Westminster Massacre.[30]

Even if that characterization was overstated, the episode at Westminster, like the Boston Tea Party, was a part of the prelude to revolution. Just a month after the "massacre," American colonists and British troops fought at Lexington and Concord, Massachusetts. Several weeks later, in May 1775, the Green Mountain Boys and Colonel Benedict Arnold's Massachusetts Militia surprised the British garrison in an early morning raid of Fort Ticonderoga in northern New York, forcing a surrender of the fort. The colonists took fifty prisoners and commandeered 120 cannons, a cache of small arms, and other supplies.[31] News of the fort's capture stunned the Continental Congress, meeting in Philadelphia at the time, which was still hoping to avoid a war with Great Britain. But events quickly overtook the Congress's caution, as spring 1775 ended with the Battle of Bunker Hill in Boston, where 140 Americans died, 301 were wounded, and 30 were taken prisoner. The casualty numbers were even higher for the British, with 1,054 killed or wounded out of 2,000 combatants.[32]

Despite his pre–Revolutionary War prominence, Ethan Allen sat out most of the war as a prisoner of the British Crown. While scouting for the Continental Army, he joined an unauthorized and ill-advised plan to seize Montreal, but anticipated reinforcements never arrived, and Allen's outnumbered troops had to surrender. He remained a prisoner for thirty-two months and later wrote a book that described his treatment, much of it in the disease-infested holds of British warships, as "malevolent cruelty."[33] Still, he avoided the death penalty, thanks to his popularity with the British public, which embraced his swashbuckling-frontiersman image. The British released him in 1778, and he returned to Vermont (by then an independent republic), where Governor Thomas Chittenden appointed him to several public posts, including liaison to the Continental Congress.

Meanwhile, as the war raged on, so did the land dispute between New Hampshire and New York. In May 1777, New York fed the fire by adopting a state constitution that included property qualifications for voting, established electoral districts that disregarded towns, and affirmed all land grants made by the State of New York, thereby invalidating all claims under the New Hampshire Grants.[34] A month later, seventy-two delegates from twenty-two towns west and twenty-six towns east of the Green Mountains convened at Elijah West's tavern in Windsor, where they changed the name of their home from "New Connecticut" to "Vermont" and agreed to hold a constitutional convention in July. At the July convention, also held in Windsor, they approved a constitution and then appointed a Council of Safety to act temporarily as Vermont's new government.[35]

The model for the Vermont Constitution was its Pennsylvania counterpart, although the two were not identical. Dr. Thomas Young, who had been a friend and mentor to Ethan Allen since Allen's boyhood, sent a letter to the delegates before the Windsor convention—along with a copy of Pennsylvania's 1776 constitution—wherein he recommended its adoption "with a very little alteration."[36] Both documents established unicameral (one-house) legislatures, an executive branch that included a governor and an advisory council, and a separate "council of censors" charged with periodically reviewing and recommending changes to both the constitution and particular statutes. But Vermont's constitution, unlike Pennsylvania's, barred property qualifications for voting and called for the governor, lieutenant governor, and the twelve executive councilors to be popularly elected instead of appointed by the legislature. The Vermont Constitution also allowed the governor and council to review legislation before it became law, which the Pennsylvania Constitution did not.[37] Vermont's was the first state constitution to outlaw owning slaves and the slave trade, reflecting the egalitarian and antiauthoritarian sensibilities of its early settlers. Furthermore, it called for compensating private landowners when government took their property for public use.[38]

Despite their passion for democracy, the drafters of Vermont's constitution centralized power within state government. They permitted successive reelections for any executive office, enabling Thomas Chittenden to serve nineteen one-year terms as governor and Ira Allen, Ethan's younger brother, to be reelected treasurer continuously until 1786. During the first eight years of the Executive Council, only twenty men served on that twelve-member body.[39] Moreover, power was centralized in practice as well as in form; from the beginning, the council drafted bills and sent them to the legislature for its concurrence, which was usually achieved because council members not only drafted the bills but also served on the legislative committees that considered and passed them. Absent both separation of powers and term limits for executive officials, the executive branch dominated state government in Vermont during and immediately after the American Revolution.[40]

Perhaps this strong executive authority reflected the delegates' keen awareness that the British Army posed a clear and present danger to Vermont's security. As they pondered the document's proposed provisions, news reached them that British forces had recaptured Fort Ticonderoga. According to the account of Ira Allen, who attended the convention (Ethan was still a prisoner), that news had prompted the delegates to consider leaving Windsor, but a severe thunderstorm delayed their departure, spurring them to return to work and approve the final draft of the new constitution.[41] Later that summer, though, American military fortunes on the northern frontier improved dramatically when New Hampshire and Vermont troops under the command of General John Stark defeated a British force at the Battle of Bennington on August 16.

Despite its name, the battle occurred six miles northwest of Bennington in East Hoosick, New York; in the fighting, Stark's undersized army of 1,800 men routed the British, of whom 200 were killed and 700 captured, about

10 percent of General John Burgoyne's army. The success at Bennington lifted American morale and facilitated Stark's greater success two months later, when his troops blocked the retreat of the weakened British forces at Saratoga, resulting in the surrender of Burgoyne's remaining army of almost six thousand men.[42] When Burgoyne surrendered on October 17, the immediate British threat to the northern frontier temporarily disappeared.[43]

By the fall of 1780, however, the military situation on the northern frontier had deteriorated considerably. After the Battles of Bennington and Saratoga, troops and provisions from forts and supply depots in the north were transferred to buttress General Washington's forces in the south. Frederick Haldimand, the Governor-General of British Quebec, hoped to capitalize on the weakened frontier and on Congress's unwillingness to grant Vermont statehood while the land dispute between New Hampshire and New York continued. He sought to persuade Vermont to reconcile with Britain in return for ending its political battles with New York and Congress and retaining its recent eastern and western acquisitions.[44] The "Haldimand Negotiations," in which Ethan Allen participated, caused a cessation of hostilities in the north. The British hoped to secure Vermont's neutrality for the remainder of the war and its eventual readmission to the British Empire as a distinct colony.[45] Meanwhile, Allen played a dangerous game, shuttling between the British and the American Congress, letting each one know only part of his discussions with the other, thereby keeping Vermont's options open and seeking to foster both its sovereignty and his family's future financial success. Happily, the negotiations produced an exchange of prisoners, among whom were the settlers who had been seized during the Royalton raid in October 1780.[46]

Ultimately, developments on the battlefield ended the negotiations. In October 1781, General Washington's army defeated Lord Cornwallis's forces at Yorktown, Virginia, capturing six thousand British regulars. As an American victory began to appear certain, the British lost interest in Vermont. In 1783 the United States and Great Britain signed the Treaty of Paris, in which the British ceded Vermont to the United States even though Congress had not yet admitted it to the union.[47] Apparently only Great Britain was willing to acknowledge Vermont's sovereignty. Congress had twice promised to admit it as a state, only to renege when New York, determined to preserve its land claims there, threatened to secede from the United States and withdraw its troops from the Continental Army if

Vermont became a state.[48] The second broken promise occurred after Vermont agreed to relinquish its claims to territory in New Hampshire and New York (see Chapter Two).[49]

The stalemate continued into the postwar era until a commission established by the New York Legislature proposed that Vermont pay New York $30,000 in compensation for surrendering its claims to Vermont land. Both states agreed to the proposal, and on March 4, 1791, Vermont became the fourteenth state.[50] At the convention in Bennington to consider statehood, the final vote was 105–4 in favor.[51] Thus ended Vermont's fourteen years as an independent republic, an uncertain status caused by the inability of New Hampshire and New York to enforce their land claims and the impotence of the Continental Congress to resolve the matter expeditiously.[52] Ethan Allen did not live to see that day, having died in 1789.

Vermont also failed to honor Abenaki land claims within its borders. The Abenakis sought to reoccupy their village as the war neared its conclusion, but Ira Allen successfully portrayed them as "Canadian Indians" with no land rights south of the 45th parallel. Foreseeing dispossession, they sought compensation for their lands after the war but were unsuccessful. Eventually, although some tribal members remained in Vermont, others resettled in Odanak, Quebec, where an Abenaki First Nation Reserve exists today.[53]

Thus, the early histories of New Hampshire and Vermont are quite different, notwithstanding the dispossession of Abenaki lands in both states. New Hampshire, first inhabited in the 1620s, was settled initially along the coast, and maritime wealth produced an aristocracy in Portsmouth akin to those in Salem, Boston, and Newburyport, Massachusetts. In contrast, European settlement did not occur in Vermont until the 1760s, and Vermont was predominantly agrarian thereafter. Consequently, as Charles Morrissey has observed, "Vermonters were upcountry people from the outset and plainly democratic in ways unlike the seaport residents."[54] Social equality characterized their relations with each other, as reflected not only in the state constitution's prohibition of slavery and guarantee of universal male suffrage but also in traditional practices, such as work bees and communal barn raisings, which later evolved into electric and food cooperatives.[55]

Politically, the early Vermonters followed the New England tradition of annual town meetings, which they had extended from churches to towns in their previous homes in Massachusetts and Connecticut. They valued democratic practices and resented the ecclesiastical and aristocratic establishments of southern New England and Great Britain. In the Vermonters' view, neither political nor religious authority should reside in any privileged or exclusive group of men.[56] A similar ethic developed in New Hampshire after 1800, thanks to the respective elections of Thomas Jefferson and Andrew Jackson to the presidency. In Vermont, which lacked a seacoast or a merchant aristocracy, an egalitarian, democratic ethic dominated public life from the beginning.

Both economic and political change came rapidly to Vermont after the Revolutionary War. The 1791 census revealed a population of 85,311, two-thirds of whom lived in the four southern counties. By the 1800 census, though, the population had swelled to nearly 155,000, making Vermont the fastest-growing state in the nation, with a population increase of 80.1 percent since 1790.[57] As of 1810, that number had grown by another 41 percent, to a total population of 212,895.[58] But the population growth dipped precipitously in the middle of the nineteenth century, making Vermont the slowest-growing state between 1840 and 1850.[59] After 1820, growth occurred only in larger towns such as Bennington, which had transitioned from subsistence agriculture to commercial farming and manufacturing.[60] During the first two decades of the nineteenth century, subsistence agricultural production gradually gave way to large-scale commercial operations that favored wealthier farmers with enough land and capital to expand production and meet market demands.[61]

Political change paralleled economic change in Vermont. The years between 1783 and 1799 saw a new flurry of political activity in the Green Mountain State, fueled by the emergence of at least sixteen weekly newspapers, with varying political slants. For example, the *Vermont Gazette*, published in Bennington, favored Thomas Jefferson's Democratic-Republican Party (a.k.a. Jeffersonians), whereas Windsor's more conservative *Vermont Journal* supported the Federalists. This tussle reflected a larger disagreement between the parties' respective world views: Jeffersonians prized the revolutionary values of competition, tolerance, and democracy, whereas the Federalists valued security, moral and spiritual unity, and political harmony. The Jeffersonians, who supported the interests of farmers primarily, accused the Federalists of advocating pro-creditor policies that favored wealthy commercial interests over those of farmers and workers.[62] In the legislature, the parties disagreed about whether, when restoring Loyalist lands confiscated during the Revolution, Vermont should compensate the settlers who bought those lands believing they had been abandoned.

Jeffersonians favored such compensation, but Federalists, viewing the settlers as trespassers, opposed it. Ultimately, responding to public pressure in 1785, the legislature approved a compromise that gave settlers half the value of improvements they had made to the land.[63]

In the presidential election of 1800, Thomas Jefferson spoiled Federalist John Adams's bid for reelection. Jeffersonian values coincided with the agrarian democratic tradition epitomized by the Green Mountain Boys and many Vermont settlers of the Revolutionary War generation. Those values reflected small farmers' distrust of commercial and religious elites.[64] Instead, they placed their trust in principles such as government by consent of the governed and the equality of citizens before the law.[65]

By 1807, in the wake of Thomas Jefferson's two presidential election victories, the Jeffersonians took control of Vermont politics, as Jeffersonian Republican Israel Smith defeated ten-term Federalist incumbent Isaac Tichenor in the gubernatorial race, and Smith's party also gained a majority of seats in the legislature. Reflecting its opposition to ecclesiastical privilege, the new majority promptly abolished the "Standing Order," which had long permitted towns to tax residents to fund the construction of church buildings and the compensation of ministers. Accordingly, Vermont became the first New England state to formally separate church and state.[66]

Another action in 1807—Congress's passage of the Embargo Act—proved to be problematic for Vermont's Jeffersonians, though, because President Jefferson favored it, but many Vermonters opposed it. The Act forbade virtually all exports from the United States to any country. Its aims were to starve Britain into accepting America's neutral trading rights and to protect American ships from harassment by warships of either Britain or France. But it was stymied in Vermont because the smugglers knew too many alternative routes and ingenious means of avoiding the authorities. The present-day site known as Smuggler's Notch and other roads that were carved out along Vermont's border with Canada offered numerous opportunities to avoid the embargo, enabling the transport of ashes, lumber, grain, pork, beef, and cheese to Canada.[67] Initially, most Vermonters opposed violating the embargo, but as residents of the Champlain Valley began to feel financial pain from it and its effectiveness was increasingly questioned, Vermonters began to look the other way while the smuggling continued. Thus, the perceptions of ineffectiveness both caused and resulted from the choice of many Vermont residents to personally refrain from smuggling while tolerating it by their neighbors.[68] The greatest beneficiaries of the illegal trade were Champlain Valley beef producers, whose product tripled in price during the war, prompting them to supply enemy troops in Canada.[69]

In 1809, Congress repealed the embargo, replacing it with the Non-intercourse Act, which barred British and French vessels from entering American ports. By 1812, as diplomacy failed, President James Madison concluded that war was unavoidable, so he sent Congress a war message on June 12 and proclaimed a state of war on June 19. The war lasted more than two years, during which one of its major confrontations—the Battle of Plattsburgh—occurred on Lake Champlain in September 1814. It lasted for two hours and twenty minutes, after which the British guns fell silent and the entire British fleet, except for its small gunboats, surrendered, ending any military threat from the north and strengthening the American position in the peace negotiations that had begun the previous month. The parties signed the Treaty of Ghent on Christmas Eve, 1814, ending the war and reaffirming America's neutral trading rights.[70]

Politically, the 1807 embargo spurred a Federalist revival in Vermont. The Federalism of this era was largely negative, featuring frustration with the embargo, fear of war, concern about a resulting depression, and a general dissatisfaction with politics and politicians.[71] By late 1814, Federalism was more popular than ever before in Vermont. But parties and candidates must show what they favor, not just what they oppose, so the Federalist wave crashed after the War of 1812 ended. By 1815, the Jeffersonians had taken full advantage of that crash to recapture the Vermont governorship. Indeed, for a decade after 1817, Jeffersonian candidates for governor of Vermont won their annual races unopposed.[72] Jefferson's party stood alone on the political mountaintop, in Vermont and nationally, during this so-called Era of Good Feelings.

Contemporaneous economic change included increases in manufacturing and commercial farming. Seeking to encourage further economic development, Kentucky congressman Henry Clay—a master of the legislative craft—proposed "The American System," a federally supported program of tariffs, "internal improvements" (roads, bridges, canals, etc.), a national bank, and sales of public lands designed to foster economic growth and finance additional improvement projects.[73] He envisioned a small protective tariff on imported wool to raise its price relative to domestic wool, thereby encouraging American farmers to raise sheep and American textile manufacturers to use the less expensive domestic wool. Congress enacted the proposal in 1824, over the opposition of Southern wool importers, and it spurred Vermont farmers to raise sheep.[74] Four years later, Congress enacted another tariff, dubbed the Tariff of Abominations by its opponents, which nearly doubled the duty on imported wool and caused the price that American farmers received for their wool to also nearly double during the next five years. The resulting "sheep craze" hastened the integration of Vermont farmers into wider markets beyond Vermont's borders.[75]

Unfortunately, the growth of commercial agriculture brought with it increasing land prices that prevented aspiring farmers from acquiring land unless they inherited it. Consequently, many of them sought employment as tradesmen, mechanics, or factory workers in larger Vermont towns or in the industrial cities of southern New England, while others migrated westward.[76] Thus, "a persistent exodus from the land" in Vermont by impoverished small farmers and their landless sons, which had begun earlier in the nineteenth century, continued into the mid-nineteenth century.[77] Even once-profitable sheep farmers suffered when, in 1846, the Democratic majority in Congress eliminated the tariff on wool, causing wool prices to plummet, along with Vermont's sheep population, which dipped by more than 600,000 between 1846 and 1850.[78] Thus, when the 1850 Census reported that 42 percent of the Americans born in Vermont were residing outside the state, the news was not a surprise.[79]

Still, by that year, Vermont was not only saying goodbye to emigrants, but also saying hello, albeit grudgingly, to immigrants, mostly from Ireland, whose arrival during the 1840s coincided with that of the railroads. By 1850 Irish people accounted for one-third of the population of Burlington and performed about 80 percent of its manual labor.[80] The railroads arrived late in Vermont because of the state's mountainous terrain, small population, and relative poverty. Passenger service began in June 1848, when the Vermont Central Railroad opened twenty-seven miles of track between White River Junction and Bethel. Service gradually expanded, but railroad-building was expensive, and Vermont did not offer enough passenger or freight traffic to ensure profitability. Later, the companies that built Vermont's first railroads merged into several corporations that connected the state to larger markets in all directions, making railroading economically viable. Ultimately, the railroads had profound economic and political effects in Vermont. Indeed, four men who built them between the 1840s and the 1860s served as governor between 1841 and 1878, respectively, and towns the railroads served grew considerably whereas towns they bypassed lost business and population.[81]

Meanwhile, the Era of Good Feelings after the War of 1812 ended in the late 1820s. By that time, the United States once again had two major political parties: the Democrats, led by Andrew Jackson of Tennessee, and the National Republicans, led by John Quincy Adams of Massachusetts. Broadly speaking, the Democrats inherited the Jeffersonian tradition, and the National Republicans inherited the Federalist tradition. Adams won the 1824 presidential election, which was decided in the House of Representatives, but Jackson triumphed in 1828. Jackson, like Jefferson before him, championed limited, frugal government and the interests of farmers. In Vermont, Democrats emphasized social and political equality among individuals and generally promoted the interests of the less well-off.[82] Frequently hostile to centers of wealth and power, many Democrats had not benefitted from economic growth following the War of 1812.[83] National Republicans were more likely to be amongst the top tenth of income earners in their respective towns, to live in towns that had prospered during the 1820s, and to be factory owners, lawyers, financiers, or commercial farmers.[84]

Despite its relative poverty, Vermont was fertile territory for the National Republicans, giving three of every four votes to Adams in his 1828 presidential rematch with Jackson, even though Jackson won the national election in a landslide.[85] After Jackson won reelection in 1832, easily defeating Henry Clay, the Democratic Party dominated politics nationally, and the National Republicans faded from the scene, replaced by the Whigs, who, essentially, were a "national anti-Jackson coalition."[86] The Whigs were ideologically diverse: from the Jeffersonians they adopted a tradition of favoring states' rights, but from the Federalists they acquired a tendency to champion financial and manufacturing interests.[87] Their large "tent" housed strange political bedfellows whose assorted grievances included Catholicism, immigration, liquor, slavery, and other single-issue causes. In Vermont, Whig candidates were most likely to succeed in wealthy towns and commercial and manufacturing centers, among economically comfortable voters who belonged to established religious denominations and favored using government to improve public morals.[88]

But slavery proved to be the Whig Party's undoing in the 1850s. Its northern and southern factions disagreed about whether to allow slavery in western territories yet to become states. In fairness to the Whigs, Congress could not agree on that issue either. Congress tried to navigate the relationship between slavery and territorial expansion by enacting the Compromise of 1850, which was largely the handiwork of Henry Clay, by then a Whig senator from Kentucky. This legislation admitted California to the Union as a free state, fixed the border between Texas and New Mexico, abolished the slave trade in Washington, DC (while permitting slavery to continue there), and strengthened the fugitive slave law by requiring citizens to assist in returning runaway slaves to their owners.[89] Tensions between North and South remained high, though, so in 1854, Congress enacted the Kansas–Nebraska Act, which organized the two territories and allowed new states to vote to enter the Union as either slave or free. This law also repealed the Compromise of 1820, an earlier example of Henry Clay's legislative skill that had long established the northern boundary of slavery (latitude 36 degrees, 30 minutes north) and balanced the number of slave and free states.[90] After the Kansas–Nebraska Act, slave states could outnumber free states in the future if the voters so chose.

Just two months after the Act passed, a coalition of antislavery Vermonters who opposed the act gathered at the state house in Montpelier and formed the Republican Party. Thereafter Vermont, which was already a strong antislavery state, became a predominantly Republican state too. In the 1860 presidential election, Vermonters cast 42,419 votes for Abraham Lincoln; 6,849 votes for Senator Stephen Douglas of Illinois (a Vermont native); and about 2,000 votes combined for other candidates.[91] Douglas's authorship of the Kansas–Nebraska Act not only doomed his candidacy among Vermonters, but also soured them on the Democratic Party.[92]

The Civil War and its Aftermath

On April 14, 1861, just weeks after President Lincoln's inauguration, Confederate troops fired on the federal garrison at Fort Sumter in Charleston, South Carolina, marking the start of the Civil War. Afterward, Vermont Governor Erastus Fairbanks received a telegraph from Lincoln, saying: "Washington in grave danger. What may we expect from Vermont?" Fairbanks's reply was equally terse and direct, promising, "Vermont will do its full duty."[93]

Indeed, it did. By war's end, in the spring of 1865, Vermont had fielded seventeen infantry regiments, a cavalry regiment and a company of cavalry to patrol the Canadian border, three artillery batteries, and three companies of sharpshooters, besides the 619 men who served in the Navy and Marines.[94] Vermonters fought at the Battles of Bull Run, Cedar Creek, Cold Harbor,

Fredericksburg, Lee's Mills, Malvern Hill, Petersburg, Spotsylvania Courthouse, and the Wilderness, all in Virginia; at Antietam in Maryland; Port Hudson in Mississippi; and most notably, Gettysburg in Pennsylvania.[95] At Gettysburg on July 3, 1863, the Second Vermont Brigade under General George Stannard occupied a central battlefield position on Cemetery Ridge when Confederate infantrymen under General George Pickett ran across a mile of open field toward the Union lines in the ill-fated "Pickett's Charge." The Vermonters wheeled and fired on the flank and rear of the Confederates, repelling their charge and thwarting their attempt to split the Union lines.[96] Later, near the end of the war, Vermont's Ninth Regiment led the Union Army into Richmond, the Confederate capital, which its defenders had abandoned.

Among the Vermonters in the Union Army were 68 members of the famous 54th Massachusetts Regiment, an African American unit, who served between 1861 and 1865. Another 150 Black Vermonters served in the Tenth Infantry US Colored Troops, the Thirty-First, Forty-First, and Forty-Fifth Infantry Regiments, and the Massachusetts Fifty-Fifth.[97] All told, 34,238 Vermont men were part of the war effort: one in every ten men in its population and more than half the total number who were eligible for military duty. Of those who served, 5,224 died in action or from wounds, diseases, or other causes.[98] Of the northern states, only Michigan lost more men per capita in the war than Vermont.[99]

After the war, many Vermont soldiers returned home only briefly, then, seeking better opportunities than their hardscrabble farms and isolated towns could offer, they took their military pay and emigrated to the cities or the West.[100] The consequences of postwar migration were evident in the 1870 Census, which showed that Vermont's population had increased by just 5 percent since 1850, whereas the American population as a whole had increased by 70 percent during the same time period. Not only had young men left Vermont in search of opportunity,[101] young women had often done the same, finding mill and factory work in the industrial cities and towns of southern New England.[102]

Two of every five Vermonters migrated out of state between 1850 and 1900. Some of them enjoyed great success in their new homes. Henry Wells of Thetford became the Wells in Wells Fargo. Frederick Billings of Royalton and Woodstock was the inspiration for Billings, Montana, because of his success during the California Gold Rush as San Francisco's first lawyer and as founder of the Northern Pacific Railroad. Elisha Otis of Halifax founded the Otis Elevator Company, and Harvey Hood of Chelsea started the Hood Milk Company.[103] Former Vermonters succeeded in politics too. Between 1850 and 1900, eighty-eight native Vermonters represented eighteen other states in Congress: fifteen in the Senate and seventy-three in the House. And Vermont natives Chester Arthur and Calvin Coolidge, both of whom had migrated elsewhere, became president on the deaths of Presidents Garfield and Harding, respectively.[104]

Peacham, a small town located in the northeastern part of the state serves as a good example of how dramatic the population decline was in some communities. Overwhelmingly agricultural in 1840, Peacham reached its peak population of 1,443 that year, at the height of wool-growing spurred by the protective tariff. By 1860, though, the population had dropped to 1,247, as raising sheep became less profitable without the tariff, competition from Midwestern farmers increased, and no fertile land was available to pass on to the next generation. Thus, migration reduced the population of Peacham to just 794 by 1900 and it continued well into the new century, leaving the town with just 543 residents in 1940.[105] Since then, however, Peacham has become a popular summer and retirement retreat for professors and authors and a bedroom community for professionals who work in St. Johnsbury, Montpelier, and elsewhere, boosting its population to 715 in the 2020 Census.

Population decline was not the only change in Vermont after the Civil War. The state transitioned from a mostly agricultural economy to one with noteworthy manufacturing, and from a rural to a more village-based society. Accordingly, 1890 marked the last time that Vermont had more sheep than people; in that year, the flock numbered 333,947 and the human population was 333,422.[106] Several Vermont towns had a single dominant manufacturer; for instance, the E. & T. Fairbanks Company in St. Johnsbury, which made world-famous platform scales, employed more than six hundred skilled workers by 1887.[107] Similarly, the quarrying and finishing of granite for use in construction, monuments, and cemetery markers dominated Barre. St. Albans became a railroad town after a new owner moved the Central Vermont Railroad's shops and administrative headquarters there from Northfield.[108] Industrial growth triggered expanded immigration, which brought Irish millworkers, French-Canadian loggers, Italian and Scottish stonecutters, and Welsh miners and quarrymen to Vermont. By 1900 more than 13 percent of the state's population was foreign-born.[109]

In agriculture, technological change in the form of new farm machinery and refrigerated transportation meant larger markets in Boston, Worcester, and other southern New England cities, which hastened a change to dairying and expanded fluid-milk production, preserving Vermont's link to economic conditions beyond its borders.[110] Attitudinal changes occurred too; public officials in Vermont came to believe that through "scientific management" government could solve an array of social and economic problems. On this point, historian Paul Searls has written, "Perhaps the most salient feature of late nineteenth century Vermont politics was the eagerness of rural legislators to cast votes toward greater and more centralized authority when it suited them."[111] Thus occurred a flourishing, during the 1880s and 1890s, of boards, commissions, secretariats, and other governmental entities charged with upgrading and managing Vermont's resources and services.[112]

A principal object of increased state attention was public education. Almost every legislative session between 1872 and 1896 enacted legislation that mandated educational reforms: more equitable taxation for schools and distribution of the proceeds, more effective training for and licensing of teachers, free textbooks, compulsory attendance, longer school terms, and the establishment of high schools in towns of 2,500 or more residents. The greatest victory for educational reform, however, was achieved in 1892, when the legislators abolished small, autonomous school districts and gave towns the sole authority to make and enforce educational policy within their borders.[113] Before these reforms, Vermont had been home to multiple tiny, independent school districts per town, often woefully underfunded and of widely varying quality.[114] In 1894, still another law facilitated the establishment of town libraries. Under this law, a town that appropriated at least $25 annually to support a local library and elected five trustees would receive a collection of books worth $100. Thanks to this incentive, twenty-one library buildings were built in Vermont by 1900, and thirty more by 1910.[115]

Professor Samuel Hand once observed that although centralization in government is generally a function of modernization and urbanization, in Vermont it was instead "driven by rural poverty."[116] Rural poverty was surely one of the two forces that spurred centralization in Vermont after the Civil War. The other was the development of specialized commercial farming, which showed farmers that legislation could influence their livelihoods and that they could benefit from government help in developing and marketing farm products.

The rural poverty that Professor Hand referenced made small, rural agricultural towns the prime movers behind state programs designed to supply and pay for services the towns had neither the funds nor the personnel to furnish themselves.[117] An example is the Highway Act of 1892, which the dairymen's association and allied interest groups championed because even when towns and counties desired improved farm-to-market roads, they often lacked the means to achieve their goals. The 1892 law required every town to elect a road commissioner and to levy a tax of twenty cents per resident to support its roads, plus a five-cent tax to be paid to the state for redistribution to the towns based on a mileage formula. Although the Act required some towns to spend more money than usual on roads, its formula ensured redistribution of funds from wealthier to poorer communities, which the latter supported wholeheartedly.[118] Thus, the Highway Act shows how state government tried to reconcile the growing needs and meager resources of Vermont communities during the late nineteenth century.

The growth of commercial farming after the Civil War also fostered centralization in government. By the end of the war, dairying had replaced sheep-raising as Vermont's principal agricultural activity, and dairy farmers—facing a loss of markets because of epidemics blamed on unwholesome milk—began to seek state inspections of their output. Their professional associations became the foremost advocates for state and federal government interventions. Recognizing the potential benefits of government aid, dairy farmers organized a dairymen's association in 1869. It used state and federal support to restrict the sale of oleomargarine that competed with the butter they produced, to protect American markets from Canadian dairy imports, and to regulate railroad shipping rates.[119]

Political leadership in Vermont was also centralized as the nineteenth century ended. In 1880, the Republican Party controlled Vermont politics, and it did so for the rest of the nineteenth century and well into the twentieth. Republicans held Vermont's three US House seats—which became two in 1882 and one in 1932—both US Senate seats, all elected statewide offices, and most of the seats in the Vermont Legislature. The Democrats had only a bare-bones organization that seemed to exist mostly for the few federal patronage positions (US attorney, US marshal, etc.) that were awarded to loyal party members during Democratic presidential administrations.[120]

The Twentieth Century and Beyond

Former State Archivist Gregory Sanford has observed that the traditional image of Vermont as featuring "a loosely knit central government overseeing a series of independent fiefdoms: each town" does not match reality. On the contrary, Vermont was among the first states to create a state highway commission, establish a public service board to regulate utilities, and publicize its tourist attractions. These actions, notes Sanford, centered "more and more responsibility and authority in Montpelier."[121]

Centralization was a key to Vermont's responses to societal changes early in the twentieth century. In 1906, Fletcher Proctor, whose family had made a fortune in the marble industry and dominated the state's Republican Party, became governor. Despite his background, he embraced government regulation of business, signing legislation that directed corporations to pay employees weekly, created a new railroad commission with expanded regulatory powers, strengthened regulations on rail transportation charges, and increased tax assessments on railroads.[122] Subsequent governors continued this trend; in 1912, Governor Allen Fletcher signed a factory inspection bill, and the following year he signed legislation establishing a maximum fifty-hour work week for women and children. In 1915 Vermont adopted a workers' compensation program that made employers legally responsible for injuries their employees sustained on the job.

The state also addressed deficiencies in public education during this era by lengthening the school year to thirty-four weeks, sponsoring teacher-training courses, setting a minimum weekly salary for teachers in rural districts (with the state providing salary supplements), and establishing vocational education programs. Beyond that, it paid transportation costs for children in poorer towns who lived more than a mile-and-a-half from school and mandated the creation of sixty-six rural supervisory unions with professionally trained administrators for each one.[123] Vermont also passed a bill that set up a direct primary election, which a subsequent referendum approved,[124] and another bill that authorized an appropriation of $7,500 to buy lands in the state's name to be administered as state forests.[125] The concern for state forests reflected Vermont's determination to use its scenic landscape to build a tourist industry that would earn it additional revenue and perhaps new residents too. Back in 1891, Vermont had established the first state publicity service in the United States, which it enlarged in 1911 into the Bureau of Publicity, just as automobiles were making the state more accessible.[126]

As the twentieth century proceeded, events continually spawned assertive responses by the state government to challenging conditions. For example, in 1927 a tropical storm in early November dumped between seven and nine inches of rain in three days, resulting in eighty-four deaths, almost ten thousand people displaced from their homes, $30 million of property damage, and miles of railroad track washed away.[127] Because towns could not afford the cost of repairs, the state assumed the towns' responsibility for repairing highways and bridges, with the state highway department in control of the work. To defray the repair costs, the governor and legislators agreed to forego their customary pay-as-you-go strategy, instead authorizing issuance of $8.5 million in bonds and enacting a flood tax to retire the bond. The expanded state responsibility for roads—especially hard-surfaced roads necessitated by the flood—hastened the creation of a modern state highway system in Vermont.[128]

No sooner had the flood waters receded than the Great Depression hit Vermont. Both events contributed to the state's decision to end its traditional reliance on a statewide property tax for most of its income and to substitute a personal income tax. The latter eased the burden on land-rich but cash-poor farmers and captured income from intangible sources (e.g., capital gains from sales of stock) that had previously escaped taxation.[129] Once again, the fiscal limitations of Vermont's small towns and agrarian economy triggered a bold state response to meet pressing needs.[130] Another tradition that ended in this era was the unwritten "Mountain Rule," whereby the governorship alternated between politicians who lived on opposite sides of the Green Mountains, and Vermont's two senators also lived on opposite sides of the mountains. The same rule applied to the lieutenant governor; an east-side resident would be elected to serve with a west-side governor, to be succeeded by an east-side governor and a west-side lieutenant governor.[131] This rule long reconciled conflicting ambitions within the Republican Party, forcing potential candidates to "wait their turn" to run. But it fell victim to improved transportation, increased integration between east and west, and the 1930 Census, which reduced Vermont to one US House seat, making the "wait your turn" dictum more difficult to enforce.

The Depression era of the 1930s belied the old joke that Vermonters were already so used to poverty that they barely noticed the economic collapse. The value of Vermont's industrial products dropped from $142,522,547 in 1928 to $86,602,968 in 1931 and to $56,623,538 by 1933. The number of industrial wage earners statewide declined from 27,421 to 15,083, and total wages fell from $33,809,987 to $12,456,113, as the tally of manufacturing plants shrank from 927 to 530.[132]

In response, the newly elected president—Democrat Franklin D. Roosevelt (FDR)—created numerous federally funded programs designed to jump-start the moribund economy. Although staunchly Republican Vermont rejected FDR in all four of his presidential elections, it took full advantage of his New Deal programs, overcoming the traditional preference for local control. Historian Richard Munson Judd writes, "The history of the New Deal in Vermont is largely a record of triumph of progressive planning over provincial inertia."[133] That record partly resulted from the leadership of George Aiken, a nursery owner and horticulturist from Putney who was governor from 1937 to 1941. He helped the federal Rural Electrification Administration succeed in Vermont by encouraging farmers to set up nonprofit cooperatives that could receive low-cost federal loans with which to expand power lines to farms and rural homes. Private companies refused to undertake this expansion because they viewed it as unprofitable.[134]

Even before Aiken became governor, though, representatives of thirteen larger towns and cities voted 12–1 to borrow from the federal Reconstruction Finance Corporation to fund highway construction by unemployed workers.[135] Young Vermont men between the ages of eighteen and twenty-five joined the Civilian Conservation Corps (CCC) and participated in forestry, parkway construction, pest and disease control, boundary surveys, trail cutting, and shelter construction. Some of them cut the state's first ski trails and built a parking lot and warming shelter at Smugglers Notch. Income from the state's leases of land to ski areas funded much of the annual budget for the state parks. Soon, ski trains from New York City brought skiers to Vermont on winter weekends, enhancing the state's reputation as a recreation destination.[136] Farmers benefitted immensely from crop-production loans and mortgage loans, production-control payments, drought relief, soil conservation payments, rural rehabilitation loans, and payments for the purchase of their surplus commodities.[137] All Vermonters benefitted from the construction and renovation completed in the state by the federal Works Progress Administration (WPA), including the building or improvement of bridges, culverts, highways and public schools.[138]

But not every New Deal–era federal program was popular in Vermont. One that failed was the Green Mountain Parkway, a proposed 250-mile road along the length of the mountain range, to be flanked by strips of protected parkland one thousand feet wide. It would have connected about one million acres already designated as state parks, including the new Green Mountain National Forest, with a large wilderness park set aside at the northernmost tip of the highway.[139] The parkway's planners believed it would reduce short-term unemployment and boost Vermont's burgeoning tourist industry. Its opponents included conservationists and many rural Vermonters who "could not reconcile their ideal of 'unspoiled' nature with a permanent, artificial structure."[140] Ultimately, the legislature asked the voters to decide the project's fate in a referendum on Town Meeting Day in 1936, and they rejected it by a vote of 43,176 to 31,101.[141] Evidently, local control still mattered, and so did preserving Vermont's wild lands. The parkway proposal presented a conundrum that still confronts Vermont: how to realize economic benefits from its natural environment without damaging that environment in the process.

In 1941, World War II replaced the Depression at the forefront of Vermonters' minds. More than 49,000 residents left the state to participate in the war, with 38,000 men and women serving on active duty and an estimated 11,000 traveling out of state to work in war-related jobs.[142] After the war, both the conflict itself and the hardships that preceded it affected Vermont politics. The most immediate effect was the 1946 Republican gubernatorial primary by Ernest W. Gibson, Jr. a charismatic forty-year-old with an outstanding war record and a progressive political philosophy. Gibson was a close political ally of George Aiken who, by 1946, was completing his sixth year in the US Senate.

Gibson's inaugural address was ambitious, and he achieved many of his goals in his first term, including a larger and better-paid corps of public school teachers and a more generous retirement program for them; annual medical and dental exams for every schoolchild; a more equitable distribution of educational funds; a Department of Public Safety, and several other proposals for reorganizing state government.[143] Although he won reelection in 1948, Gibson soon tired of battling the more conservative members of his party, who often rejected his second-term proposals. As a result, halfway through that term, he resigned the governorship to accept an appointment to a federal district judgeship in Vermont.[144] Gibson's frustration reflected conservative dominance in the Vermont House, where each municipality, regardless of size, was allotted one representative. This rule, which existed until 1965, enabled conservative rural communities to outvote larger, more progressive ones by giving the former greater voting power.

The 1950s witnessed important changes in Vermont that signaled things to come. For example, in the 1952 gubernatorial election, the Republican incumbent won by the narrowest margin ever for the Republican Party. Democrat Robert Larrow campaigned more actively than Democratic candidates usually did and won sixty thousand votes, suggesting changing voter loyalties and an invigorated Democratic Party.[145] In 1958, William Meyer, a little-known forester from Bennington County, won Vermont's lone US House seat, becoming the first Democrat to win a statewide election in the Green Mountain State since 1853.[146] The 1950s also witnessed economic changes, as 1957 brought a major corporation, IBM, to Essex Junction, and the first experiment in snowmaking to Mt. Ascutney Ski Area in Windsor County.[147] Snowmaking hastened Vermont's transformation into a three-season recreation hub, offering skiing, second homes, summer resorts, hiking, fishing, and foliage tours.[148] That transformation, spurred primarily by construction of the interstate highways, boosted state revenues and population, but also caused economic dislocation for native Vermonters who could no longer afford to live in their hometowns. This problem was acute in ski-resort towns, where real estate values skyrocketed. In Warren, the site of Sugarbush Ski Area, the grand list of residential and commercial property values rose from $6 million in 1960 to more than $400 million by the mid-1970s.[149]

The 1960s brought dramatic political changes, beginning with the 1962 election of Philip Hoff, a Burlington lawyer and former legislator, as the state's first Democratic governor since 1853. He won by just 1,348 votes out of the 121,389 cast, thanks to the support of disaffected progressive Republicans who rejected the conservative Republican incumbent.[150] Hoff served three terms as governor. His administration can best be described as progressive for its willingness to use government to improve social and economic conditions for ordinary people.[151] Hoff's achievements include the transfer of responsibility for public assistance from individual towns to the state, a college-loan-guarantee program for Vermont students, an increase in per-pupil spending to get Vermont closer to the national average, the establishment of an educational television network at the University of Vermont, a law prohibiting billboards on roads and highways, and the elimination of a poll tax for voting.[152]

The most consequential achievement during the Hoff years, though, came in his second term. A federal court had ruled in July 1964 that both legislative chambers were malapportioned contrary to the Supreme Court's governing mandate that each legislator in each chamber must represent an equal number of constituents. In May 1965, after an emotional debate, the legislators voted 163–62 to reduce the size of the house from 246 to 150 members, thereby toppling the old rule that called for one representative per municipality. They also reapportioned the state senate, established a procedure for periodic reapportionment of both chambers, and set up another procedure for electing members to a reapportioned house.[153]

The results were dramatic. Burlington and Winooski, which previously had one vote each, had fifteen between them after reapportionment; conversely, nine Northeast Kingdom towns were consolidated into one single-member district.[154] The Democratic Party benefitted because its voters were concentrated in the larger towns and cities, where the voting power now lay. The Republican Party suffered because its voters lived in more rural communities with less voting power. In the 1966 election, more Democrats were elected to the Vermont House than ever before.[155] Vermont was undergoing a political transformation from a one-party state to a two-party state.

Progressivism continued in Vermont state government long after the Hoff administration ended. Republicans George Aiken, Ernest Gibson, and Republican-turned-Independent Jim Jeffords (congressman, 1975–89; senator, 1989–2007) were often progressive, but more Democrats than Republicans held progressive views after 1970.[156] In that year the state began regulating large-scale land development by assessing its impact on natural, cultural, and historic resources. In 1985, Vermont supplemented the 1970 law by enacting legislation designed to promote land-use planning by towns, regional entities, and the state. In 1997, it revamped its system of funding public education, greatly reducing the role of property wealth in financing schools. In 2000, it enacted a "civil union" law that enabled same-sex couples to enjoy the benefits that married heterosexual couples enjoyed. In 2009, it became the first state to legalize same-sex marriage by legislation instead of a court order. More recently, it has enacted gun-safety laws, generously subsidized early childhood education, and passed major legislation designed to expand the supply of affordable housing.

Conclusion

Vermont's state-centric political culture has four historical roots. First, a deep belief in social equality, derived from its agrarian tradition, has long prompted collective action toward the common good. Second, the historic settlement pattern produced many small, relatively poor farming towns that could not meet their growing needs for services after the Civil War, spawning an increased reliance on state assistance. Third, the transition from subsistence to commercial farming caused farmers to recognize the benefits of state financial and technical assistance. Finally, migration from metropolitan areas during the twentieth and twenty-first centuries increased the population, intensified the demand for services, and brought to Vermont many newcomers who favored active, progressive government.

Such government is expensive and prescriptive, though, so Vermonters may not continue to support the accompanying taxes and regulations. Thus, if the challenge for New Hampshire is to fund enough state government to meet future needs, the challenge for Vermont is the opposite: to ensure that the demands on state government do not outstrip Vermonters' capacity to fund it and willingness to support it.

CHAPTER FOUR

The Individualistic Twin

Politics in Contemporary New Hampshire

"Live Free or Die" as Political Culture

RECALL FROM CHAPTER ONE a Canadian visitor's memory of crossing the Connecticut River in 1970 from Vermont into New Hampshire, leaving "green rolling hills" behind and encountering instead "a big billboard announcing that New Hampshire had no sales tax."[1] Today—more than fifty years later—at least some Granite State politicians still like to trumpet their state's lack of a sales or income tax as the New Hampshire advantage.

That antitax reputation prompted the libertarian Free State Project to announce in 2003 that New Hampshire had won the group's poll to choose the most libertarian-friendly state in the United States. According to a Free State spokesperson, New Hampshire "boasts the lowest state and local tax burden in the continental United States, the leanest state government in the country . . . a citizen legislature, a healthy job market, and perhaps most important, support for our movement."[2] By 2016, the Free Staters' plan to move to New Hampshire gained 2,500 new signatories, putting the group over the 20,000-signature mark, which triggered a concerted effort to convert the signatories into Granite Staters. Many did move, enabling the group by 2019 to claim twenty state legislators among its ranks, along with numerous municipal officials. The votes of Free Staters helped the New Hampshire Legislature eliminate licensing requirements to carry loaded, concealed firearms; abolish criminal penalties for possessing small amounts of marijuana or hashish; legalize same-sex marriage; and expand school choice.[3]

Some libertarians, who usually serve in the legislature as Republicans, risked their lives for their ideology during the COVID-19 pandemic. In November 2020, after winning control of both chambers, Republican legislators exhibited their commitment to individual freedom by gathering indoors at a ski resort, mostly without face masks, to choose their leadership. After realtor Dick Hinch praised his colleagues for not wearing masks, they chose him as their party's candidate for speaker of the house. Sadly, after leading the house for just over a week, Hinch died on December 3, 2020, a victim of the coronavirus. Only five days later, the federal government made the first shipment of the new coronavirus vaccine available to the American public.[4]

For a time, the Free Staters were especially influential in the Town of Grafton in west-central New Hampshire, which had 1,385 residents during the 2020 Census. Although unable to withdraw Grafton from the regional school district or eliminate funding for the town library, the Free Staters succeeded in cutting the town's $1 million budget by 30 percent and in denying funding to the county senior citizens' council. And despite failing to abolish the town planning board directly, they got themselves elected to the board, then effectively disbanded it.[5] They extinguished most of Grafton's streetlights to save on electricity bills, discontinued long stretches of dirt roads to save on highway maintenance, and defunded the town's annual Christmas lights and July Fourth fireworks. Ironically, though, their hostility to government spawned frequent disputes that caused Grafton's legal expenses to increase ninefold between their 2004 arrival and 2011. Thus, the same people who sought to save the town money ended up costing it money.[6] Eventually, their influence waned because many of them, who were predominantly single men, got restless and left Grafton.

But Grafton is not the only New Hampshire town that the Free Staters have tried to dominate. Croydon, a town of 800 residents located twenty-three miles southwest of Grafton, has also seen an influx of Free Staters in recent years. In March 2022, at the annual town meeting, residents approved the town budget in the morning, then in the afternoon, turned their attention to the proposed $1.7 million school budget, which covered the operations of a K–4 school and the cost of tuition for older students to schools out of town. When a resident who was a Free Stater moved to reduce the school budget to $800,000, his amendment passed by a vote of 20–14 at the lightly attended meeting.[7] That tally was potentially catastrophic for Croydon's school because an $800,000 budget would have resulted in nearly half of the jobs in the school either being lost or outsourced.

But the small vote was not the end of the story. New Hampshire law permitted those who objected to that vote to petition for a special meeting during which it could be overturned if at least half of Croydon's voters were present and voted. Some 379 residents appeared for the revote in May 2022, and 377 of them voted to restore the original budget. This episode prompted political scientist Wayne Lesperance to observe that citizens of a democracy have obligations as well as rights, and that "when we don't fulfill our obligations, we often end up with results we don't like."[8] It also calls to mind the aphorism: "Ninety percent of life is showing up."

Taken together, the Grafton and Croydon examples show that the Free Staters have not always prevailed in New Hampshire, but they are heard, and their ideas are often followed because the state is generally friendly to their small-government philosophy. Numerous illustrations exist from a wide array of policy contexts. Despite an unhealthy number of human conflicts with black bears during the 2000s, New Hampshire lawmakers waited until 2013 to consider a bill to reduce these conflicts by requiring owners of bear-attracting garbage to store or dispose of it in bear-proof dumpsters and garbage cans. The objection cited most often by opponents of the bill was that trash haulers and property owners should not be expected to pay for such expensive containers. Therefore, two months after the New Hampshire House took up the bill, the committee considering it voted it down 14–0.[9]

In a similar vein, New Hampshire's government was the last in New England, and one of the last in the United States, to issue a mask mandate during the coronavirus pandemic in 2020, and the first in New England to lift it. The mandate, which lasted from November 2020 until April 2021, required persons ages five or older to wear masks in public, indoors or outdoors, when they could not maintain six feet of separation from individuals outside their household. But New Hampshire declined to restrict gatherings between households, prohibit indoor dining at restaurants, ban in-person religious gatherings, or close bars. Instead, besides imposing a lockdown in the spring of 2020, New Hampshire asked residents to restrict their travel, practice social distancing, and quarantine voluntarily if informed by close contacts that they had tested positive for the virus.[10]

The libertarian spirit is also evident in New Hampshire's gun-safety policies. In 2017, Governor Chris Sununu, a Republican, signed a law making the Granite State a "constitutional carry" state, eliminating the gun owner's need to apply for a permit to carry a concealed firearm. In 2019, when they enjoyed a majority, Democratic legislators passed bills that (1) required background checks for all gun sales, including sales made at gun shows; (2) barred individuals from carrying guns on school property; and (3) established a three-day waiting period for gun purchases. Governor Sununu vetoed all three bills, saying they would violate New Hampshire's "culture of responsible gun ownership and individual freedom." In 2020, Sununu also vetoed a "red flag" law sponsored by Democratic legislators, which would have authorized courts to order the temporary confiscation of guns from persons whom the courts had determined were threats to themselves or others.[11]

Another example of New Hampshire's distaste for regulation is its response to climate change, which has been notably less robust than those of its fellow New England states. A 2022 study by the University of New Hampshire's Sustainability Institute and the Union of Concerned Scientists found that New Hampshire is "the only New England state that has yet to adopt legislation that would transition the state away from using fossil fuels and towards renewable energy adoption."[12] The report concluded that political leaders in New Hampshire focus on the economic costs of actions aimed at climate change mitigation and adaptation instead of the benefits of such actions and the costs of inaction. It concluded further that because New Hampshire lacks an adequate strategy for building climate resilience statewide, municipalities and regional planning commissions "are left to take the lead on local-scale climate adaptation efforts," with mixed, often inequitable, results because of the localities' widely varying capacities to undertake such efforts.[13]

Besides a hostility to regulation, the Live Free or Die ethos manifests itself in a reluctance to spend public dollars. That reluctance was front and center in a 2011 study of New Hampshire's fiscal policy conducted by the Federal Reserve Bank of Boston's New England Public Policy Center. Admittedly, the data cited in the study are old, hence less reliable today than formerly, but the study's findings are still valuable for what they reveal about the philosophy behind taxing and spending choices in New Hampshire.[14]

The study found that New Hampshire's state and local governments raised and spent considerably less money than their New England counterparts. Census data for Fiscal Year (FY) 2007 showed that governments in New Hampshire collected 22 percent less revenue per capita than the average for the six New England states and spent 20 percent less money per capita than the regional average.[15] At that time, New Hampshire ranked at or near the bottom of the New England states in most spending categories, including the two largest ones for states and localities: public welfare and elementary and secondary education. New Hampshire's per capita spending on public welfare (chiefly Medicaid) was the lowest in New England and more than 31 percent below the regional average. Its per-capita spending for public education was lower than that of all other New England states except Maine, though it was only about 7 percent below the regional average. Taken together, New Hampshire's frugal spending on public welfare, public education, and public hospitals accounted for more than half of the overall spending gap between it and its New England neighbors, according to this study.[16]

Looking beyond the numbers, the study's author observed that spending variations between states can reflect both deliberate choices and their varying circumstances, such as geography, demographics, and socioeconomic conditions. For example, the wealthier a state's population is, the less money the state is likely to spend on Medicaid. Because New Hampshire is a relatively wealthy state, typically ranking in the top ten for per-capita income, its residents are less needy than the residents of most other states, which partially explained its expenditure gap with its neighbors. Indeed, the study's author calculated that reduced need accounted for 41 percent of the spending gap between the Granite State and the rest of New England, with 59 percent accounted for by other factors. Those other factors include the choices states make about which services to provide and the varying degrees of efficiency with which they provide them. Because efficiency across states is difficult to assess, the study focused instead on comparing New Hampshire's services to those of its neighbors.[17]

Regarding Medicaid, New Hampshire's per capita spending was by far the lowest in New England: 47 percent below the regional average. Its enrollment in the program as a percentage of the state's population was also lower than that of any other New England state, just 10.9 percent, compared to a range from 15.2 percent (Connecticut) to 26.6 percent (Maine) across the region. But its spending per Medicaid enrollee ranked fourth among the six New England states, just 6 percent below the regional average. To the study's author, the disparity between New Hampshire's low overall spending on Medicaid relative to its population and its somewhat higher spending per enrollee suggested that its relative wealth—reflected in a low Medicaid enrollment—was the major factor behind its low Medicaid spending compared to neighboring states.[18]

Still, the study did not give New Hampshire a free pass concerning Medicaid spending choices. Indeed, it found that New Hampshire's Medicaid program set "particularly strict criteria" for parents relative to those set by the other New England states. In July 2006, New Hampshire capped Medicaid income eligibility for unemployed parents at 45 percent of the Federal Poverty Level (FPL) and for working parents at 56 percent of FPL. In other words, unemployed parents who earned more than 45 percent of the FPL and working parents who earned more than 56 percent of FPL were not eligible for Medicaid in the Granite State. In contrast, eligibility limits for these groups in other New England states at that time ranged from 133 percent to more than 200 percent of FPL, making many more parents eligible for Medicaid in those states than in New Hampshire. New Hampshire's eligibility criteria for pregnant women and the elderly, blind, and disabled were also among the strictest in New England, although by a smaller differential than applied to parents.[19] Thus, New Hampshire's reduced need for Medicaid because of its relative wealth, coupled with its stringent financial criteria for eligibility, help the state to balance its annual budget without broad-based income and sales taxes.

The study also used higher education spending to illustrate New Hampshire's fiscal philosophy. In this context, New Hampshire has reduced its need for tax revenue "by shifting costs away from current taxpayers without necessarily providing fewer or less comprehensive services than its regional peers."[20] More specifically, the state funds a smaller share of spending on higher education than its New England neighbors, which means that tuition and other charges account for a higher percentage of institutional revenue at New Hampshire's public colleges than at their regional counterparts. Public higher education is different from public welfare, public safety, or even public elementary and secondary education because it relies heavily on income from "charges," meaning fees tied to the use of a particular government service. Those charges include tuition and fees, along with payments for services such as room and board. The more that a state relies on such charges, or on nonstate revenue sources such as federal aid, to fund public colleges and universities, the more it shifts the costs of higher education away from state taxpayers, at least those who neither attend a public institution nor finance a student's attendance.

The study found that New Hampshire ranked high among its New England peers in the share of revenue its public institutions obtained from the two largest charges: tuition and fees, on the one hand, and the sales and services of "auxiliary enterprises" (dormitories, cafeterias, and bookstores) on the other. It also found that the state's low appropriations for public higher education were largely a matter of choice because a reduced need for financial assistance by a relatively wealthy population accounted for only about 12 percent of the spending gap between New Hampshire and other New England states. Thus, at least as of 2011, New Hampshire balanced annual budgets without a sales or income tax through favorable demographics and conscious policy choices—specifically, stringent eligibility criteria for benefit programs and a practice of shifting costs away from current taxpayers when possible. Still, the study's author cautioned that New Hampshire's fiscal model might not work for other states because of needier populations or because strict eligibility criteria and cost-shifting could conflict with the values and policy preferences of their residents.[21]

More recent data confirm the findings of the study by the Federal Reserve Bank of Boston; New Hampshire's fiscal policy, which continues to shun broad-based sales and personal income taxes, remains unusual, albeit not unique, among the states. Census data from 2021 show that general sales and gross receipts taxes, on the one hand, and individual income taxes, on the other, were the largest sources of state tax revenues during that year. States raised $369.7 billion in sales tax revenues and $503.6 billion in individual income tax revenues that year; the former represented 29.3 percent and the latter 39.9 percent of total state tax revenues in 2021.[22] To be sure, New Hampshire spends most of its money on the same items that other states do. According to the census data, "public welfare" (including Medicaid) consumed the largest share of state government funds ($856.4 billion, or 36.6 percent) in 2020, followed by education (32.8 percent) and transportation (7.9 percent).[23] Similarly, in its Fiscal Year (FY) 2024–25 budget, covering July 1, 2023 through June 30, 2025, New Hampshire devoted 44 percent of its expenditures to "health and social services," 23 percent to education, and 10 percent to transportation.[24] Although the spending categories from the census do not match the state's categories exactly, they are comparable enough to show that New Hampshire allocates most of its spending to the same objectives as other states do.

Nevertheless, because it refuses to impose either a sales tax or a personal income tax, New Hampshire does not collect as much tax revenue per capita as most other states do. For example, in FY 2021, Vermont raised more tax revenue per capita ($6,342) than any other state, well above the national average of $3,802, whereas New Hampshire raised just $2,316, which ranked it above only Florida, Texas, and Alaska in revenue collection. A different picture emerges, though, when measuring state and local taxes per capita; by that measure, New Hampshire ranked twenty-fifth among the states in FY 2021, at $5,409.[25] New Hampshire ranks higher when local taxes are included in the mix because local property taxes account for 56 percent of total state and local tax revenues in the Granite State. In other words, New Hampshire counterbalances its lack of a sales or personal income tax with relatively high property taxes. In FY 2021, New Hampshire ranked fourth among the states, just below New Jersey, New York, and Connecticut, in state and local property tax revenue per capita, at $3,046, which is well above the national median of $1,898.[26] Property tax receipts in that year were 59 percent of the revenue collected by New Hampshire municipalities.[27]

A 2019 study by the Carsey School of Public Policy at the University of New Hampshire stated, "Compared to other states, New Hampshire has chosen to raise less revenue and spend less on public investments and services. State and local government spending make up a smaller share of the state's economy than they do in all but one other state, and spending is low at both the state and local levels."[28] In 2016 New Hampshire and its localities together spent $12.6 billion, which was 16.1 percent of the state's gross domestic product (GDP), placing it forty-ninth in spending as a share of GDP, ahead of only Georgia.[29] The Carsey School study acknowledged that "high local taxes and other revenue sources partially offset low state taxes, but noted that "local governments in New Hampshire have fewer resources available than their counterparts in other states because they receive less from their state government than do local governments in all but three other states."[30] Such conditions, the study observed, reflect conscious choices by state policymakers. "The people of states with higher spending and revenue as a share of GDP," it emphasized, "are choosing to collect and allocate a higher share of the resources available in the state to public purchases and investments—in education, parks, infrastructure, etc." It added that "states with lower spending and revenue as a share of GDP are making the opposite choice."[31]

Several examples illustrate New Hampshire's fiscal choices. In July 2018, Governor Chris Sununu signed sweeping legislation that preserved government-paid health insurance coverage, via Medicaid, for more than fifty thousand low-income adults through 2023. Absent the compromise that made the legislation possible, the insurance coverage would have expired at the end of 2018. Sununu's support for the final bill was a reversal of his prior vote, as a member of the state's Executive Council, against a previous contract for Medicaid expansion in New Hampshire. At that time, he criticized the program's complexity and the uncertainty about the source of future state matching funds for its continued operation. In 2018, though, he supported a compromise that enabled New Hampshire to avoid the direct use of any state taxpayer dollars for the expansion by earmarking 5 percent of the net profits from sales at state-run liquor stores for this purpose. Previously, all the profits from liquor sales had been deposited in the state's Alcohol and Drug Abuse Prevention and Treatment Fund. Sununu also insisted that Medicaid applicants be employed, seek employment, or pursue schooling or job training.[32] The choice of a funding source reflected New Hampshire's practice, whenever possible, of shifting costs away from taxpayers generally to a subset who pay a designated fee to obtain a particular product (higher education, liquor, etc.).

The use of liquor sales as a funding source is another means by which New Hampshire balances its budget and funds services and programs without a broad-based sales or personal income tax. The Carsey School's 2019 study of fiscal policy in New Hampshire found that as of 2016, the state raised 5.3 percent of its annual revenue from liquor sales, the highest percentage of state revenue from that source of any state.[33] Liquor sales are one of several nontax sources of revenue from which New Hampshire benefits; by far the largest one is federal grants, which all states receive. Others include turnpike tolls, Lottery Commission sales, and the state's Unemployment Compensation Fund.[34]

The state also imposes an array of narrowly based taxes directed at specific sectors of the economy or users of certain services. The major taxes include the following:

1. Business Profits Tax: This is New Hampshire's version of a corporate income tax. Businesses must file a BPT return if they have more than $50,000 of gross income in a particular tax year. It draws most of its revenue from relatively few large businesses, minimizing its impact on small businesses, but increasing its volatility according to economic trends. Set at 8.5 percent in 2015, the BPT was lowered to 7.5 percent in 2023, where it remains, at this writing, in the fall of 2025.[35]

2. Business Enterprise Tax: The BET collects revenue from a broader base than the BPT, including for-profit and nonprofit entities, except for entities exempt from tax under section 501(c)(3) of the federal tax code. Its revenue source is the "enterprise value tax base," which includes wages and salaries paid, interest and dividends earned, fees, bonuses, commissions, etc. It rises and falls with changes in economic cycles and the labor market, but it tends to be less volatile than the BPT because it draws from a larger base of taxpaying businesses. The BET was set at a higher rate (0.75 percent) in 2015, was lowered to 0.55 percent in 2023, and remains there as of the fall of 2025.[36]
3. Statewide Education Property Tax: Known as SWEPT, this tax collects from local property taxpayers statewide to help fund public primary and secondary education. Chapter Seven will discuss this tax in detail.[37]
4. Meals and Rentals Tax: Commonly (though erroneously) referred to as the "Rooms and Meals Tax," this revenue device collects money from certain restaurant or catered meals, hotel or lodging rentals, and automobile rentals. Its proceeds go to the state's General Fund and the Education Trust Fund.[38]
5. Tobacco Tax: Although levied on customers who purchase tobacco products, in practice, the tax is often paid by wholesalers who affix stamps to tobacco packages and sell the stamped packages to customers. New Hampshire uses its lower tax rate on cigarettes as a means of economic competition with neighboring states for smokers' business. The proceeds are divided between the General Fund and the Education Trust Fund. This tax is likely to be a declining source of revenue in the future, though, because of a downward trend in cigarette sales in recent years.[39]
6. Real Estate Transfer Tax: Collected from both buyer and seller in property sales. The proceeds are divided between the General Fund and the Education Trust Fund. Its revenue tends to fluctuate with the condition of the economy more dramatically than other sources of revenue because its receipts are correlated with property sales and property prices.[40]
7. Insurance Premium Tax: The IPT is collected from insurance companies, with the proceeds going to the General Fund and the New Hampshire Health Protection Trust Fund. It is a tax on premiums paid for health and accident insurance. A company can claim a credit

against its IPT bill for BET taxes paid or against its BET bill for IPT taxes paid.[41]

8. Motor Fuels Tax: More commonly known as the "road toll," this tax is collected on every gallon of automobile fuel. Its proceeds go to the Highway Fund, with set-asides for certain transportation-related obligations, but the state constitution requires that they be used for highway-related purposes only (e.g., road resurfacing, bridge rehabilitation, debt service for the I-93 expansion project). Its revenues are subject to change as driving habits change, cars and trucks become more fuel efficient, and drivers increasingly purchase electric vehicles.[42]
9. Medicaid Enhancement Tax: This is a tax on charges that hospitals impose for their services minus deductions for charity care, bad debts, or other discounts. The proceeds are deposited in the Uncompensated Care and Medicaid Fund and are used to pay hospitals for uncompensated care, particularly care provided to uninsured patients and Medicaid recipients.[43]
10. Communications Services Tax: This tax is collected from retailers of communications services, including telephone, paging, and specialized radio services. It does not apply to the Internet, though, which likely explains its lackluster performance as a revenue source. The declining use of landline telephones and the shift of more communications services to Internet-based technologies suggest that this tax will continue to decline as a source of revenue.[44]
11. Utility Property Tax: Created to help support the Education Trust Fund, this tax is levied on real estate, buildings, structures, machinery, poles, and pipelines associated with the generation or transmission of electric power, natural gas, or petroleum owned by regulated utilities. It has proved to be a stable, indeed growing, revenue source.[45]
12. Interest and Dividends Tax: Historically, this tax has been levied on individual and certain corporate income from bonds, bank accounts, debt payments, and dividends, but it was repealed on January 1, 2025. The repeal could be problematic because it will cause New Hampshire to lose a revenue source that yielded $184.1 million in FY 2024.[46]

Thus, New Hampshire relies on many revenue sources, including taxes collected from a relatively small universe of individuals or entities and nontax sources such as profits derived from liquor and lottery ticket sales.

Together these sources are designed to substitute for broad-based taxes, principally a general sales tax and a personal income tax.

New Hampshire's tax structure has both advantages and disadvantages as an instrument of fiscal policy. Its advantage lies in having a variety of funding streams, thereby avoiding dependence on a few large sources of revenue, which could result in budgetary shortfalls if one tax or another underperformed during a given year.[47] But it depends on revenue sources (e.g., motor fuels tax, tobacco tax, communications services tax, liquor sales, etc.) that are susceptible to decline amid changing demographics and habits, along with recessions and changes to federal grant programs.[48] And although it depends less on the ebbs and flows of personal incomes than the tax structures of other states do, it relies on the continued growth of industries and revenue sources that do not necessarily grow along with the economy or population. Therefore, the nonpartisan New Hampshire Fiscal Policy Institute has observed that "as New Hampshire's economy and demographics change, this lack of flexibility may present long-term challenges, as declining funding sources may erode future revenue without policy changes."[49] Additional revenue challenges seem likely to result from recent reductions in the rates of the BPT and the BET and the 2025 repeal of the Interest and Dividends Tax.

One major policy consequence of New Hampshire's aversion to taxes generally and broad-based taxes particularly is its low spending in the field of public higher education. Recall the study by the Federal Reserve Bank of Boston, which noted New Hampshire's habit of keeping its spending in this category lower than that of its neighbors by shifting costs away from the taxpayers generally to the students and their parents in the form of high tuition and fees.[50] A 2023 report by the New Hampshire Fiscal Policy Institute shows that the Granite State continues to fund its public colleges less generously than other states do. The report used three metrics to assess this matter. The first metric showed that for every one of its residents, New Hampshire budgeted $106 for public higher education in FY 2023, the lowest amount of any state. For a comparison, note that the next lowest contributor, Pennsylvania, budgeted $153 per capita for this purpose. Nationwide, state government support for public higher education that year averaged $358 per capita.[51]

The second metric compared state funds appropriated for public colleges per $1,000 of personal income among the state's residents. It showed that in 2022, New Hampshire appropriated $1.43 per $1,000 of personal income to fund public higher education. Therefore, a New Hampshire household that earned the median income in 2022 ($89,992) would pay $128.69 toward funding the state's public colleges. In the same year, the national average among the states was $5.22 per $1,000 of personal income.[52] The final metric examined the amount of money appropriated per full-time student enrolled at a public institution of higher education in every state. It revealed that New Hampshire appropriated the lowest amount of all fifty states in FY 2022: $3,699 per fulltime student. The national average was $10,237.[53]

Therefore, it is no surprise that New Hampshire's public colleges relied on tuition for 72 percent of their revenue in FY 2022, compared to a national average figure of 42 percent. After all, the money to pay professors, clean laboratories, and keep lights on in the library must come from somewhere; if state appropriations are insufficient, tuition and fees are the most likely alternatives. Tuition and fees can create debt, though, and a 2020 study by The Institute for College Access and Success (TICAS) found that graduates of New Hampshire's colleges and universities who had higher education loan debt had the highest average debt, at $39,950, compared to graduates of public colleges in other states. That study also found that New Hampshire ranked second in the United States for the percentage of graduates with student loan debt, at 70 percent.[54] It is fair to question a funding structure that makes out-of-state colleges financially competitive with New Hampshire colleges, even for New Hampshire residents, and saddles students with debt loads that may force them to leave the state after graduation to find more lucrative job opportunities elsewhere. Neither result will benefit the state's economic future.[55] Both results, though, flow from New Hampshire's small public investment in higher education, a reflection of its Live Free or Die political culture.

Do Changing Demographics Threaten New Hampshire's Political Culture?

Though political culture continues to influence public policy in New Hampshire, that culture, in recent years, has been subject to major changes in the state's demographic makeup and political party competition. As demographer Kenneth Johnson and political scientists Dante Scala and Andrew Smith have explained, reality belies "the image of the taciturn Yankee with deep roots in New Hampshire" because the state's population "is among the most mobile in the nation: two-thirds of residents aged 25 and over weren't born in the state."[56] Indeed, only 41 percent of the state's American-born residents were born in the Granite State, compared to a national average of 66 percent. Only five other states and the District of Columbia have smaller percentages of native-born residents. Because of New Hampshire's high percentage of recent migrants, more than 20 percent of the voters eligible to vote in its presidential primary in 2020 were either not old enough to vote in 2016 or were living outside the state at that time.[57]

Migrants are essential to New Hampshire's current well-being, and they are likely to be essential to its future too, as they comprise 53 percent of the current population. And even before the arrival of the coronavirus pandemic in 2020, deaths exceeded births annually in New Hampshire, which has an aging population and a low fertility rate, making migration necessary to maintain a productive workforce and a vibrant economy.[58] "Migration" is relocation from one American state to another by persons who were born in the United States; it is distinct from "immigration," which refers to relocating from one's country of origin to the United States. Immigration was important to New Hampshire's population growth during the state's early history, but it has not been a major part of New Hampshire's growth for the past half-century. Today, only 6 percent of New Hampshire residents are foreign-born, compared to 13 percent nationwide.[59]

The "natural" population increase (more births than deaths) in New Hampshire peaked in the 1980s, when births exceeded deaths by 7,200 annually. But even then, migration accounted for most of the state's population increase. Indeed, even during the 1970s, when New Hampshire's population ballooned by almost 25 percent, migration comprised nearly three-quarters of the increase. The slowdown in population growth that occurred in the state during the 1990s resulted primarily from dwindling migration.[60] Migration tends to dwindle during difficult economic times, when increased unemployment, diminished retirement accounts, and housing slumps may make relocating to another state difficult. Accordingly, New Hampshire enjoyed a net migration gain of 8,600 residents annually between 2000 and 2003 but suffered a net loss during the recessionary years (2007–10) of more than 2,100 migrants annually.[61] Migration to New Hampshire recovered after the recession, and the annual population gains between 2014 and 2018 were nearly as large as between 2000 and 2003.

From July 2016 to July 2018, New Hampshire grew by 7,000 residents, a 50 percent increase over the same period from 2014 to 2016. Migration accounted for nearly all the gain.[62]

Population increases in New Hampshire have been "spatially uneven"; the southern and central parts of the state have grown the fastest, whereas the northern part of the state and the Connecticut River Valley have either grown more slowly or have lost population in recent years.[63] Demographer Kenneth Johnson analyzed data from the 2020 Census and found that in the two fastest-growing counties—Rockingham and Strafford—more than 80 percent of the population gain between 2010 and 2020 resulted from migration, as both counties benefitted from the "outward sprawl" of the Boston metro area.[64] Seven of the state's ten counties added population, while three—Cheshire and Sullivan in the lower Connecticut River Valley, and Coos in the North Country—lost people. In Coos, the decline of the wood and paper products industry prompted young adults to seek employment opportunities elsewhere, resulting in fewer births to offset the deaths among its large elderly population. Thus, the overarching demographic truth about New Hampshire is that, in Johnson's words, "migration is critical to the state's future."[65]

More recent data analyzed by Professor Johnson, regarding the time between April 1, 2020, and July 1, 2023, tell the same story; New Hampshire gained 24,500 residents, an increase of 1.8 percent, during that period. The increase occurred even though New Hampshire had 6,600 more deaths than births during that period, because nearly 31,000 more people moved in than moved out, almost 80 percent of them migrating from within the United States.[66] The largest gain during those years occurred in Carroll County, which has long lured retirees and outdoor recreation enthusiasts away from large cities because of its rural character and outdoor amenities (hiking trails, ski areas, etc.).[67]

Although New Hampshire is among the oldest and whitest states, migration has diversified it, particularly in regard to age.[68] Recent migrants have been younger than the established residents. For example, 61 percent of those who arrived between 2010 and 2020 were under age fifty, compared to just 40 percent of established residents. On balance, the migrants were also better educated and earned higher incomes than the former residents they replaced, thereby increasing New Hampshire's human capital.[69] Compared to residents born in-state, both migrants and immigrants to New Hampshire are more likely to have a bachelor's degree and nearly twice as likely to have a graduate degree. They help to explain New Hampshire's relatively high rate of college graduates in its population (36.9 percent), which exceeds the comparable figure for the United States by nearly 5 percent.[70] Between 2013 and 2017, about 16,000 people with at least a bachelor's degree moved to New Hampshire annually, whereas approximately 11,500 people with similar academic credentials left the state.[71] Thus, the migrants are just what the doctor ordered for New Hampshire's aging labor force.[72]

When surveyed, recent migrants cited as their top reasons for moving to New Hampshire: family (i.e., proximity to relatives); the natural environment; the quality of life (i.e., safety, small-town atmosphere, slower pace of life); employment; taxes; culture and lifestyle; and the economy. Only 20 percent of recent migrants cited taxes and just 10 percent cited the economy as a major reason for moving to New Hampshire; similarly, the same percentages of established residents cited those factors as major reasons for staying.[73] These figures belie the conventional wisdom that people move to and remain in New Hampshire primarily because of low taxes; the survey data show that a low tax burden makes New Hampshire attractive to some people, especially higher-income migrants, but family, employment, the natural environment, and the quality of life are stronger motivators for most migrants. A related bit of conventional wisdom that the migration data challenge is that migrants to New Hampshire are mostly former residents of Massachusetts pursuing lower taxes. To be sure, more migrants to New Hampshire come from Massachusetts than any other state (nearly 44 percent in 2021 and 2022). But the data show that in 2021–22 they also came from other northeastern states (14 percent), the South (14 percent), the West (ten percent), and the Midwest (3 percent), and their reasons for migrating varied.[74]

New Hampshire has also diversified racially in recent years because of migration, immigration, and the natural life cycle. Data from the 2020 Census show that during that period the state's minority residents, meaning those who were other than non-Hispanic whites, reached 176,900, an increase of 74.4 percent, making them 12.8 percent of the state's population as of 2020. Ten years earlier, minority residents had represented just 7.5 percent of New Hampshire's population. "Hispanic/Latino" residents reached 4.3 percent, making them the largest minority group in the state. The respective percentages of racial groups in New Hampshire following the 2020 census were as follows:

White, non-Hispanic:	87.2%
Black, non-Hispanic:	1.4%
Native American or Some Other Race alone:	0.6%
Asian alone:	2.6%
Multiracial, non-Hispanic:	4.0%
Hispanic/Latino:	4.3%.[75]

The greatest racial diversity in New Hampshire exists among its children. The population of minority residents under age eighteen reached 20.2 percent by 2020. Their ranks increased by 16,800, or 47.9 percent, between 2010 and 2020. In contrast, the percentage of non-Hispanic white children in New Hampshire declined by 18.7 percent between 2010 and 2020. The increased diversity of New Hampshire's children is most evident in Manchester and Nashua, where minorities constitute 43.1 percent and 45.4 percent, respectively, of the children living in those cities.[76] These changes have occurred because the population of white women of child-bearing age has declined, whereas the population of minority women in that age group has increased, in the United States generally and New Hampshire particularly.

Migration and generational change have combined to produce closer electoral competition between Democrats and Republicans in New Hampshire during the past three decades. As Chapter Two explained, New Hampshire was one of the most Republican states in this country between the Civil War era and the 1990s. In their 2015 book *The First Primary*, University of New Hampshire researchers David Moore and Andrew Smith noted that since the Civil War, New Hampshire had elected only three Democrats to the United States Senate, seventeen Democrats to Congress, and seven Democrats governor. They added that Republicans held a majority of seats in the State House of Representatives and the State Senate "for all but a handful of years since the Civil War."[77] The tectonic plates under New Hampshire politics began to shift, though, in the 1990s, as Democrat Jeanne Shaheen, a longtime political campaign operative and a former state senator, won the governorship in 1996, 1998, and 2000. Building on Shaheen's success, the Democrats also gained control of the State Senate from 1998 until 2002. Then, after a brief interlude between 2002 and 2004, when Republican Craig Benson held the governorship, Democrat John Lynch reclaimed the governorship for the Democrats, winning an unprecedented four times: in 2004, 2006, 2008, and 2010. In 2006, the Democrats also won both congressional seats and majorities in both houses of the state legislature for the first time since 1872.[78]

Moore and Smith have observed that the migrants who settled in New Hampshire during these years "did not change their political allegiance when they moved to the Granite State; instead, they began changing the political landscape of the state itself."[79] For example, about one-third of the New Hampshire electorate in the 2008 elections comprised different people than the 2000 electorate; 21 percent of the 2008 voters were migrants and another 11 percent were newly eligible voters. Both groups were much more likely to identify as Democrats than were the established voters of New Hampshire: 52 percent of the migrants and 53 percent of the young (previously ineligible) voters identified as Democrats, whereas only 43 percent of the established voters did.[80]

More recent data, also compiled by University of New Hampshire researchers, showed that nearly 34 percent of young voters (who turned eighteen after 2015) classified themselves as liberal, as did 28 percent of migrants (who moved to New Hampshire after 2015), and 26 percent of established voters (who were eligible to vote in New Hampshire in 2015 and still lived there at the time of the survey). Conversely, the established voters were more likely to identify themselves as conservative (31 percent), as compared to young voters (25 percent) and migrants (26 percent).[81] Among the recent migrants surveyed, 31 percent self-identified as Republicans, compared to 35 percent of young voters and 36 percent of established voters. Approximately the same proportions of the respective groups self-identified as Democrats. The migrants, however, were more likely than the other two groups to be Independents.[82]

Discussing party identification in New Hampshire is tricky, though, because voters there can conceal their party identification by registering as "undeclared." These voters are often described as "Independents," but most of them favor a particular political party. As of 2019, only 17 percent of young voters were registered as Democrats, but 44 percent favored that party. Similarly, only 13 percent of young voters were registered as Republicans, but 35 percent of them favored that party. This circumstance results from a New Hampshire rule that only requires voters to register with a political party when they wish to vote in a primary election and allows them to reregister as "undeclared" immediately after voting, just before leaving the polling place. Thus, the percentage of undeclared voters does not accurately reflect the presence of true political independence in the New Hampshire electorate.[83]

In any event, New Hampshire's shift to close two-party competition has been part of a larger political realignment in New England during the past three decades. The impetus for this realignment has been the national Republican Party's increasing social conservatism (e.g., opposition to abortion, gun regulations, same-sex marriage, and transgender rights, etc.) which has helped the party in the South and parts of the Midwest and West, but cost it dearly in New England, including New Hampshire.[84] The Republican Party has lost support in New Hampshire in the past generation because its voters are more likely to be economic conservatives than social conservatives; they are more interested in keeping government small and taxes low than in banning abortion or repealing same-sex marriage.[85] In other words, the Republican electorate in New Hampshire differs considerably from its counterparts in the South and West because it is not particularly religious and lacks evangelical Protestants.[86] To be sure, the party is still competitive and often holds a majority in the state legislature, but it has changed from a rural party to a party of the suburbs and exurbs, with strongholds in the two most populous southern counties—Hillsborough and Rockingham—which abut Massachusetts.[87]

The Democrats, on the other hand, maintain urban strongholds in Manchester and Nashua, along with more rural ones in the Hanover/Lebanon area in Grafton County and in Durham and parts of the Seacoast Region. Professor Scala writes, "As long as the populous counties along the Massachusetts border remain closely divided, the more sparsely populated counties of New Hampshire hold the balance of power because the Democrats dominate most of them." Accordingly, he characterizes New Hampshire as a "Democratic-tilting swing state."[88] But New Hampshire Democrats are divided by social class, income, occupation, and education. Suburban areas surrounding the state's larger cities are home to well-educated, well-to-do, socially liberal professionals who are friendlier to business than traditional working-class Democrats. The latter, conversely, are often less friendly to business but more socially conservative than the professionals in the Democratic electorate.[89]

A major consequence of the close competition between the two parties is that moderation is essential to success for gubernatorial candidates in New Hampshire today. For example, Jeanne Shaheen won the governorship in 1996, the first Democrat to do so since Hugh Gallen in the early 1980s. Governing as a moderate, she opposed the introduction of an income tax, vetoed a bill to abolish the death penalty, and was reelected in 1998 and 2000. In the latter year, Mark Fernald, a state senator who advocated the adoption of an income tax, challenged Shaheen in the Democratic gubernatorial primary but lost. Two years later, when Shaheen ran for a US Senate seat, Fernald captured the Democratic nomination for governor but lost badly to Republican Craig Benson, whose one term (2002–04) interrupted an eighteen-year string of Democratic governors in New Hampshire.[90] In the legislature during these years, the majority seesawed between the Democrats and Republicans, with each party often being up or down depending on national electoral trends, especially in presidential election years. The Republicans lost control in 2008 and 2012, when Democrat Barrack Obama won the presidency, but regained it in the 2010 and 2014 midterm elections. Party competition was largely absent from the congressional delegation until 2006, when Democrat Carol Shea-Porter won the First District seat, which she proceeded to win intermittently three more times, alternating in office with Republican Frank Guinta.[91] In 2012, Democrat Anne McLane Kuster won the Second District seat, defeating moderate Republican incumbent Charlie Bass and holding the seat for twelve years before retiring in January 2025.[92]

Jeanne Shaheen's two Democratic successors as governor also governed from the center. Neither one supported a broad-based tax, which undoubtedly made possible John Lynch's four terms (2004–12) and Maggie Hassan's two terms (2012–16) in office. Hassan, a former majority leader in the State Senate, positioned herself from the start of her first campaign as fiscally cautious, pledging to invest in job creation and education, but to veto a state income tax if one ever reached her desk. She defeated Republican Ovide Lamontagne, a social conservative, winning 54.6 percent of the vote. For Lamontagne, the loss was his second in a gubernatorial race, having lost to Shaheen back in 1996. Governor Hassan was reelected in 2014 with 53 percent of the vote.[93]

A better example of close partisan competition was the 2016 US Senate race between Maggie Hassan and the Republican incumbent, Kelly Ayotte. Ayotte served six years as New Hampshire's attorney general, an appointed office, and then in 2010 defeated Congressman Paul Hodes, a Democrat, for the Senate seat long held by retiring Republican Judd Gregg. Before defeating Hodes in the general election, Ayotte bested Ovide Lamontagne in the Republican primary, showing once again that social conservatism was not a winning ticket in elections for statewide or federal office in New Hampshire.

The Hassan–Ayotte Senate race offered voters a welcome choice between two candidates with ample leadership experience in the public arena. Although both candidates were women, Hassan benefitted from a gender gap in the electorate, which was 52 percent women, as she won among women voters (55–42%), narrowly outpacing Ayotte's advantage (53–41%) among men voters. Hassan also benefitted from a racial gap, as nonwhite voters—who were just 8 percent of the electorate—favored her by a significant margin (57–38%). Meanwhile, Hassan and Ayotte battled to a tie among white voters, with each candidate garnering 48 percent of that vote. Finally, young voters also helped to fuel Hassan's victory; voters under the age of thirty—who were 21 percent of the electorate—favored her by nine points (51–42%). The town of Durham—home to the University of New Hampshire—experienced a record-breaking voter turnout and gave Hassan a 3,300-vote win. She won by similar margins in the state's other college towns.[94] Despite such advantages for Hassan, the final tally was extremely close, as Hassan prevailed by just 1,023 votes out of the 738,420 cast.[95]

Maggie Hassan enjoyed an easier path to reelection in 2022, winning by nine points over retired Army Brigadier General Don Bolduc. Bolduc and the Republican candidates who ran for the two US House seats from New Hampshire that year either failed to learn or chose to ignore the message of earlier elections that social conservatism is unhelpful when running statewide or in a federal election in New Hampshire. That maxim is especially true when the opponent is experienced, capable, and moderate. All three Republicans embraced former President Donald Trump's "Big Lie" that President Biden and the Democrats had somehow stolen the 2020 presidential election from Trump, along with what political scientist Christopher Galdieri has termed "strident and, at times, ham-fisted opposition to legal abortion rights and transgender rights."[96] Consequently, incumbent Democratic Congressman Chris Pappas defeated Republican Karoline Leavitt in the First District race by eight points, and Pappas's Democratic colleague, Second District Congresswoman Anne McLane Kuster, defeated Republican Bob Burns by just under twelve points.[97] Evidently, the Trump "Make America Great Again" (MAGA) message of hostility to immigration, neo-isolationism in foreign policy, and a general social conservatism can still win a Republican primary in New Hampshire, especially when the candidates are neither well-known nor well-funded. But the MAGA message handicaps a Republican nominee in a general election there, which should not be surprising, as Granite State voters rejected Mr. Trump's presidential bids in 2016, 2020, and 2024.[98]

The parties were more closely competitive in state legislative races and had been so for years. The Democrats seized control of the legislature and the Executive Council in the 2006 midterm elections, and the Republicans reciprocated in 2010. The Democrats recaptured the majority in 2012, but the Republicans took it back in 2014, another midterm election in which dissatisfaction about national political trends likely affected local results. During the 2000s, the party out of power in Washington, DC, has often gained seats in the New Hampshire Legislature in midterm elections. In the 2018 midterms, true to form, the Democrats won control of both houses of the legislature and of the Executive Council, besides gaining more than sixty seats in the State House of Representatives.[99] For the first time in history, then, a Republican governor—Chris Sununu, who had won a seven-point reelection victory over former state senator Molly Kelly—faced a legislature and a council controlled by Democrats.[100]

Four years later, Republicans eked out a bare majority among the four-hundred representatives, as several elections were decided by single-digit margins. Special elections held throughout 2023 to fill seats vacated by resignations or deaths pared the Republicans' margin to 199–198 by January 2024. But the best news for Republicans from the 2022 elections was the reelection to a fourth term of Governor Chris Sununu, who defeated his Democratic opponent, state senator Tom Sherman, by fifteen points.[101]

Although New Hampshire Republicans, including Governor Sununu, are best known for their fiscal conservatism, the continued competitiveness of Republicans in state elections has enabled social conservatism to succeed from time to time, at least temporarily. For example, in 2023 Governor Sununu signed House Bill (HB) 544, championed by Republicans, which restricted what teachers in public schools could say to their students about discrimination.[102] According to its sponsors, this "divisive concepts" bill was an antidiscrimination measure designed to ensure that all students were treated equally. But in the view of the federal district court that invalidated it, the legislation, which teachers could lose their licenses for violating, was so vague that teachers had "virtually no way of knowing whether a lesson that touches upon the banned concepts violates [it]."[103] Therefore, the court concluded that the law was unconstitutional based on its vagueness.

In 2024, Governor Sununu signed HB 1205, also pushed by Republicans, which requires public schools to designate their athletes by sex and prohibits people assigned male at birth from participating on female sports teams. One's biological sex would be determined by the sex designated on the student's official birth certificate or a certificate issued at adoption. The law's sponsors hailed it as a means of protecting the integrity and the survival of female sports programs. Nevertheless, one day after the law went into effect and shortly before the start of the 2024–25 school year, a federal district judge granted a transgender female who wished to play on her high school's soccer team a temporary restraining order (later extended) against the law's enforcement. The same court later granted the plaintiff's motion for summary judgment, reasoning that the challenged law discriminated based on sex stereotypes. The state could not justify it by arguing that transgender girls created safety issues or enjoyed an athletic advantage, especially when, as in this case, they had "developed physiological traits associated with female puberty."[104] This ruling shows the far-reaching consequences of party politics and election outcomes for individuals' daily lives. A legislature controlled by Democrats would presumably not have passed, and a Democratic governor likely would not have signed, a bill banning transgender athletes in female sports, making a legal challenge unnecessary.

Small Government, Big Challenges: Prospects for New Hampshire's Future

The changing partisan patterns examined here have not changed New Hampshire's devotion to small government. No Democratic governor has proposed an income or sales tax. And the responses of Democratic governors to court orders requiring that public schools be funded equitably—like those of Republican governors—have been to direct more aid to the neediest districts, not to revamp the funding system to make it less reliant on regressive property taxes. In the short run, then, New Hampshire will face its economic and social challenges with a small-government ethos that may hamper its ability to respond.

New Hampshire's taxes may not be broad-based, but its biggest challenges surely are because they affect a wide swath of the state's families and businesses in multiple ways. One such challenge concerns the availability and affordability of childcare services. Demand far exceeds supply; for example, between 2018 and 2022, on average, New Hampshire experienced a shortage of 8,400 childcare slots. Childcare workers are also in short supply. In March 2023, for example, the state's Department of Health and Human Services reported a vacancy rate for childcare workers as 26 percent statewide. And the average annual price of care for an infant and a four-year-old had risen

12 percent, from $28,340 to $31,868, between 2022 and 2023.[105] Therefore, a married couple earning the median income in New Hampshire ($145,000) in 2022 could expect to spend nearly 20 percent of it on child care for an infant and a four-year-old, even though the federal Department of Health and Human Services defines "affordable" child care as costing no more than 7 percent of household income.[106] Such costs affect employers as well as families; for example, in 2024, an average of nearly 17,300 New Hampshire residents each month were not in the labor force because they were caring for children who were neither in school nor daycare.[107]

Meanwhile, as parents struggle to pay for childcare, the providers try to keep their tuition rates within a range that local families can afford, which often means that childcare workers are paid an amount that reflects what funds remain after other expenses are covered. In 2023, for example, preschool teachers in New Hampshire earned a median annual salary of $37,641 or approximately $12,000 less than the median income for all New Hampshire occupations.[108]

To its credit, the state government has begun to respond to these conditions. For example, the FY 2024–25 budget allocated $15 million for distribution to childcare providers for the support of teachers, administrators, and other staff members. The funds are to be used for wage increases or sign-on bonuses, student loan repayments for teachers, credits toward health insurance plans, or deposits into Health Savings Accounts or Flexible Spending Accounts with which to pay for healthcare.[109] The state has recently expanded family income eligibility for its childcare scholarship program to 85 percent of its median income and has limited the cost share for participants in the program to no more than 7 percent of their household income.[110] Under the new rules, a family of four that earns up to $124,595 annually and a family of three that earns up to $104,660 annually may qualify for financial aid to cover childcare costs. And beginning in 2026, a two-year program will allow earlier access to scholarship funds for daycare while families—after an initial screening—complete the application process. A recent critique of childcare policy in New Hampshire applauds these efforts but recommends continuing (rather than one-time) investments, such as childcare scholarships for the children of early childhood educators; free childcare for families who earn 400 percent or less of the federal poverty level; and $2,000-per-semester stipends for childcare professionals pursuing advanced degrees in early childhood education.[111]

Another contemporary challenge for New Hampshire is the future health of its outdoor recreation industry in the face of climate change, which continues to alter the state's natural environment. Outdoor recreation is responsible for more than thirty thousand jobs in New Hampshire, representing 3.2 percent of the state's gross domestic product (GDP) from both in-state and out-of-state visitors. And this industry has enjoyed a dramatic increase in visitors in recent years, partly because of the coronavirus pandemic, which made outdoor recreation both accessible and relatively safe. Under those conditions, outdoor recreation in the White Mountain National Forest in northern New Hampshire increased by nearly 50 percent between 2015 and 2020.[112]

Simultaneously, though, a changing climate is taking a toll on the state's outdoor recreation industry. For example, in the past fifty years, New Hampshire has lost approximately three weeks of snow-covered days, and the dates when the ice has fully melted on Lake Winnipesaukee average eight days earlier than they used to.[113] Providers are especially aware of the changes, such as less vibrant fall foliage, longer and hotter summers, warmer and shorter winters, and fewer days of snow and ice. Beyond those changes, more intense and frequent storms, featuring rain and wind, have strained the resources of providers, who must not only cover annual maintenance costs, but also find extra funds for emergency repairs.[114] When surveyed, providers were more aware than visitors of the challenges and more pessimistic about the future, but responses from both groups reflected wariness about what lies ahead. One provider stated,

> To put it plainly, I'm not sure how much longer operating in New Hampshire in the winter is going to be viable. We have already begun looking for opportunities elsewhere.[115]

Similarly, a visitor stated,

> I've been reconsidering season passes at ski areas for my kids and myself due to the shorter winter season and poorer snow conditions.[116]

To complicate matters, many state parks and protected areas in New Hampshire depend for their funding on visitor fees, which may become a double-edged sword for the outdoor recreation industry. A recent report explains that the visitor-funded model "may exacerbate climate-related issues because additional funding to combat climate impacts would presumably have to come from increased visitation, which would worsen the overcrowding problem."[117] A change in the funding model seems unlikely in the face of the parks' traditional self-sufficiency and New Hampshire's small-government ethos. Alternatively, the 2024–28 Statewide Comprehensive Outdoor Recreation Plan (SCORP) recommends:

1. Designing and redesigning outdoor recreation areas to be adaptable to seasonal shifts and to minimize the impacts that visitors have on the natural environment.
2. Fostering stewardship of outdoor recreation areas (i.e., volunteer participation) through education messaging and programs.
3. Strengthening interagency relationships within state government to develop a shared set of guiding principles for sustainable management of outdoor recreation sites.[118]

Only time will tell whether the public and private providers of outdoor recreation in New Hampshire adapt to or mitigate the environmental and financial consequences of climate change. Outdoor recreation is economically and culturally important to the state's future, so providers will have strong incentives to preserve the vitality of sites and programs. The prevailing political culture, though, will likely dictate that they be self-sufficient in obtaining the necessary funds and judicious in using them.

The two challenges to New Hampshire's future that this book will devote the most attention to, however—in Chapters Six and Seven, respectively—are affordable housing and public school finance. This attention is warranted because these issues affect a large segment of New Hampshire society and have triggered policy responses that reflect the state's political culture. Because later chapters will examine both issues in detail, the current discussion will merely introduce them.

The housing challenge is daunting because the demand is high, but the supply is quite limited. The median sale price of a single-family home in New Hampshire rose by 82 percent between March 2017 and March 2023, and the comparable figure for a condominium during the same period increased by 89 percent.[119] By June 2025, anyone looking to buy a median-priced single-family home in New Hampshire faced a $565,000 price tag.[120] The spike in home prices caused rental rates to rise too; indeed, for a two-bedroom apartment, the cost of rent and utilities shot up from just over $1000 per month in 2011 to $1,600 by 2022. Higher monthly rents, in turn, caused a steady drop in vacancy rates for rental units, from 3.5 percent in 2011 to an eye-popping 0.3 percent in 2022.[121] New Hampshire Housing, the state's housing finance authority, estimated in 2023 that New Hampshire needed 23,500 new housing units immediately (and 90,000 by 2040) to create a market better balanced between supply and demand.[122]

Without a better-balanced housing market, New Hampshire's productivity will likely suffer. As older workers retire, employers will not be able to attract younger people to replace them if the latter cannot find affordable housing. By the same token, retirees looking to downsize to smaller homes will pressure the housing market by competing with younger residents for those homes.[123] State government's response to these concerns is worth exploring because of New Hampshire's traditional preference for local solutions and the historic dominance of local institutions nationwide regarding land-use regulation. Chapter Six will assess how New Hampshire and Vermont have responded to a lack of affordable housing.

Unlike the availability and affordability of housing, which is subject to the decisions of local planning and zoning boards, the funding of public education results from decisions by state government because state constitutions generally guarantee their citizens free public education. The constitutions of New Hampshire and Vermont both include that guarantee.[124] In New Hampshire, the school-funding conundrum reflects a policy choice linked to the state's political culture, which favors minimal taxation, low spending, and local solutions to public needs. Accordingly, New Hampshire school districts rely on their own property taxes for 61 percent of their revenue, with state grants supplying just 21 percent.[125] Even if one includes in the state's share the 10 percent that comes from statewide property tax revenue raised and retained by localities, then the state's contribution increases to just over 30 percent, still the smallest state share nationwide. Under these circumstances, a recent report observes that "by directing more resources to districts with lower property values and students with lower incomes, the state could help address issues of education inequity and strengthen New Hampshire's future workforce."[126]

But directing more state resources to poorer school districts may no longer suffice. Such supplemental distributions have been the state's preferred solution since the late 1990s, resulting in on-again–off-again litigation ever since, because the state has failed to revamp a funding mechanism long ago held unconstitutional. The litigation's latest iteration features new plaintiffs, who are residents of property-poor school districts, seeking to end the reliance on property taxes to fund public schools. Late in 2023, a trial court held that the school funding mechanism still violates the state constitution. In 2025, the state supreme court agreed but declined to order legislators and the governor to provide the constitutionally required funding.[127] In short, the saga continues. Chapter Seven will compare the school funding mechanisms of New Hampshire and Vermont.

Conclusion

New Hampshire's Live Free or Die ethos is reflected in policy choices to delay imposing a mask mandate during the coronavirus pandemic, allow the concealed carry of firearms without a permit, and spend sparingly on public welfare, education, and hospitals. Low spending has helped the state to balance its budget without a sales tax or income tax. Considerable migration and demographic change during the past three decades have turned New Hampshire from a reliably Republican state into a competitive two-party state, but the small-government ethos survives. The Granite State continues to occupy last place in the nation regarding the percentage of state funds per capita spent on public schools.

The question remains, then, whether New Hampshire can meet its current challenges, particularly housing and public school finance, while maintaining its small-government tradition. Both issues threaten the state's future economic viability. Chapter Six will compare the responses of New Hampshire and Vermont to the housing crisis, and Chapter Seven will compare their respective school funding mechanisms. But first, Chapter Five, which follows, will discuss contemporary Vermont politics.

CHAPTER FIVE

The Community-Minded Twin

Politics in Contemporary Vermont

"Freedom and Unity" as Political Culture

ACCORDING TO TRADITION, ETHAN Allen's entrepreneurial brother Ira devised Vermont's motto, "Freedom and Unity," but authorship remains unconfirmed, as Ira was uncharacteristically silent on the matter. In any event, the motto reflected Vermont's tenuous position from 1777 to 1791, proclaiming its freedom from Great Britain and New York, while simultaneously hoping for admission to statehood. Today, Freedom and Unity can be seen as a continuing invitation—even an admonition—to balance the inevitable tensions in society between individual interests and community aspirations.[1] The motto also encourages Vermonters to embrace the possibilities of the future, while preserving, says historian Paul Searls, "those traditions worth saving."[2]

Befitting its motto, "Vermont doesn't fit the usual patterns," argues Frank Bryan, as it combines "ruralism with technology, fiscal conservatism with a social-welfare mentality, not much wealth with a lot of services [and] local democracy with an effective state government," among other contradictions.[3] These contrasts reflect an "independence of thought" that triggered opposition to the Alien and Sedition Acts in the late 1790s, the Green Mountain Parkway in the 1930s, and Senator Joseph McCarthy's Communist-hunting in the 1950s as governmental intrusions on individual freedom. But the same independence of thought prompted support for land-use controls in the 1970s, same-sex civil unions in the late 1990s, and gun regulations in the 2000s, as protections for both individual freedom and community well-being.[4] Seeking to balance those two goals, Vermont has long exhibited, writes political scientist David Plazek, a "willingness to go it alone" in matters of public policy.[5]

The Alien and Sedition Acts, passed in 1798 during the administration of John Adams, responded to threatening behavior by France and an American society bitterly divided between political supporters of France and England. French privateers were seizing American ships on the high seas, and agents of the French Foreign Minister informed American envoys that France would only negotiate an end to the seizures if the Americans paid a bribe, loaned money to the French government, and apologized for disparaging remarks that President Adams had made about France.[6] In this dangerous atmosphere, Congress passed and President Adams signed the Alien and Sedition Acts. The former restricted the rights of legal aliens and eligibility for citizenship, whereas the latter made it a crime to "write, publish, or utter anything of a false, scandalous, or malicious nature against the government, Congress, or the President of the United States." Violations of the Sedition Act were punishable by a fine of up to $2000 and a prison term of up to two years.[7]

Adams supporters in Vermont did not have to look far to find a target for prosecution. Vermont congressman Matthew Lyon, a Jeffersonian firebrand, had excoriated Adams just prior to passage of the Sedition Act, charging him with "a continued grasp for power" and "an unbounded thirst for ridiculous pomp, foolish adulations and selfish avarice."[8] Accordingly, within two days of Lyon's newly established newspaper, *The Scourge of Aristocracy*, becoming available, a grand jury in Rutland indicted Lyon for sedition in October 1798. After a short trial, Lyon was convicted of sedition by bringing "the President and Government of the United States into contempt."[9]

Although a pariah to Federalists who supported Adams, Lyon was a hero to Vermont's Jeffersonians, who reelected him to Congress while he was in prison, enabling him to win a runoff election by almost six hundred votes. Beyond Vermont, Jeffersonian politicians raised money with which to pay his fine. When he was released from jail in Vergennes in February 1799, an enthusiastic crowd of supporters greeted him, and he was driven to Middlebury in a sled drawn by four horses and followed by a long procession of well-wishers.[10] Lyon went on to play a crucial role in the defeat of the Federalists in 1800, casting the decisive vote in the House of Representatives, on the thirty-sixth ballot, that made Thomas Jefferson—rather than Federalist Aaron Burr—president of the United States.[11] Opposition to the Alien and Sedition Acts in Vermont made the state fertile ground for Jeffersonians after 1800; by 1807, the party held both the governorship and a majority in the state legislature, and it enjoyed substantial representation in Vermont's congressional delegation too.[12]

Vermont demonstrated its independence of thought and commitment to free speech again in the 1950s when rejecting the efforts by Senator Joseph McCarthy (R-WI) to identify and punish reputed Communists and former Communists who held prominent positions in the United States. To make his case, McCarthy relied largely on suggestion, innuendo, and supposed "lists" of known Communists, which he declined to make public. In 1953, while McCarthy was popular and influential, Senator Ralph Flanders of Vermont, fed up with his colleague's useless grandstanding, which ruined careers without enhancing national security, introduced a resolution to remove McCarthy from his committee chairmanship. The resolution was later converted to a motion of censure, which passed the Senate in 1954 by a vote of 67–22, with both Flanders and his Vermont colleague, George Aiken, in the majority. That result diminished McCarthy's public support considerably and hastened his political demise.[13] For his part, Senator Flanders showed the Vermont independence of thought when it was most needed by standing up for freedom of conscience against a bully who would have crushed it in the name of a false patriotism.

In the late 1990s, Vermont again showed its independence of thought and its sensitivity to both individual rights and community welfare. The Vermont Supreme Court declared that the Vermont Constitution protects same-sex relationships but left to the legislature the choice of whether that protection should extend to marriage or be limited to civil unions. All five members of the Court agreed that the state constitution protected same-sex relationships, but four of them chose not to legalize same-sex marriage for fear that doing so would trigger an ugly backlash against gay and lesbian Vermonters.[14] In the same vein, barely an hour after the court issued its ruling, Governor Howard Dean announced, "It's in the best interests of all Vermonters, gay and straight, to go forward with the domestic partnership act and not the gay marriage act. And that's what I intend to do."[15] And when he signed the subsequent civil unions law in the spring of 2000, Dean did so in a private ceremony, fearing that a large public celebration of the new law would pour salt into the emotional wounds of its political opponents.[16]

To be sure, the civil unions law had plenty of opponents, who often complained that they no longer recognized the Vermont in which they had been raised. Said newspaper editor M. Dickey Drysdale of rural Orange

County, "We've gone, over fifteen or twenty years, from one of the more rural, conservative states in the country to one of the more liberal, and there have been a lot of people who have been hurt."[17] Taken together, the civil unions law and a major overhaul, two years earlier, of Vermont's public school funding mechanism, fueled a "Take Back Vermont" movement, centered in Orange County, that sought to punish politicians who had supported one or both changes. In the 2000 election, seven senators and twenty-nine representatives who had voted for the civil unions law either retired or were defeated for reelection, and Republicans took control of the House, although Howard Dean was reelected.[18]

Nine years later, Vermont became the fourth state to legalize marriage for same-sex couples, enabling them to enjoy all the benefits of marriage, not just those that a civil union afforded. Moreover, Vermont was the first state to legalize same-sex marriage by statute rather than by court order; previously, state supreme courts had validated it in Connecticut, Iowa, and Massachusetts. In Vermont, although Governor Jim Douglas, a Republican, vetoed the Marriage Equality Act, a legislative supermajority (100–49 in the house and 23–5 in the senate) overrode his veto, and the new law took effect on September 1, 2009.[19] Opposition to it was considerably less vocal than opposition to civil unions, suggesting that if Vermonters were not entirely supportive of same-sex marriage, they were at least resigned to it and would accept it.[20]

More recently, Vermont's independence has been evident in the realm of firearms regulation. Recall from Chapter One that in 2018, the Vermont Legislature passed and Governor Phil Scott, a Republican, signed into law legislation that expanded background checks for gun purchases, banned bump stocks (add-on devices that can make semiautomatic weapons fully automatic) and high-capacity magazines, and raised the legal age to purchase a gun.[21] In 2023, Governor Scott signed S.3, which banned paramilitary-style training camps. One such camp, in southern Vermont, had long been the subject of litigation over zoning violations and threats to neighbors by the property's owner. Scott also signed S.4, the primary purpose of which was to conform state laws on "straw" (third party) purchases of guns and serial number tampering to federal law on these subjects.

A third bill, H. 230, sought to implement safe storage rules for firearms, broaden red flag laws, (which prohibit potentially dangerous persons from having firearms), and establish a 72-hour waiting period for gun purchases.[22] Scott allowed this bill to become law without his signature because of his concern that its waiting-period provision will not survive constitutional scrutiny in court. His concern comes from the United States Supreme Court's decision in *New York State Rifle & Pistol Association v. Bruen*, which held that for a firearm regulation to be constitutional, the government must show that it is consistent with the United States' "historical tradition" regarding the regulation of firearms.[23] To be sure, Vermont may have difficulty showing that a waiting period to purchase a firearm is a long-standing tradition in America. Still, Scott allowed the bill to become law because he anticipates that a court—most likely, a federal court—will eventually resolve the matter.[24] In any event, despite its long tradition of hunting and gun ownership, Vermont in recent years has balanced the freedom of gun ownership with the responsibility to protect public safety by restricting access to firearms for persons likely to misuse them.

Meanwhile, the continuing tradition of annual town meetings appears to preserve both freedom and unity by giving everyone who wishes to speak a chance to do so, including conservative voices less likely to be heard in statewide debates.[25] To be sure, reverence for the town-meeting tradition extends well beyond Vermont and Vermonters. The eminent essayist, philosopher, poet, and abolitionist Ralph Waldo Emerson observed that town meeting reveals "the great secret of political science" and solves the "problem" it entails: how to "give each individual his fair weight in the government."[26] In town meetings, Emerson recalled, "the rich gave council, but the poor also; and, moreover, the just and the unjust . . . every opinion had its utterance, every fact, every acre of land, every bushel of rye, its entire weight."[27] Similarly, the French diplomat and political philosopher Alexis de Tocqueville, whose famous book, *Democracy in America*, reported the findings from his 1831 visit to this country, noted, "Town Meetings are to liberty what primary schools are to science; they bring it within the people's reach, they teach men how to use and enjoy it."[28]

In today's fast-paced society, where people work outside the home and frequently commute to an out-of-town workplace, attendance at town meetings, traditionally held during the daytime, is typically small, limiting their value as an instrument of democracy. Indeed, during the 1,435 Vermont town meetings that Frank Bryan and his students attended between 1970 and 1998, the average attendance was just 20.5 percent of the registered voters in town.[29] But dual-income households and long commutes are not the only factors depressing town meeting attendance. Indeed, Bryan found that the most powerful influence on town meeting attendance was the size of a particular town; a higher percentage of residents attended town meetings in smaller towns than larger ones because, Bryan concluded, "the people who live in these [smaller] places know they are more powerful decision makers than people in larger towns."[30] And although daytime meetings might dissuade workers employed out of town from attending, nighttime meetings can also depress attendance, if not from fatigue, then from frigid temperatures, snow, sleet, or ice storms, all of which are as traditional to March in Vermont as Town Meeting itself.[31]

To improve participation in townwide votes, many Vermont towns have abandoned the traditional daylong town meeting featuring floor voting on the agenda items in favor of an evening "informational meeting" that identifies the list of items to be voted on the following day by Australian ballot. This is a written ballot prepared ahead of time that allows residents to vote at a polling place before or after work instead of sitting through a long deliberative meeting. Ironically, although the Australian ballot mechanism aims to make participation easier, Professor Bryan discovered an average of only 15.6 percent of residents voted in the towns that used an Australian ballot, compared to 26.6 percent in towns that did not use it. Thus, he concluded that attendance was best when the Town Meeting was held during the day on a Tuesday and did not use an Australian ballot.[32]

Nonetheless, even if modern conditions depress attendance at Town Meeting, the institution remains a powerful tool for democratic education. After all, its small numbers make addressing the group a less daunting prospect for a young person or a newcomer than facing a large assembly would be. And most Vermont towns are still diverse enough economically that Town Meeting will offer, in Bryan's words, "an accurate approximation of the ranges of status groups in the community," no small feat at a time when Americans associate mostly with their socioeconomic peers. Besides, he notes, Town Meeting teaches one "how to suffer damn fools and to appreciate the fact that from time to time you too may look like a damn fool in the eyes of people as good as yourself."[33] Occasionally, it can even inspire bold—if only symbolic—action, as occurred in 1982, when more than 150 Vermont towns passed resolutions that called for a freeze on the development of nuclear weapons by the United States and the Soviet Union.[34]

One cannot know, of course, whether Vermonters had freedom and unity in mind when considering the Alien and Sedition Acts, Senator Joseph McCarthy's allegations, the legalization of same-sex relationships, or the regulation of firearms, or whether they contemplate it when evaluating the items before their Town Meeting. Still, the scenarios described above suggest continuing efforts, however imperfect, to reconcile individual freedom and community welfare, consistent with the state motto.

Vermont's small population surely fosters both freedom and unity, as former governor Madeleine Kunin (1985–91) has observed. She recalled that, when governor, "it took me a long time to do my grocery shopping because people would stop and talk to me. We're accessible to one another."[35] She added that Vermont attracts people who love the outdoors and the "sense of community" present in the state.[36] Sometimes, regrettably, Vermont attracts people who do not value community. In 2018, for example, Vermonters were angered, embarrassed, and forced to do some soul-searching when the first African American woman elected to the state legislature resigned her seat amidst racist threats made against her. The threats ranged from rants on social media to vandalism at her home by a Bennington man who espoused white nationalism.[37] By and large, though, the values that Governor Kunin cited predominate and continue to be reflected in Vermont's public policy choices.

A more recent example of Vermont's orientation toward community welfare was the legislature's decision, in the spring of 2023, to invest more than $120 million annually in the state's childcare system. Although Governor Scott vetoed the childcare bill, then known as H. 217, because he objected to the 0.44 percent payroll tax that was part of it, both houses of the legislature, which had Democratic supermajorities, overrode the veto by comfortable margins.[38] The new law, now known as Act 76, roughly doubles the public funds that Vermont spends on early childhood education.[39]

Vermont's childcare system was suffering when Act 76 was enacted because the coronavirus pandemic took a heavy toll. By November 2023, Vermont had 182 fewer active childcare providers than four years earlier, a decrease of more than 16 percent. Because of a drop in providers and a decline in available slots amongst the remaining providers, the state reported approximately 3,315 fewer childcare slots than had existed before the pandemic, a decrease of 11 percent. This shrinkage occurred everywhere in the state except in populous Chittenden County, where capacity among childcare providers increased by about 4 percent, or slightly more than four hundred slots.[40]

Under these circumstances, childcare experts praised Act 76 as "a great down payment on a childcare system that works for parents and providers" but "not the full investment."[41] Their qualified praise reflects the multipronged dilemma faced by the childcare community in Vermont.

First, childcare requires a low ratio between adults and children, so it is a labor-intensive, costly service. Second, most families must pay directly for this service, so providers need to set their tuition rates well below the true cost of care. Finally, those tuition rates are still difficult for many families to pay, so providers' income suffers, and childcare workers' wages leave them unable to support themselves.[42]

Act 76 seeks to address these conditions in two ways: (1) by greatly expanding the number of families eligible for government subsidies to assist them in paying tuition and (2) by increasing by 35 percent the rate at which the state reimburses providers who participate in the subsidy program.[43] As of October 2024, families earning up to 575 percent of the federal poverty level—meaning $172,000 for a family of four—became eligible for partial subsidies. This development extended state help to an estimated 80 percent of Vermont families, a greater share of the population than any other state covers.[44] Providers have also received assistance, including readiness payments in fall 2023. These payments were designed to help providers repair their facilities, invest in additional teaching materials or other resources, and increase the wages and benefits of their employees. Then, in January 2024, providers began receiving increased reimbursements.[45]

The payroll tax makes this financial restructuring of the childcare industry possible by expanding the number of families eligible to receive subsidies to pay for childcare and by paying providers more to serve those families. Vermont employers pay a 0.44 percent tax on wages paid, with an option to withhold up to 25 percent of the tax from their employees. Self-employed Vermonters pay a tax of 0.11 percent on their incomes.[46] Before Act 76, the per-child reimbursement rates that the state paid to providers were based on market surveys of the rates that providers charged families. But because providers could not charge families the true cost of care, the state reimbursements to providers did not reflect that cost either. Now, because of Act 76, the state's reimbursement rates are based on "cost of care" surveys that reflect the true cost of care. If the reimbursement rate is higher than the tuition a provider charges to families, the provider can keep the difference, which was not possible under the previous system.[47] These changes likely help to explain why, in the first quarter of 2024, more childcare programs opened than closed in Vermont for the first time since 2008.

Still, Act 76 is not a panacea for all that ails childcare in Vermont; concerns remain. For example, will providers raise their prices at the same rate as their reimbursements? If so, the new subsidies will not reduce families' out-of-pocket costs by much, if at all. And the new law does not require providers to raise wages for their employees, although it states that they may do so in the future. Will the funds provided by Act 76 be sufficient to solve the workforce shortage in early childhood education? This question remains open. Finally, recall that childcare experts have characterized Act 76 as a "down payment" toward an appropriate system; some estimates of the total annual cost of a system comparable to what other industrialized countries provide approach $700 million.[48] Thus, the cost and availability of childcare will likely continue to demand the attention of Vermont policymakers in the years ahead.

Bold state interventions such as Act 76 are often expensive, causing some Vermonters to argue that they limit freedom and undermine unity. Governor Phil Scott's opposition to the use of a payroll tax to fund new childcare subsidies reflects this view. He contends that the Democratic supermajority of recent years taxed Vermonters excessively to fund its progressive agenda. Conservative critiques of liberal fiscal policies are nothing new in Vermont; indeed, these critiques were evident, though not dominant, in the "Pulse of Vermont," a 2010 quality-of-life study produced by the Vermont Business Roundtable. The researchers surveyed 407 Vermonters by telephone and a separate sample of slightly more than 500 Vermonters via the Internet.[49] Although the data are not current, they reveal differences of opinion about public spending that remain sharp today.

The respondents' answers reflected a mixture of economic insecurity and a desire to maintain Vermonters' historic concern for both their neighbors and the natural environment. Their public priorities ranked as follows:

	Priority	*Percentage of Support*
1.	Creating more good jobs	28
2.	Maintaining family farms and local agriculture	17
3.	Helping those who can't help themselves	13
4.	Preserving clean air and water	11
5.	Improving educational opportunities	8
6.	Maintaining access to recreational land	6
7.	Maintaining a low crime rate	5
8.	Limiting sprawl	5
9.	Improving transportation and communication	4
10.	Preserving scenic views	2[50]

Fifty percent of the respondents said they were willing to pay an extra $250 in local taxes to preserve open land in their towns, 49 percent would do so to improve public transportation in their towns, and 42 percent would do so in support of improved schools and police and fire protection.

Generally, income did not affect the responses, but gender and political ideology did; women and people who described themselves as "liberal" were "significantly more supportive" of such policy goals. Specifically, women were about 10 percent more ready than men to provide additional financial support for schools, public transportation, and police and fire protection. Except for police and fire protection, self-described liberals were 15 to 22 percent more ready to pay extra for such public services than self-described conservatives.[51]

When the respondents were asked whether they thought life in Vermont was "getting better, worse, or staying the same," the most frequent response (46 percent) was "staying the same." But the respondents who thought life was getting worse had steadily increased since the first survey in 1990, reaching 41 percent in the 2010 survey. They tended to be men born in Vermont, with a high school education or less, and older but not yet retired. Fifty-four percent of them described themselves as conservative, 50 percent were "worried about paying bills," 47 percent said that their financial situation was "worse" than it had been five years earlier, and 46 percent reported that they lived outside of Chittenden County, which encompasses the Burlington metropolitan area.[52]

The distinction between respondents born in Vermont and those born elsewhere was a powerful predictor of economic circumstances and political ideologies. Part of the stark difference between the two groups was that the native-born Vermonters constituted only 28 percent of all the Vermonters with a college degree, meaning that 72 percent of the Vermonters who held a college degree in 2010 were born elsewhere.[53] Predictably, educational differences correlated with income differences. The study found that 74 percent of the respondents whose household income was less than $25,000 annually were born in Vermont, whereas only 38 percent of those whose household income exceeded $100,000 annually were born in Vermont.[54]

The Pulse of Vermont study paints a picture of Vermont as a highly desirable place to live, but a challenging place to earn a living, especially for residents without a college education. It shows that those residents, particularly older men who are still working, often perceive government initiatives such as Act 76 as making Vermont unaffordable for them by increasing their tax burden. But such initiatives will likely continue in the Green Mountain State because the political culture fosters a state-centered fiscal policy and a willingness to spend public dollars to meet human needs.

Vermont's willingness to spend public dollars is evident in data compiled by the Urban Institute for FY 2020. The data compared Vermont's state and local per capita spending to that of the New England states as a whole and the United States in seven program areas. The results were as follows:

	Program Area	*Per Capita Expenditure*
1.	Elementary and Secondary Education	VT: $3,750
		NE: $2,500
		US: $2000
2.	Public Welfare (Includes Medicaid)	VT: $3,000
		NE: $2,750
		US: $2,500
3.	Higher Education	VT: $1,500
		NE: $750
		US: $1,000
4.	Roads and Highways	VT: $1000
		NE: $500
		US: $500
5.	Health and Hospitals	VT: $700
		NE: $500
		US: $1,000
6.	Police	VT: $500
		NE: $500
		US: $500
7.	Corrections	VT: $250
		NE: $250
		US: $250

Thus, in four of the seven program areas, Vermont spent significantly more money per capita in FY 2020 than both the New England states as a whole and the United States. In two areas, Vermont's spending equaled that of the two larger entities. Only with respect to health and hospitals was Vermont's per capita spending less than that of the United States, although it exceeded that of the New England states as a group.[55]

Spending depends on revenue, though, so an examination of Vermont's revenue structure is in order. Data provided by the Vermont Legislature's Joint Fiscal Office in March 2023 will aid in that task. Vermont is a taxation unicorn among the states in that it collects most of its tax revenue at the state level rather than the local level, and it is the only state to collect a significant amount of revenue from a statewide property tax.[56] Revenue from the statewide property tax is spent only on elementary and secondary education. Like other states, Vermont can increase its revenue only by (1) increasing existing taxes; (2) expanding the bases of existing taxes so that they apply to more goods, services, or human activities; and (3) creating new taxes. Like New Hampshire, Vermont spends the biggest portions of its funds on human services and public education, which accounted for 35.8 percent and 31 percent, respectively, of Vermont's FY 2023 budget.[57] And like New Hampshire, Vermont typically uses federal funds to cover about one-third of the cost of its state programs.

Unlike New Hampshire, however, Vermont has broad-based income and sales taxes that generate considerable revenue; the income tax accounts for approximately one-third of non-property-tax revenues annually. The Joint Fiscal Office projected in 2023 that in FY 2024, proceeds from the income tax would account for 37 percent of total revenues and 56 percent of General Fund revenues. The sales tax and the rooms and meals tax raise less money, but are important too. The entire proceeds from the sales tax and one-quarter of the proceeds from the rooms and meals tax enter the Education Fund annually.[58]

Thanks to data furnished by the Joint Fiscal Office for FY 2020, one can compare New Hampshire and Vermont on the revenue side of the ledger. On a measure of total state and local tax revenue raised, Vermont ranked tenth among the states, having raised $6,446 per capita; whereas, New Hampshire ranked twenty-fifth, raising $5,128 per capita. The average figure across the fifty states was $5,616, so Vermont was well above that amount, and New Hampshire was well below it.[59] On a measure of state and local sales tax revenue, Vermont ranked twenty-sixth, having raised $1,526 per capita; whereas New Hampshire, which lacks a broad-based sales tax, but has taxes on beer, liquor, and rooms and meals, ranked forty-seventh, raising only $393 per capita via sales taxes. The United States average was $1,643 per capita, so both Vermont and New Hampshire were below average in their sales tax proceeds.[60]

Moving to personal income tax revenue, Vermont ranked eleventh, raising $1,906 per capita, a bit above the United States average of $1,525 per capita. New Hampshire, which lacks a broad-based income tax, but nonetheless includes wages and salaries paid in the Business Enterprise Tax levied on employers, ranked forty-second, raising just $107 per capita.[61] The two states were close together, though, on a measure of state and local property tax revenue per capita, reflecting New Hampshire's reliance on property taxes to offset its lack of a broad-based income or sales tax. New Hampshire ranked third among the states on this measure, raising $3,283 per capita; whereas Vermont ranked sixth, collecting $2,858 per capita in property tax revenue. The United States average was $1,810 per capita.[62] The other revenue measure on which New Hampshire ranked above Vermont was corporate income tax revenue per capita; New Hampshire was first, raising $728 per capita, reflecting proceeds from its Business Profits Tax and its Business Enterprise Tax. Vermont was fifteenth, raising $258 per capita. The United States average was $272 per capita.[63]

Finally, the Joint Fiscal Office report highlighted one expenditure measure for the fifty states: direct government expenditures per capita. Direct government expenditures are expenditures required by law. The most familiar examples are entitlements, such as the federal Medicare, Medicaid, and Social Security programs. On the state level, direct government expenditures feature payments to individuals, businesses, state agencies, and local governments. For example, Vermont's payments to consumers and providers of childcare under Act 76 are direct government expenditures. In FY 2020 Vermont ranked seventh among the states, spending $14,882 per capita in this manner; whereas New Hampshire ranked fortieth, spending $10,287 per capita on direct payments to Granite Staters. The United States average was $12,751 per capita.[64]

The data cited above reflect Vermont's continuing commitment to support public goods, such as vibrant schools, accessible libraries, and land conservation. The state's recent investment in its childcare system is a prime example of that support.

Do Changing Demographics Threaten Vermont's Political Culture?

In his January 2023 inaugural address, Governor Phil Scott included a shortage of workers on a list of serious problems facing Vermont.[65] Scott was not the first governor to sound the alarm about Vermont's demographic challenges, though, as Jim Douglas had done the same in 2005. Douglas told a reporter:

> I think the data are indisputable. We've seen a dramatic shift demographically, and it's at both ends of the chronological spectrum. It presents a real challenge for us to have fewer people in the traditional work force, and more older people to take care of.[66]

Demographic challenges remain front and center for Vermont today. The state's population of 647,464 reflects the following changes that occurred between July 1, 2020, and July 1, 2023:

1. a decrease of about four thousand children (three percent) under age 17;
2. an increase of about two thousand people (almost two percent) ages 25–39;
3. a decrease of about 6,100 people (almost six percent) ages 55–64;
4. an increase of 10,800 people (more than ten percent) ages 65–79; and,
5. an increase of about 2,600 people (almost ten percent) over 80.[67]

As a result, the share of Vermonters in the prime working years (25–64) dropped from 51.3 percent in 2020 to 50.4 percent in 2023. Note the respective increases in the populations of Vermonters ages 65–79 and over 80; the former group now makes up 17.5 percent of Vermont's population.[68] Thus, even though Vermont saw a net gain of about 4,500 residents between July 1, 2020, and July 1, 2023 because of pandemic-era migration, the data presented above show that the worker shortage continues. Thus, if Vermont is to grow its overall population and its share of working-age residents substantially, it must compensate for its low birth rate by attracting migrants, both foreign and domestic, to the Green Mountain State.[69] That low birth rate is itself symptomatic of Vermont's demographics because the state has high percentages of non-Hispanic white women and women who hold at least a bachelor's degree. Both groups have lower birth rates than other cohorts in the American population.[70]

Without migration, adverse policy consequences are likely to flow from Vermont's demographic profile. One such consequence, as Governor Douglas identified two decades ago, is pressure on working-age Vermonters to help support the youngest and the oldest Vermont residents, who may be unable to support themselves adequately. A related consequence is that as the state's large cohort of baby boomers, born between 1946 and 1964, ages out of the workforce, Vermont's income tax collections may decline. Its sales tax revenues may shrink too, as older Vermonters shift their spending away from goods and toward services, such as health care, which are either untaxed or taxed lightly.[71]

To make matters worse, Vermont is one of the major victims of the annual "college graduate brain drain," along with some other small states, such as West Virginia and New Hampshire, that lack urban areas with ample job opportunities for new graduates. In fact, Vermont ranks dead last on this unenviable list, losing 57.5 percent of its graduates annually, just below West Virginia's 52.6 percent figure and New Hampshire's 50.6 percent.[72] Admittedly, even if all graduates remained in Vermont after completing their studies, the state would still fall short of the approximately 19,000 new workers it needs each year. Under those circumstances, though, the challenge of recruiting workers would surely be less daunting than it is today.[73]

When population growth plateaus or declines, participation in the workforce tends to level off too. According to data from the 2020 census, Vermont's population grew by only 2.8 percent during the previous decade, whereas the population of the United States grew by 7.4 percent in the same period.[74] The percentage of Vermonters over age 65 grew by 40.5 percent between 2010 and 2020; by 2030 Vermont will likely have more residents over age sixty-five than under age twenty. Together, slow population growth and a large cohort of senior citizens will tend to exert a gravitational pull downward on economic activity in Vermont.[75] The large cohort of senior citizens will lower the workforce participation rate, thereby narrowing the base from which to derive revenue, potentially triggering either higher tax rates to make up for the revenue shortfall or a decrease in services. After all, paychecks not only produce income tax revenue, but also spur consumer spending, which in turn generates business income and sales tax revenue. And older people who are not employed frequently need more services than other individuals, such as Medicaid and other safety-net assistance, which add to governmental costs.[76]

One can assess the economic impact of an aging population by using the age dependency ratio, which measures the ratio of the traditional working-age population (ages 18–64) to the combination of the young (under age 18) and older (over age 64) people in a particular population. The ratio is created by dividing the combined populations of people under age 18 and over age 64 by the total population.[77] From 1900 until 1950, Vermont enjoyed a relatively stable age dependency ratio of just under 60 percent, meaning that the combined under-18 and over-64 age groups comprised slightly less than 60 percent of the state's total population. The dependent population increased between 1960 and 1970, but declined in the 1990s to about 50 percent before increasing again in 2010 to 54 percent, as compared to a nationwide average of 59.1 percent. By 2022, Vermont's age dependency ratio had climbed to 60.1 percent, and it is expected to reach 70 percent by the 2030s.[78] If that expectation is realized, seven in every ten Vermonters will be either a child or a senior citizen, hence not of prime working age. Under those circumstances, Vermont policymakers will face a double whammy of reduced tax revenues and increased demand for government programs, as many Vermonters transition from being net contributors to those programs to net beneficiaries of them.[79]

In the near term, though, this demographic challenge manifests itself as a shortage of workers for Vermont employers. In October 2023, according to the federal Bureau of Labor Statistics, Vermont workplaces had 2.7 job openings for every unemployed Vermonter, meaning a resident who was without work but actively seeking work. Vermont's ratio of job openings to job seekers was nearly double the nationwide ratio at that time.[80] To be sure, positive signs existed too, as November 2023 was the thirteenth consecutive month when the number of people employed in Vermont increased. The combination of workers and job seekers rose to 351,080, smaller than the pre-pandemic workforce of 355,000, but still the highest total since April 2020.[81] The bottom line, however, is that "Vermont still has more jobs than people."[82]

In this environment, it is understandable that the Vermont Futures Project, a nonprofit entity that seeks to improve Vermont's economic health relative to other states, argues for an increase in the state's population to

802,000 people by 2035. This number is easy to remember because it mirrors Vermont's lone telephone area code—802. According to the Futures Project, Vermont's Department of Labor estimates approximately 14,800 retirements per year through 2030, which the annual entry of young workers into the state's workforce does not come close to offsetting. More precisely, the Vermont workforce needs an additional 13,500 new workers each year to keep pace with retirements. Considering the relatively low number of high school seniors in Vermont (5,300 in 2022–23) and the college graduate brain drain noted earlier, much of the entering workforce will have to be migrants. To complicate matters, the need for more workers will exacerbate Vermont's already chronic housing shortage, which Chapter Six will address. The Futures Project estimates that the state will need approximately 350,000 new non-seasonal units to house the new workers it will require in the years ahead.[83]

The title of this section asks whether changing demographics threaten Vermont's political culture. Political cultures take a long time to develop and do not yield to change easily, as is evident in New Hampshire's long-standing individualism and resistance to broad-based taxes. Vermont's more state-centered, community-oriented political culture is sturdy too, but just as a housing shortage and a school-funding dilemma challenge New Hampshire's traditional frugality, a worsening age dependency ratio challenges Vermont's generous support for programs such as childcare and education. If, in the 2030s, as the Vermont Futures Project warns, only 30 percent of the Vermont population is helping to support the 70 percent who are either children or senior citizens, resentment, fueled by a high tax burden on the payors, could undermine Vermont's communitarian ethic. If the Pulse of Vermont study is an accurate predictor, native-born Vermonters without a college degree (particularly men) are likely to resent the tax burden associated with the need to support children and seniors. In any event, the near term will surely test the capacity of the state's political process to reconcile the powerful demographic and economic forces shaping Vermont's future.

Compromise or Continued Conflict? Prospects for Vermont's Future

Demographics will affect not only the issues that Vermonters face in the future, but also the selection of officials who must resolve those issues. If present conditions hold, most of the elected officials who will confront

Vermont's public policy challenges in the near term will be Democrats, except for Governor Phil Scott, who won reelection to a fifth term in 2024. Scott, a Vermont native, was first elected in 2000 to the State Senate, where he served five terms. He later served three terms (2011–17) as lieutenant governor before being elected governor in 2016. Like other recent Republican governors of Vermont, Scott is aptly described by author and environmental activist Bill McKibben as "fiscally and temperamentally cautious and disinclined to engage in any culture wars."[84] He has declined to support any of Donald Trump's presidential candidacies and has kept the Republican Party, especially the national party, at arm's length.

As Scott's lengthy gubernatorial tenure suggests, two-party competition and periodic alternation in office between Democrats and Republicans are alive and well in Vermont's executive branch. But they were long missing from the legislative branch. As late as election day 2024, the thirty-member Vermont Senate held twenty-one Democrats, seven Republicans, one Progressive, and one vacant seat.[85] That was no anomaly, as the Democrats had controlled this chamber continuously from 1996 through 2024.[86] Similarly, the 150-member Vermont House of Representatives held 107 Democrats, 37 Republicans, 2 Progressives, 1 Libertarian, and 3 Independents. The Democrats controlled the house from 1992 through 2000, lost control to the Republicans after the enactment of civil unions in 2000, then regained control in the election of 2004 and have retained it ever since.[87]

In the 2022 elections, the Republicans lost five seats in the Vermont House, giving the Democrats a record-breaking supermajority. Indeed, the Republicans fielded candidates for just 88 of 150 house seats. Meanwhile, in the senate, the Democrats and Progressives retained their combined twenty-three-seat supermajority.[88] After Scott, who won his race with 71.3 percent of the vote (an improvement over his 68.5 percent tally in 2020), the biggest vote-getter among statewide Republican candidates was lieutenant-governor hopeful Joe Benning, who won 43 percent against incumbent David Zuckerman's 54 percent. No other statewide Republican candidate garnered more than 35 percent of the vote. In the federal races, neither the Republican House nor Senate candidate won more than 30 percent of the vote.[89]

During the 2023–24 legislative session, Governor Scott and the Democratic supermajority were often at odds, especially regarding taxation, education funding, and environmental issues.[90] Scott telegraphed this discord in his January 2023 inaugural address, in which he identified the most pressing problems facing Vermont—the effects of climate change, a lack of affordable housing, a need for more childcare and prekindergarten programs, and a worker shortage. He then suggested resolving them through regulatory changes, executive-legislative teamwork, and a reallocation of funds the state already spends, instead of imposing more or larger taxes on Vermonters.[91] Discord was certainly a major theme of the session, which two Vermont journalists attributed to a "deepening partisan chasm in Montpelier."[92] The best indicators of that divide were the dubious distinctions the governor and the legislators acquired during the session: no governor in Vermont history had issued more vetoes than Phil Scott, and no legislature had overridden more vetoes in a single day than Vermont's Democratic lawmakers did in June 2024.[93]

The legislators overrode Scott's veto of the Yield Bill, the annual measure that sets average property tax rates statewide to fund public education, because he opposed the significant increases in property taxes it would trigger. But even though the bill was associated with a projected increase in property taxes of 13.8 percent on average, the house overrode the veto by a vote of 102–43, and the senate did the same by a 22–7 tally.[94] All told, the legislators overrode six vetoes, covering: (1) reform of Act 250, Vermont's longstanding land-use-planning statute; (2) an expansion of the state's restorative justice program; (3) the creation of a new renewable energy standard designed to reduce carbon emissions by utility companies; (4) a pilot program designed to prevent drug overdoses by establishing safe injection sites; and (5) a ban on certain insecticides, called neonicotinoids, to protect pollinators.[95]

A commentary on the 2023–24 legislative session noted that a significant philosophical conundrum underlay the vetoes and overrides: the extent of government's proper role in the lives of Vermonters and Vermont businesses in the name of social and scientific progress.[96] Democratic legislators want to use government to help Vermonters have safer, healthier lives with more economic opportunities, but Governor Scott and Republican legislators counter that the taxes and regulations associated with the Democrats' aspirations make life unaffordable for older, rural, and low-income Vermonters. Accordingly, Governor Scott, campaigning for reelection in 2024, sought to persuade voters that vetoes and overrides would continue unless more Republicans or even moderate Democrats were elected to the legislature for the 2025–26 session.

Despite the recent partisan conflict, both Governor Scott and the Democratic legislators supported a first-in-the-nation law, enacted in 2024, to hold fossil fuel companies liable for the weather impacts of climate change precipitated by fossil fuel use. This law may succumb to a legal challenge, which is process as of early 2026, but it still reflects bipartisanship and Vermont's historic boldness in meeting big problems head-on.[97] And regardless of the state's image as a Democratic stronghold, Republicans have regularly won gubernatorial elections in Vermont. Indeed, since 1968, every time a Democrat has retired from the governorship, the successor has been a Republican, and vice versa. Thus, Phil Scott is the latest in a long line of Republican governors who have replaced a Democrat. The list is as follows:

Name	*Party*	*Term of Service*
Phil Scott	Republican	2017–
Peter Shumlin	Democrat	2011–2017
Jim Douglas	Republican	2003–2011
Howard Dean	Democrat	1991–2003
Richard Snelling	Republican	1977–1985; 1991
Tom Salmon	Democrat	1973–1977
Deane Davis	Republican	1969–1973
Phil Hoff	Democrat	1963–1969[98]

Moreover, besides regularly alternating in the governorship, the two parties have sometimes been closely competitive in individual elections, to the extent that neither party's candidate won a majority of the vote. For example, in 2002, Jim Douglas won 45 percent of the vote, Democrat Doug Racine captured 42 percent, and Independent Cornelius (Con) Hogan garnered 10 percent. Similarly, in the 2014 governor's race, Democrat Peter Shumlin received 1.1 percent more votes than Republican Scott Milne without winning a majority of the vote.[99] In such circumstances, the Vermont Constitution directs the legislature to select as governor the candidate who won the largest number of votes in the election, which is what happened in both cases. Following the constitutional prescription, the legislature—dominated by Democrats, chose the Republican Douglas in 2002 and the Democrat Shumlin in 2014.[100]

Regarding Vermont voters' practice of alternating between Democratic and Republican governors, author and former Vermont journalist Chris Graff observes that they "have done more than just alternate between parties"; rather, they "have chosen governors so that a period of expansion follows a period of retrenchment, which, in turn, follows a period of expansion."[101] The word "retrenchment" may be too strong in this context because the Republicans on the above list have generally been moderate. For example, Deane Davis championed Act 250 in 1969, and Phil Scott has twice signed significant regulations on firearms during his time in office. Neither man tried to undo all or even most of his predecessor's accomplishments. Nevertheless, as Governor Scott's recent vetoes illustrate, a Republican governor is likely to be more cautious in pursuing social change and more reluctant to impose new or increased taxes or regulations on Vermonters than a Democrat. Thus, Chris Graff rightly sees alternating partisanship in the governor's office as reflecting Vermonters' periodic wish to slow a ship of state they think is moving too far too fast or, alternatively, speed up one that fails to respond to new circumstances.

The 2022 elections in Vermont were noteworthy not only for state contests but for federal contests too. For the first time since 1974, Patrick Leahy was not a candidate for the US Senate, having decided to retire after serving eight terms in office. Leahy was just thirty-four years old when he first won the Senate seat, and his only electoral experience was running locally in Chittenden County, where he had been the chief prosecutor for eight years. Besides, he was Catholic and a Democrat at a time when Vermont was still largely Protestant and Republican. Despite such apparent disadvantages, Leahy prevailed over Republican congressman Richard Mallary by 4,406 votes, becoming "the first Democrat and the youngest person ever elected to the U.S. Senate from Vermont."[102] Nearly a half-century later, he retired as the third-longest-serving senator in American history, having cast more than 17,000 votes and served under nine presidents.[103]

Senator Leahy left a colossal legacy in Vermont and nationally. In 1975, as a member of the Senate Armed Services Committee, he cast the deciding vote in the committee to end funding for America's participation in the Vietnam War.[104] A quarter-century later, he voted against funding American participation in the Iraq War, having become convinced that President George W. Bush and his advisers "were not telling the truth about [Iraq's possession of] weapons of mass destruction."[105] Leahy's efforts also spurred passage of temporary moratoria on the production, export, and use of land mines by the United States and the creation of a War Victim's Fund, which provides financial assistance to persons who have incurred serious injuries from land mines.[106] Furthermore, Senator Leahy: (1) created a small-state minimum amount in budget bills, which brought billions of dollars to Vermont; (2) supported a certification law for organic food; (3) spearheaded environmental protection for Lake Champlain; (4) supported the Violence Against Women Act (VAWA); and (5) helped to preserve thousands of acres of wilderness in Vermont.[107]

He was a master at securing federal dollars for projects and programs to be implemented in Vermont. In the spring of 2020, for example, he secured $125 billion from the Coronavirus Relief Fund. And in 2022, his last full year in the Senate, he secured $167 million for numerous Vermont nonprofit organizations and schools. The largest portion was $10 million to build a new center in Burlington to train the next generation of aviation technicians at the Burlington Technical Center's aviation and aerospace program. In that same year, he obtained $24.3 million for the University of Vermont. The largest portion of that amount, $9.3 million, establishes an Institute for Rural Partnerships designed to meet the transportation, workforce, and infrastructure needs of rural communities.[108] Thus, Patrick Leahy wielded enormous moral and political influence on Capitol Hill for decades, and Vermont benefitted immensely from his visibility and clout.

Senator Leahy's decision not to seek reelection in 2022 sparked a spirited game of musical chairs in Vermont politics, as Congressman Peter Welch vacated his post to seek Leahy's seat, and both State Senate President Becca Balint and Lieutenant Governor Molly Gray left their positions to pursue Welch's US House seat. In winning the Senate seat, Welch revived a longstanding Vermont tradition of the sitting representative replacing a retiring senator. In 2007, Bernie Sanders, after serving sixteen years in the House, replaced Senator Jim Jeffords, just as Jeffords, after serving fourteen years in the House, had succeeded Senator Robert Stafford in 1989.[109] The only break in this tradition occurred in 1974, when, as previously noted, Patrick Leahy defeated Congressman Richard Mallary in a bid for the Senate seat being vacated by George Aiken.

Becca Balint's victory in the 2022 House race, in which she won both the Democratic primary and the general election with 60 percent of the vote, gave Vermont its first congressional delegation to include a woman and member of the LGBTQ community and three members who had been born outside Vermont.[110] The reconstituted delegation reflects the demographic change that has occurred in Vermont during the past fifty years, primarily through migration. Other notable results from the 2022 elections include the voters' approval of two amendments to the state constitution, one to guarantee reproductive rights and the other to explicitly outlaw slavery. The former garnered 73 percent of the vote, and the latter received 82 percent, including approval in every town.[111]

In the 2024 elections, Governor Phil Scott was reelected easily, winning 70 percent of the vote. He also succeeded in creating a legislature more supportive of his policy goals, as the Republicans captured the lieutenant governorship, gained eighteen seats in the house, and added six seats in the senate. Therefore, the partisan lineup in the house at the start of the 2025–26 legislative session was eighty-seven Democrats, fifty-six Republicans, and seven Progressives/Independents.[112] Similarly, after defeating four Democratic incumbents and capturing two open seats, the Republicans changed the partisan split in the senate to sixteen Democrats, thirteen Republicans, and one Progressive as the 2025–26 session opened.[113] In this new environment, as Chapter Seven will discuss in detail, Governor Scott's plan to transform the organization, governance, and funding of public education in Vermont was enacted with bipartisan support in June 2025, albeit after an intense and protracted debate in both legislative chambers.[114]

On the federal level in 2024, Senator Bernie Sanders and Representative Becca Balint were reelected by large margins, Sanders winning a fourth term and Balint a second term. Sanders's rags-to-riches political story is even more unlikely than Patrick Leahy's rise to power. In the 1970s, Sanders ran for governor and US senator under a third-party banner without success, garnering only a single-digit vote tally each time. Vermont was evidently not ready for a blunt-spoken socialist with a gravelly Brooklyn accent. But by 1980, at least the voters of Burlington had warmed to him, electing him mayor and reelecting him twice. In 1990, Sanders easily ousted incumbent Republican Peter Smith from his US House seat and proceeded to serve an improbable sixteen years in the House. He began as a "backbench gadfly" ranting against "greedy millionaires and billionaires" and "multinational corporations." But he gradually learned to build coalitions with other members of Congress and enact legislation to benefit the "working families" who are the heart of his constituency.[115] In 2007, when Jim Jeffords retired,

Sanders was elected to the Senate, where he continues to serve. Once the ultimate outsider, Sanders is now a senior member of an exclusive club.

As a senator, he has championed progressive causes such as a single-payer healthcare system, a $15 minimum hourly wage, and free tuition at public colleges. These proposals earned him a sizeable following beyond Vermont, fueling his campaigns for the presidency in 2016 and again in 2020. He came up short each time, but in 2016 gave Hillary Clinton a scare, essentially tying her in the Iowa caucuses, defeating her soundly in the New Hampshire primary, and winning primaries in Michigan and Wisconsin, thanks largely to small-dollar donations made online. Eventually, Clinton prevailed by winning primaries in the South by large margins, and Sanders ended his campaign shortly before the Democratic Convention. Similarly, in 2020, Sanders did well in Iowa and won in New Hampshire and Nevada, but Joe Biden won more primaries and more delegates, and Sanders was forced to end his campaign in April, as the coronavirus took hold, trailing Biden by more than three hundred delegates.[116] Still, he built a political movement that continues to influence the Democratic Party and American politics. And like Patrick Leahy, Bernie Sanders has enabled Vermont to exercise a measure of political clout that belies its small size.

Conclusion

Vermont's motto—Freedom and Unity—is evident in policy choices to restrict firearms sales, expand eligibility for childcare subsidies while increasing reimbursements to childcare providers, impose a mask mandate and restrict out-of-state travel during the coronavirus pandemic, and approve a constitutional amendment guaranteeing reproductive freedom. Yet Vermont continues to exercise moderation, as the 2024 election results and the state's long-standing practice of alternating parties in the governor's office show. Vermont's challenge for the future is to balance freedom and unity wisely by using public funds to meet human needs without requiring a greater financial sacrifice from Vermonters than they can afford. Chapter Six will address the specific challenge—for both Vermont and New Hampshire—of ensuring affordable housing for their citizens.

CHAPTER SIX

Policy Consequences of Political Culture

The Case of Land-Use Regulation

Introduction: Broadly Similar Responses to a Shared Challenge

NEW HAMPSHIRE AND VERMONT face comparable challenges in the twenty-first century because of their demographic similarities: relatively few working-age adults but many retirees and prospective retirees. One shared challenge is a housing shortage, which boosts housing prices for both buyers and renters. Yet migration is crucial to replenish the workforce because, in both states, deaths exceed births each year. Thus, unless New Hampshire and Vermont can overcome their housing shortages, they risk becoming economic backwaters unable to attract and retain the workers needed to support a population increasingly dominated by senior citizens. To overcome those shortages, though, they will have to reconcile housing goals with both the local nature of zoning and with municipalities' traditional preference for single-family homes. The following discussion will highlight the broadly similar but nonetheless distinct ways in which the Twin States have confronted the housing crisis, reflecting their respective political cultures.

New Hampshire

Historical Patterns

As settlers streamed inland from the New Hampshire coast in the late eighteenth century, land-use patterns changed from the Natives' nomadic hunting and trapping to activities such as grazing livestock and draining wetlands for pastures. Before European colonization, an estimated five thousand Native inhabitants lived in what became New Hampshire, but by the start of the American Revolution in the mid-1770s, the total number of white and Native inhabitants had grown to sixty thousand, all of whom subsisted primarily on the native wildlife.[1] A century later, after decades of farming, agriculture had largely surrendered to the rocky soil, and reforestation was occurring in southern New Hampshire. Meanwhile, deforestation was just beginning in the North Country, where the timber barons reigned supreme. An 1867 state law that required the sale of New Hampshire's public lands unleashed fifty years of deforestation that did not peak until 1907.[2] The timber barons got their wish, though, as the state's production of lumber tripled between the 1860s and 1900. Only the complaints by downstream mill owners about the resulting floods and by innkeepers and their customers about unsightly hillsides stemmed the carnage of excessive logging.

The timber barons had to accommodate the innkeepers because tourism had become a major industry in the North Country by the late nineteenth century, and it was incompatible with the slash-and-burn tactics commonly practiced in the woods.[3] Railroads made the North Country accessible to tourists, which allowed the tourism industry to develop. They worked with the hotels to advertise the latter, and they coordinated schedules to afford greater convenience for would-be travelers. The railroads also encouraged North Country entrepreneurs to build resorts that would attract an affluent clientele.[4] As a result, elegant destination hotels featuring fine cuisine and ample recreational activities sprouted in northern New Hampshire during the late nineteenth century.[5] The railroads, a product of industrialization, like the disposable income of their clientele, transported travelers from the cities to the hotels, which sometimes stood on the abandoned farms of men and women who had migrated south or west in search of greater economic opportunity.

The abandonment of farming in New Hampshire had begun well before the Civil War, but it intensified after the war, as factories in Manchester, Nashua, and Massachusetts, and more fertile land in the Midwest, beckoned scores of young people to leave struggling farms in the Granite State. Over time, the farmland reverted to forest, and New Hampshire's tourism industry benefitted from the wooded landscape and outdoor recreation amenities for which the state became known.[6] Thus, by the end of the nineteenth century, industrialization—along with its many byproducts—had dramatically altered the landscape and land use in New Hampshire.

Of all the byproducts of industrialization, the most consequential ones for New Hampshire might have been developments in transportation, especially the railroads and, later, automobiles. Each one unleashed colossal economic, social, and environmental changes and, says author Richard Ober, "for the most part, caused the demise of what previously existed."[7] The railroads not only transported tourists to the White Mountains but also made East Coast cities accessible to young people seeking an alternative to farm life. They also gave farmers and manufacturers access to larger markets and consumers access to a wider array of goods. And their economic strength brought them political clout to shape legislation and legal muscle to protect their interests in court.

As the nineteenth century yielded to the twentieth, automobiles began to supplant railroads, creating a new role for state governments in the process. New Hampshire began registering automobiles and licensing drivers in 1911; such licensing had been unnecessary in the era of horse-drawn wagons and stagecoaches.[8] The rise of the automobile happened quickly: New Hampshire registered just 704 vehicles in 1905, but ten years later, it registered 13,449.[9] Like railroads, automobiles influenced both travel habits and land use. Unlike railroads, though, which concentrated populations close to stations and tracks, automobiles and their road networks dispersed population, facilitating the growth of suburbs and, later, of seemingly endless car-friendly shopping centers and other commercial enterprises, sprawled out alongside major highways.[10]

If automobiles invited sprawl, their younger cousins—the bus and the truck—spurred the adoption of zoning. Trucks freed heavy industries from having to locate their facilities alongside downtown railroad stations and docks. They also enabled manufacturers to leave downtown areas in favor of building on less costly land in residential districts. And in the 1920s, the advent of buses gave apartment developers the option to build outside the immediate vicinity of trolley tracks.[11] Thanks to these new transportation options, economist William Fischel wrote, a "vacant lot in a partially developed single-family neighborhood could now easily be sold to a nonresidential user or an apartment developer."[12]

To prevent the cheek-by-jowl proximity of private homes and manufacturing plants, cities began to engage in comprehensive zoning after 1910. By putting every acre of land in one zone or another, a city could control the future use of its land instead of having to resolve scores of private land-use disputes case-by-case, without any binding rules.[13] Instead, writes Professor Fischel, "home-owners and builders could read in a public record what the zoning allowed and they knew that, if a developer sought to change what was allowed, neighbors and other citizens would have some influence on the political process by which the change was made."[14]

After all, zoning divides a community into districts or "zones" in which certain uses of land are permitted, and others are prohibited. Each zone specifies the permitted uses, along with pertinent regulations, such as height limits and dimensional and placement requirements for buildings.[15] Put another way, zoning and related land-use regulations "control the development of private land through use, density design, and historic preservation requirements."[16] Local governments establish zoning rules under state law and enforce them by means of approval processes for individual building projects overseen by planning commissions or other local government entities. Those processes can protect communities from ill-conceived or underfinanced ventures, but they can also frustrate developers and builders because of the time and the costs they may require.[17]

Zoning is commonplace today, but it was controversial early in the twentieth century, as reflected in the nearly even split among state supreme courts regarding its constitutionality. In 1926, in a case titled *Village of Euclid v. Amber Realty*, the United States Supreme Court upheld Euclid, Ohio's, zoning ordinance, the stated purposes of which were to promote the "safety and security of home life, decreased noise, and a better environment for raising children." In the Supreme Court's view, those aims were reasonably related to the city's "police power"—its power, under the Constitution, to promote health, safety, morals, and the general welfare.[18] Accordingly, the Supreme Court rejected the realty company's claim that the zoning ordinance was unconstitutional because its restrictions on the use of the company's land destroyed the land's marketability for industrial, commercial, and residential uses.[19]

In the decades after *Euclid*, automobiles, suburbanization, and zoning proliferated, bringing profound changes to American life. By the 1950s, automobiles were Americans' favorite mode of transportation, as reflected in Congress's passage of the Interstate Highway Act in 1956, and subsequent construction of the interstate highway system. That system included I-89 and I-93 in New Hampshire, begun in the late 1950s and largely complete a decade later, altering the physical landscape dramatically and greatly increasing the year-round volume of visitors to the Granite State.[20] Ownership of automobiles ballooned from 59 percent of households in 1950 to 82 percent of households by 1970.[21]

The increased accessibility of automobiles and highways spawned a movement of employers and jobs to the suburbs, to the disadvantage of city residents who lacked automobiles. Meanwhile, suburban residents became increasingly concerned about their quality of life and wary of potential zoning changes that might affect it. For many suburban homeowners, "quality of life" meant a large lot in a middle- or upper-middle-class neighborhood, protected from higher-density housing and less affluent neighbors. Therefore, three-acre-minimum lot sizes that had previously been regarded as "holding zones" to later be rezoned for greater density, froze, according to Professor Fischel, "into a permanent cast that kept the poor and higher-density development at bay."[22] These trends occurred nationwide. New Hampshire experienced them too, as the proliferation of large lots in suburban grid patterns, especially in the southern towns close to Massachusetts, increasingly altered a once-rural landscape.[23]

The proliferation of single-family homes occupying large lots has had some unfortunate consequences in New Hampshire and elsewhere. By the 1970s, as Professor Fischel notes, federal and state fair-housing laws had made racial discrimination in housing illegal, even by informal means, such as "steering" racial minorities to less desirable neighborhoods. But the same purpose could be achieved, with respect to either racial minorities or low-income groups, by the seemingly neutral method of mandating that residential districts emphasize single-family homes on large lots.[24]

Admittedly, zoning is susceptible to abuse, though it is not inherently nefarious. As Professor Fischel notes, zoning and associated land-use controls "are necessary to manage the intimacy of urban life, but they also can be applied so strenuously that we become strangers to one another."[25] Industrialization and population growth brought incompatible uses of land closer together than ever before, necessitating zoning.[26] In New Hampshire, the state supreme court empowered communities to keep incompatible uses apart in 1928, when it upheld zoning as a valid exercise of the police power.[27]

Zoning's trademark segregation of land uses kept the chemical plant away from the elementary school, but it also tended to segregate residents by race and socioeconomic status. For example, in Manchester—New Hampshire's largest city—zoning laws have essentially maintained the residential arrangement established by the Amoskeag Company in the late nineteenth century, keeping the impoverished neighborhoods in the center of the city and the affluent enclaves in its North End.[28] Manchester adopted its first zoning ordinance in 1928. At the time, the first tier of housing was single-family residences, which encompassed just 2 percent of the city, all in the North End and were the most expensive type of housing. The second tier, which comprised more than 80 percent of the city, allowed both single-family and two-family homes; the latter were common to immigrant communities in mill towns of the Northeast early in the twentieth century. Finally, the third tier, which was limited to 2 percent of the city, allowed multifamily housing, almost all of which sat near the textile mills on both sides of the Merrimack River. This arrangement prevented the poverty in the city's center from expanding outward, and it preserved the North End as an enclave of affluence.[29]

The Great Depression and World War II restricted development, so the full impact of zoning was not felt until the postwar era. That was a time of rapid growth in New Hampshire, especially between 1960 and 1990, when census data showed a growth rate exceeding 20 percent in each decade. Municipalities began to fear that the explosive growth would greatly increase public school enrollments, triggering expenditure increases far above the additional property tax revenue produced by new housing. Many New Hampshire cities and towns responded to this anticipated shortfall by adopting "growth management zoning," which meant using single-family zoning to restrict population growth.[30]

In Manchester, by 1965, single-family zoning had expanded from 2 percent of the city (in 1928) to 70 percent, effectively preventing—absent permission from the zoning board—construction of more of the two-family homes that had been popular at the start of the twentieth century. Therefore, the amount of land in the city that was available for the building of two- and three-family homes declined from 80 percent to just 10 percent, with only 1 percent left for apartments, almost all of it in the city center. After 1965, zoning changes gradually made more parts of the city available for the construction of multifamily homes, although the established pattern of high-density housing in the city center and low-density housing elsewhere has largely continued. Between 1965 and 2000, Manchester deemphasized single-family homes slightly, as their reach dropped from 70 percent of the city to 67 percent. Meanwhile, medium-density housing—two- and three-family homes—increased from 10 percent to 13 percent, and multifamily units inched up from 1 percent to 3 percent of Manchester's homes.[31] These trends continued after 2000. Indeed, by late 2021, according to an updated zoning map, the area reserved for single-family zoning had declined from 67 percent of the city to 54 percent, and the area open to medium-density housing had dropped from 13 percent to approximately 7 percent. In contrast, the area zoned for multifamily housing had expanded from 3 percent to nearly 10 percent, the largest share of land allocated to such housing in Manchester's history. And the multifamily zone had come to include several neighborhoods outside the city center.[32]

The impetus for these changes was the New Hampshire Supreme Court's 1991 decision holding that municipalities with zoning ordinances must provide "realistic opportunities" for the development of housing that is "affordable" for low- and moderate-income families. The court reasoned that municipalities are responsible for sharing the burden of population growth; hence, they are not allowed to create obstacles—such as single-family zoning and large minimum-lot sizes—designed to keep certain aspiring residents out.[33] In the court's view, zoning should ameliorate problems of "uncontrolled growth," not deny access to a city or town "by outsiders of any disadvantaged social or economic group."[34]

That decision was not a cure-all for exclusionary zoning in New Hampshire, though. Indeed, the housing market did not improve during the decade and a half that followed because municipalities continued to draft ordinances that discouraged the building of multifamily homes. In response, state legislators enacted a workforce housing law in 2008 that required municipalities to comply with the court's 1991 decision by providing "reasonable and realistic" opportunities for the development of workforce housing, including multifamily rental housing.[35] Still, progress has been uneven because zoning decisions are fundamentally local choices made by municipal zoning boards. Statewide legislative mandates for more inclusionary zoning often face resistance from town officials and residents eager to preserve "local control" in land-use matters.[36]

The maintenance of traditional zoning patterns has become problematic in recent years, as New Hampshire has faced a severe shortage of workforce housing, which threatens its ability to attract a new generation of workers to replace a flood of retirees. Critics charge that traditional zoning patterns also perpetuate racial segregation and environmentally unsound uses of land. The following section will address current conditions in New Hampshire regarding land use.

Current Practices and Problems

As the previous discussion shows, New Hampshire municipalities have long favored owner-occupied, single-family homes.[37] Many municipalities have also favored restricted-age housing (e.g., senior-citizen housing) as a means of expanding their property tax base, while resisting apartment buildings and multifamily housing likely to add children to the school population, thereby increasing property tax bills.[38]

To counter such exclusionary zoning, New Hampshire, in recent decades, has enacted laws designed to encourage inclusionary zoning—meaning alternatives to single-family homes—to expand the availability of affordable housing. New Hampshire law defines inclusionary zoning as "land use control regulations which provide a voluntary incentive or benefit to a property . . . to induce the property owner to produce housing units which are affordable to persons or families of low and moderate income."[39] The state seeks to pursue this goal while honoring its traditional preference for local control. Therefore, it offers incentives rather than imposing requirements; for example, it allows developers to build more dense housing than is typically permissible, if they agree to set aside a fixed portion of the units for affordable housing.[40] Inclusionary zoning thus links the creation of affordable, below-market-rate housing units with new development, thereby fostering affordable housing and more racially and socioeconomically inclusive communities.[41]

One tool New Hampshire has used to combat exclusionary zoning is its Workforce Housing Law. This law defines "affordable" as "housing with combined rental and utility costs or combined mortgage loan debt services, property taxes, and required insurance that do not exceed 30 percent of a household's gross annual income."[42] It also defines "multi-family housing," within the context of workforce housing developments, as "a building or structure containing 5 or more dwelling units, each designed for occupancy by an individual household."[43] And it defines "workforce housing" as housing for sale that is affordable to a household "with an income of no more than 100 percent of the median income for the metropolitan area or county where the housing is located," or rental housing that is affordable to a household "with an income of no more than 60 percent of the median income for a 3-person household for the metropolitan area or county where the housing is located." Housing developments that exclude minors from more than twenty percent of the units, or in which more than half the units have fewer than two bedrooms, are, by definition, not workforce housing under New Hampshire law.[44]

Under the Workforce Housing Law, municipalities must enact land-use regulations that provide "reasonable and realistic opportunities for the development of workforce housing, including rental and multi-family housing."[45] They must also allow workforce housing to be present in "most, but not necessarily all" of the land area within their boundaries that is zoned to permit residential uses. But they are not required to permit multifamily housing in most of that land area.[46]

Another example of New Hampshire's statutory effort to promote inclusionary zoning is its law concerning accessory dwelling units (ADUs). This law defines an ADU as a residential living unit that is inside of or attached to a single-family home and offers independent living facilities for one or more individuals, "including provisions for sleeping, eating, cooking, and sanitation on the same parcel of land as the principal dwelling that it accompanies.[47] An ADU can house a caregiver on the same property as a homeowner who requires care, house a renter whose rent provides supplemental income for a homeowner, or house an elderly relative who receives care from a homeowner.[48] The ADU often takes the form of a basement apartment, backyard cottage, or converted garage.

Owners of single-family homes frequently oppose ADUs, usually because of concerns that they will increase traffic, damage neighborhood character, or lower property values. Therefore, some communities prohibit them, and others allow them only through special permitting processes.[49] But ADUs can help to combat restrictions on the number of units permitted on a single lot, which are commonplace in the United States. In the present era of housing shortages, therefore, legalizing ADUs has been the most common method by which states have sought to make additional lower-cost housing feasible to build, usually as additions to single-family homes.[50]

New Hampshire's ADU law, enacted in 2017, requires municipalities to permit the construction of ADUs, but it nevertheless provides considerable leeway for local control. Specifically, it allows municipalities to require that the homeowner live on the premises, that off-street parking be provided for the ADU occupant, and that applications for ADU permits be subject to discretionary reviews by zoning authorities instead of being granted as a matter of right.[51] One recent commentary on this law, despite criticizing such requirements, has acknowledged that many Granite State communities have welcomed ADUs. The authors hypothesize that the state's high median home price and the housing shortage in its "southern tier" have created enough of a crisis to make ADU construction highly desirable despite the conditions that municipalities may impose on it.[52] They note that New Hampshire's high median age contributes to the attractiveness of ADUs, which are often built when an elderly homeowner sells a home and uses the proceeds to build an ADU at a younger relative's house, where the elderly person plans to live.[53]

New Hampshire's most recent efforts to foster inclusionary zoning are reflected in several bills enacted into law during the 2025–26 legislative session. For example, H.B. 577 amended the existing ADU law by permitting property owners to construct detached ADUs on their land. It requires municipalities to allow either attached or detached units, provided that other zoning rules are met. Another bill, H.B. 631, requires local zoning committees to permit multifamily residential developments to be built in commercial areas, thereby fostering "mixed-use" development, provided that adequate roads, water services, and sewer connections exist for residents. And S.B. 284 bars municipalities from mandating more than one parking space per unit (previously 1.5) for residential construction.[54]

Laws on affordable housing and accessory dwelling units are not the only means by which New Hampshire seeks to make housing more available and affordable to its residents. For example, another state law authorizes municipalities to use innovative land-use controls, such as requiring that housing be built in timed phases, collecting "impact fees" from developers to cover the costs of necessary infrastructure improvements, and facilitating construction of "cluster developments." In cluster developments, homes are spaced closer together than in a traditional subdivision, in exchange for protecting shared open space.[55] State law has also created a three-member Housing Appeals Board to hear appeals of decisions by local planning and zoning boards regarding housing and housing development, including but not limited to, decisions about the use of innovative land-use controls and growth-management devices. After a hearing, the board must render a decision within sixty days, making it a speedier alternative to a trial court; still, the party that loses at the board level may appeal to the state supreme court.[56]

New Hampshire has also spent money—albeit federal money—to boost the availability of affordable housing. In 2022, Governor Chris Sununu used $100 million in federal pandemic-relief funds to spur residential construction, including $60 million in grants to developers and $40 million in grants to municipalities. Two years later, state officials reported that demolition grants from the program facilitated the demolition of more than 2,300 dilapidated units. Meanwhile, grants designed to encourage towns to approve new affordable housing helped to create more than 1,900 units, and another grant program aimed at promoting affordable housing helped to fund more than 1,600 units. Many of the housing developments involved were works-in-progress that the state grants nudged across the finish line. In the future, the investment will continue, yet on a smaller scale, as the state has set aside $15 million from its general fund to spur the construction of more housing.[57] More state efforts will likely be necessary for New Hampshire to solve its housing crisis.

The Housing Crisis and the Challenge Ahead

In 2023, New Hampshire Housing, a self-supporting public corporation that seeks to "promote, finance, and support housing solutions" in New Hampshire, published a report that underscored the gravity of the state's housing shortage. According to this report, the state needs 60,000 more housing units by 2030 and nearly 90,000 units by 2040, based on estimated population growth.[58] The shortage is reflected in the high cost of buying or renting a home in New Hampshire, which rose by 50 percent between 2019 and 2022, reducing the prospects for even middle- and high-income renter households to become homeowners.[59] Remaining a renter is also expensive. The Granite State's extremely low vacancy rate elevates rents, making rental properties unaffordable for many, especially lower-income individuals and families.[60]

Both buyers and renters in New Hampshire face a market in which price increases have long exceeded wage growth. Between 2000 and 2020, New Hampshire's sale and rental prices for housing increased dramatically—by 111 percent for sales and 94 percent for rents—while household incomes rose by just 73 percent.[61] The tight housing market, accompanied by an expected increase in the state's median age, will likely make finding a home even more difficult in the future because older adults may be forced to "age in place" instead of selling their homes and moving to a smaller living space.[62]

In this environment, the rental-vacancy rate in New Hampshire dipped from 2.8 percent in 2015 to a stunning 0.5 percent in 2022. The decline in the availability of rental options was the product of several influences, including an increase in second-home purchases, investment activity, and a spike in short-term rentals.[63] The latter are properties leased as accommodations, in return for payment, for less than thirty days, often through entities such as Airbnb or VRBO.[64] As of early 2023, these conditions caused some 23,000 renters in New Hampshire to pay a higher rent than was affordable for their income level.[65] According to a July 2023 survey by New Hampshire Housing, to afford the statewide median rate for a typical two-bedroom apartment, including tenant-paid utilities, a renter had to earn more than $70,600 per year.[66]

New Hampshire Housing also surveyed a variety of occupations to determine which ones paid a median wage that enabled a worker to afford New Hampshire's median rent, which was $1,510 per month at the time of its report. Of the professions surveyed, only electricians, engineers, "patrol officers," and registered nurses who earned the median salary for their respective professions could afford the median New Hampshire rent without being cost burdened (i.e., spending more than thirty percent of one's gross monthly income on housing). Among the occupations surveyed whose practitioners could not afford the median rent in New Hampshire were: (1) assemblers and fabricators; (2) cashiers; (3) childcare workers; (4) construction laborers; (5) fast food and counter workers; (6) truck drivers; (7) home health and personal-care aides; (8) janitors and cleaners; (9) office clerks; (10) retail salespeople; and (11) servers.[67]

The shortage of affordable housing has profound consequences for New Hampshire's economy. As of December 2023, the state's workforce numbered approximately 750,000, which is the lowest figure since 2021 and represents a decline of about 3 percent compared to pre-pandemic levels. The workforce participation rate—the share of people ages twenty-five to fifty-four in the labor force—in 2023 was at 64.6 percent, which is a historic low and a trend "likely influenced by the state's aging workforce."[68] Replacing retiring workers is also problematic because of the lack of affordable housing. Statewide, the median price of a home sold during the first three-quarters of 2022 was $430,000, up from $285,975 in 2019, a 50 percent increase in just three years.[69] By late June 2025, according to the New Hampshire Association of Realtors, that price had climbed to $565,000.[70]

Scholars and practicing planners offer numerous remedies for the housing crunch that plagues New Hampshire and other states. Among them are banning single-family-only zoning; permitting multifamily housing in more places than it currently is allowed, including adjacent to transit stops; and eliminating minimum-parking requirements.[71] Happily, zoning reform is bipartisan, attracting the support of both free-market conservatives who favor limiting government regulation and liberals eager to reduce homelessness and combat socioeconomic segregation in housing.[72] The bipartisan support reflects the gravity of the housing crisis. New Hampshire's Granite State Poll found in June 2024 that 36 percent of respondents identified housing as "the most important problem facing New Hampshire." The second most important problem was education, according to 7 percent of the respondents.[73]

Still, as Professor Fischel noted, "zoning is preeminently the product of local initiative."[74] Reflecting that reality, New Hampshire's record in making housing more available and affordable has been mixed. For example, regarding the Workforce Housing Law, New Hampshire Housing explains that "many communities have responded by making changes to their land use regulations in an effort to comply with the law's obligations while many other communities have made little or no progress."[75]

Examples of this mixed record abound. An economic development director in Exeter said during a webinar on the housing crisis sponsored by the *NH Business Review* that towns possessed "carrots" to encourage the building of affordable housing but few "sticks" to prevent overreliance on single-family housing. He identified Seacoast communities that imposed two-acre-minimum zoning and barred municipal sewer and water systems, thereby precluding construction of anything other than expensive single-family homes.[76] Most of the eighty-five communities that have adopted workforce housing ordinances are in southern New Hampshire (including the Seacoast), the Mount Washington Valley and the Upper Connecticut River Valley, where housing cost-pressures are the greatest. But only fifty-two of them have added to their ordinances an inclusionary-zoning clause that permits a developer to construct units of greater density than would otherwise be allowed in exchange for designating a specific percentage of units (usually between 10 and 20 percent) as affordable. The relaxed-density provision can be just the incentive a developer needs to build affordable housing.[77]

A mixed record also characterizes the implementation of New Hampshire's Accessory Dwelling Unit Law. Of the state's 234 municipalities, 211 have adopted a provision in their zoning ordinances to regulate ADUs since the state law went into effect in 2017. But of these 211 municipalities, 179 require the principal dwelling or the ADU to be owner-occupied.[78] On the other hand, in 2024, fifteen communities modified their ordinances to allow ADUs in structures that are detached from the principal dwelling unit, and in 2025 the legislature modified the ADU law to permit the construction of ADUs (including detached ones) by property owners throughout the state. Beyond that, seven communities that had required anyone seeking to build an ADU to first obtain a conditional-use permit or a special exception from the pertinent town board changed their rules in 2024 to allow ADUs by right.[79]

More broadly, thirteen New Hampshire communities adopted zoning changes in 2024 designed to lower regulatory hurdles to development of a diverse array of housing types. Examples of the changes that the new rules will facilitate are: (1) conversion of existing single-family homes to multifamily housing; (2) greater maximum-density allowances for duplexes and multifamily housing; (3) the allowance of residential uses in commercial districts (now allowed by state law); (4) removing minimum-square-footage requirements for single-family homes; and (5) permitting duplexes in all residential districts.[80] Still, some towns, albeit a minority, amended local zoning ordinances to further restrict housing development, such as by setting a minimum lot size of 1.5 acres for detached ADUs, retaining owner-occupancy and parking requirements for ADUs, and rejecting other housing-friendly zoning changes.[81]

Besides zoning reform, scholars and practicing planners encourage local officials to educate the public about workforce housing by providing examples of the income groups and professions likely to benefit from it and of workforce housing developments that have succeeded in New Hampshire.[82] Key to this educational effort is informing communities that the impact of affordable housing developments on schools is likely to be much less than is feared, because family sizes have shrunk considerably in recent decades. Besides, additional students may help school districts that face diminished state funding because of declining enrollments.[83] Furthermore, the use of large minimum-lot sizes to discourage an influx of families with children results in residential sprawl that relegates open space to areas that cannot be developed, such as wetlands, steep slopes, and bodies of water.[84] Sprawl, in turn, increases commuting times and road-maintenance costs and degrades air and water quality.[85]

Finally, the experts recommend three additional steps municipalities can take to increase the likelihood that their zoning reforms will make housing more available and affordable. One is to monitor social media when a workforce housing ordinance or project is proposed so that town authorities can counter false or misleading claims advanced online. Another is to regulate the short-term rental market, especially in tourist towns, perhaps by levying fees on the landlords and allocating the proceeds to a local fund to support the development of workforce housing.[86] A third recommendation is for municipalities to form partnerships with public or private entities to manage affordable-housing developments so that small towns are not required to bear that responsibility.[87]

New Hampshire has made noteworthy progress in zoning reform in recent years. But to achieve a balanced housing market, which, in New Hampshire Housing's view, features a 5 percent rental-vacancy rate and a 2 percent owner-vacancy rate, the state must add almost 88,400 new units, including some 58,000 owner-occupied units and 30,000 rental units.[88] Considering the local variability of zoning decisions and New Hampshire's localist political culture, that will likely be a daunting task.

Vermont

Historical Patterns

In Vermont, which was settled by colonists in the 1760s and 1770s, the customary land-use patterns that developed over time included a village center with commercial establishments and private homes, surrounded by farms and forests. Contemporary Vermont law seeks to maintain those patterns, despite improvements in technology and transportation that push residential development farther from town centers.

In 1921, coincident with the advent of the automobile and the growth of government services and responsibilities, the Vermont Legislature authorized municipalities to create planning commissions. The commissions could propose plans for public improvements, such as schools or libraries, but lacked authority over privately owned projects. Ten years later, after the

United States Supreme Court's *Euclid* decision that authorized municipal zoning,[89] the legislature permitted towns to establish zoning commissions to create bylaws and boundaries for various zoning districts and boards of adjustment to hear appeals of individual zoning decisions and grant exceptions to the regulations.[90] The lawmakers waited forty-seven years to revise this law, by which time the interstate highway system had spawned economic development and concern for environmental protection and growth management. In 1968, they amended the law to establish purposes for planning and zoning and to outline the contents of municipal plans.[91]

That year also brought news that the International Paper Company planned to build a large development of vacation homes on twenty thousand acres of hilly land in the southern Vermont town of Dover. This news was alarming because previous housing developments in southern Vermont, poorly planned and incompatible with the terrain, had resulted in soil erosion and sewage problems. For its part, the state was promoting tourism, and towns such as Wilmington and Dover had become popular skiing destinations. Suddenly, they faced the prospect of hundreds of second homes and condominiums being built within their borders, often on mountainsides with thin soil prone to erosion. Jim Jeffords, who was Vermont's attorney general from 1969 until 1973, summarized the situation well. "Development was going on all over the place, with no concept of how the sewage was going to get down into the ledge and not run all over . . . it was a mess."[92]

After viewing some of the "mess," Governor Deane Davis, a Republican, was dismayed, because he knew Vermont had almost no environmental regulations or land-use controls.[93] Fortunately for Governor Davis, public opposition to the massive development was considerable, and his background as a corporate executive smoothed his relations with International Paper. Consequently, his request that construction be delayed was granted, and he used the hiatus to create the Governor's Commission on Environmental Control in May 1969.

The Commission held hearings throughout the state, after which it recommended to legislators several environmental laws, primarily a new statewide system for evaluating and regulating large-scale, environmentally sensitive construction projects. In the spring of 1970, the legislature passed the Land Use and Development Law, better known as Act 250, which the state's website describes as providing "a public, quasi-judicial process for reviewing and managing the environmental, social, and fiscal consequences of major subdivisions and developments in Vermont."[94]

Act 250 review applied when a commercial development project planned to use ten or more acres of land, and when a residential development project planned to construct ten or more housing units within a five-mile radius. An Act 250 permit was also required for construction intended to occur more than 2,500 feet above sea level; for communication or broadcast structures that measured twenty feet or more; and for oil and gas drilling. But the construction of improvements related to farming, logging, or forestry did not require an Act 250 permit.[95] The Natural Resources Board, an independent entity in the executive branch of state government, was authorized to administer and enforce Act 250 by supervising the work of nine district environmental commissions, each comprised of volunteer members appointed by the governor and supported by professional staff in regional offices throughout Vermont.[96]

Act 250 still requires that a permit application be filed and that one or more public hearings on the project be held before the relevant district commission. Members of the public may attend, but because the process is quasi-judicial, one must have "party status" to offer evidence or present an argument for one side or the other. The applicant, the municipality and its planning commission, the regional planning commission, and any affected state agencies have party status under the law. The district commission may grant such status, in a particular case, to individuals, citizens' groups, or property owners likely to be affected by the commission's decision. Under the original law, an applicant, municipality, or regional or state entity disappointed in the outcome could appeal the commission's decision to the State Environmental Board; later, the law was amended to assign this appellate authority to the Superior Court's Environmental Division. A subsequent appeal to the Vermont Supreme Court is also permitted under the law.[97]

District commissions must review development projects according to their likely effects on a set of specific criteria named in the law, which concern "the value of the state's natural resources [e.g., air, water, soil, etc.] and the health of its environment, its scenic beauty, and its historic patterns of orderly and sustainable development."[98] For each project, applicants must persuade the commissioners that their plans will not unduly strain local natural resources or community (e.g., school or governmental) resources.[99]

Act 250 has been controversial. Developers and the Vermont Business Roundtable have long argued that it discourages development by lengthening the approval process for projects and increases their associated costs. But supporters have countered that the complaints are unwarranted because most permit applications are granted. They add that the law is not intended to limit or prevent development, but instead, to enable municipalities to control their own development rather than being left to respond as best they can to corporate construction plans. In other words, Act 250 enables cities and towns to develop in ways that fit their goals, not just the goals of the developer or its client.[100] It therefore confers a distinct economic benefit on Vermont by helping to preserve the state's traditional landscape—largely free of billboards and unsightly strip development—which, in turn, fuels its tourist industry and businesses such as Ben & Jerry's.[101]

Absent Act 250, Vermont may well have fallen victim to the strip development that characterizes the landscape in states to its south and west. Instead, because of Act 250, Walmart was unable to open its Bennington store—the giant retailer's first in Vermont—until September 1995, after a five-year battle and considerable compromise. At 50,000 square feet, the new store was half the size of the average Walmart and occupied a preexisting building downtown, consistent with Act 250's preference for downtown development.[102] A previous attempt by Walmart to build a store in Williston and a subsequent attempt to build one in St. Albans both failed because of Act 250. The intended size of the Williston store was incompatible with existing stores in the vicinity, as the store and its parking lot would have consumed forty-four acres of land. And the St. Albans store would have so damaged existing businesses as to burden the city's tax base instead of benefitting it.[103]

Still, Act 250 is far from perfect, as even its supporters recognize. The acreage and mileage minimums that trigger its jurisdiction mean that only about 40 percent of development projects in Vermont are subject to this law's review process; hence, the ability of Act 250 to prevent sprawl and restrict the growth of the second-home market are limited. Another criticism has been that the law is ineffective at protecting historical sites.[104] Nevertheless, Act 250 puts a modern cast on "local control" by enabling municipalities—supported by evidence and expertise—to take charge of their own development and to push back against poorly designed projects, by means that are unavailable to residents of other states.[105] In classic Vermont fashion, it marries new methods to an old idea.

Vermont enacted several other land-use laws in the wake of Act 250. In 1988 came Act 200, which encouraged coordinated planning between municipalities, regions, and the state. It identified a set of state planning goals to be considered in local and regional planning and a list of required subjects or "elements" that must be addressed in municipal and regional plans.[106] First on the list of the goals was to "plan development so as to maintain the historic settlement pattern of compact village and urban centers separated by rural countryside."[107] Under Act 200, then, economic growth was to be encouraged "in locally designated growth areas, or employed to revitalize existing village and urban centers, or both."[108] Act 115, Vermont's permit-reform legislation, followed in 2004. It eliminated the Environmental Board as the entity that heard appeals of Act 250 decisions by the district commissions, assigning that role instead to a new Environmental Court. It also created the Natural Resources Board to oversee the district commissions and to develop rules and standards for issuing Act 250 permits.[109] Finally, Act 183, Vermont's Smart Growth Law, was enacted in 2006. Smart growth "generally refers to land-use planning that focuses a larger share of regional growth within central cities, urbanized areas, inner suburbs and areas already served by infrastructure."[110] A part of smart growth is "the new urbanism," which "promotes walkable, neighborhood-based development as an alternative to sprawl."[111]

Thus, between 1970 and 2006, Vermont addressed the threats posed to its traditional landscape by population growth, suburbanization, and the burgeoning tourism industry by enacting a comprehensive system of land-use regulations. Act 250 and its three progeny, taken together, comprise a regulatory scheme with two distinct features: (1) a statewide permitting process for obtaining approvals for large projects through Act 250, and (2) local planning and review of development projects by municipal planning commissions and development review boards, consistent with the goals of downtown revitalization and smart growth.[112] The recent housing crisis has strained Vermont's system of land-use regulation, as employers, housing advocates, and the general public have clamored for more available and affordable housing. A discussion of the state's response follows.

Current Practices and Problems

Like New Hampshire, Vermont has faced a major housing shortage in recent years. In a 2021 survey by the Vermont Housing Finance Agency (VHFA), 102 of the 242 reporting municipalities noted a price-to-income ratio that exceeded the 30 percent figure that defines affordability. In other words, residents of those communities who earned the median income in their area spent more than 30 percent of their gross monthly income on housing.[113] High housing costs are a function of low supply; one in four Vermont homes were built before 1939, and the number of houses in the state over eighty years old exceeds the total number built between 1990 and 2021. Meanwhile, the state's population has increased by about 12 percent since 1988, and living alone is the most common housing pattern today; both factors exacerbate the housing shortage.[114] To complicate matters, municipalities often impose density limits on housing, allowing only three or fewer houses per acre, which restrains efforts to build multifamily housing.[115] Thus, the VHFA concluded that a slowdown in homebuilding in recent decades, modest population growth, a decrease in household size, and wage stagnation have caused the price of either renting or owning a home to exceed the financial capacity of more than one-third of Vermonters.[116]

Consequently, Vermont will need to make at least thirty thousand homes available by 2030 to match its population growth and "normalize" its housing market.[117] Such numbers have put considerable pressure on state lawmakers to facilitate the production of housing by modifying state and local regulations, one of the few factors in the housing equation that they can affect.[118] To reach the goal for 2030, Vermont must add between 5,000 and 6,700 units to its primary home market each year, far more than the approximately 2,000 it has produced recently.[119]

Toward that end, the Vermont Legislature enacted the Housing Opportunities Made for Everyone (HOME) Act (Act 47), which Governor Phil Scott signed in June 2023. It also passed the Community Resilience and the Biodiversity Protection Through Land Use Act (Act 181) one year later. Scott vetoed it, but the legislature overrode his veto with the necessary two-thirds vote. A cosponsor of the bill that became Act 47 identified the regulatory problems that limit the construction of affordable housing in Vermont. He observed: "Large lot sizes, excess parking requirements, excess setbacks, and height limitations all drive up costs and make it harder for low- and even moderate-income people to be able to live in the communities in which they work." [120]

Perhaps the most noteworthy provision of Act 47 effectively bans exclusive single-family zoning in residential areas served by municipal sewer and water facilities. In these areas, the Act provides that "the lot size for residential uses shall be 1/5 of an acre or less and building dimensional standards shall allow 5+ dwelling units per acre." Furthermore, density standards for multi-unit dwellings "shall not be more restrictive than density standards for single-family dwellings."[121] Thus, although single-family homes may be constructed in these locations, they no longer are the only dwellings that may be constructed there, and their lot sizes are restricted. A related provision states that "multi-unit dwellings with four or fewer units shall be a permitted use (unless the district requires multi-unit dwellings to have more than four units)." Similarly, in all residential areas, "duplexes are an allowed use with the same dimensional standards as single-unit dwellings."[122]

Act 47 also relaxes the minimum parking-space requirements imposed by municipalities, which developers often find costly because they sacrifice potential housing units to make room for unnecessary parking spaces.[123] It provides that in residential areas with municipal sewer and water services, "regulations may only require one parking space per dwelling unit [i.e. house or apartment], except in areas located more than one quarter-mile from public parking. In the latter locations, the regulations may require 1.5 parking spaces per dwelling unit for duplexes and multi-unit dwellings."[124]

Act 47 addresses Accessory Dwelling Units too. Except in areas prone to flooding or riverbank erosion, "single-family dwellings *with* ADUs are subject to the same requirements as single-family dwellings without ADUs."[125] The Act also covers affordable housing, providing that in residential areas with municipal sewer and water services, local zoning bylaws "shall permit affordable housing developments to exceed density limitations by 40% and height limitations by one floor" (so long as the building complies with the fire safety code). The lot size for affordable housing in such locations "cannot exceed 6,222 sq. ft., and multi-unit dwellings can have four floors and seven units per acre.[126] Act 47 even includes a temporary modification of Act 250. Under Act 250, review of a project is ordinarily triggered when a developer seeks to build ten housing units within five years' time and a five-mile radius.[127] Under Act 47, though, until July 1, 2026, Act 250 jurisdiction will not apply unless a developer seeks to construct more than twenty-five units of housing in a downtown or a village center within a five-mile radius and a five-year period.[128] Thus, Act 47 gives developers a temporary reprieve from Act 250 to encourage them to build affordable, multifamily housing in or close to downtown.

Finally, the Act prevents opponents of affordable and multifamily housing from derailing it by appealing a local decision approving the project based on a claim that it "changes the character" of the area where the project is to be located. The Act states that an appeal "shall not include the character of the area affected if the project has a residential component that includes affordable housing."[129] This provision seeks to prevent residents who are hostile to multifamily housing from barring it by charging that it intrudes on their neighborhood of single-family homes. Thus, Act 47 takes on Vermont's housing shortage by ending a long-standing entitlement for single-family homes in residential settings, offering instead equal treatment for ADUs, affordable housing, and multifamily housing to hasten their construction, especially downtown and in village centers.

In June 2024, the Vermont Legislature bolstered Act 47 by passing Act 181. The latter eased Act 250 requirements in downtown and village center locations to promote the development of compact housing there. But it also enhanced Act 250 protection in ecologically sensitive areas. The ecological focus prompted the veto by Governor Scott, who thought the legislation mistakenly prioritized land conservation over housing construction, especially in rural areas.[130] Previously, Act 250 jurisdiction flowed from the size of a project, such as commercial construction that planned to use ten or more acres of land or a residential development that aimed to construct ten or more housing units within a five-mile radius. Instead Act 181 establishes "location-based jurisdiction" that applies different rules within three major locational "tiers," to "promote housing within well-planned smart growth areas, while reducing harm to critical natural resource areas and wetlands."[131]

In Tier 1A, which encompasses larger downtown areas, no Act 250 permits will be required for residential, commercial, or industrial development, provided these locations have municipal planning and land-use bylaws, public water and sewer infrastructure, adequate professional planning staff, and flood-hazard and river-corridor bylaws in place. In Tier 1B locations (smaller downtowns), permanent zoning, subdivision regulations, and the capacity for growth exist, but municipal regulations, infrastructure, planning staff, and administrative capacity fail to meet the standards required by Tier 1A. Act 250 permits will not be required in Tier 1B for the construction of projects with up to fifty housing units located on ten acres or fewer.[132]

In Tier 2, which consists of "natural resource areas, working farms and forests, and low-density development areas," the preexisting Act 250 rules remain in place, along with one new addition, a revised "road rule," which aims to encourage placing houses close together while leaving ample undeveloped land for common use. Specifically, the new rule requires Act 250 review "for the construction of a single private road longer than 800 feet, or a network of combined roads and driveways greater than 2,000 feet."[133] In Tier 3, which includes the state's "most critical natural resource areas," such as "river corridors, headwater streams, habitat connectors of statewide significance, riparian areas, pristine waters, and certain natural communities," development is possible, but it will require Act 250 review.

Besides these substantive changes to Act 250 regulations, Act 181 includes an important procedural change: replacing the Natural Resources Board, which is comprised of volunteers, with a new Land Use Review Board (LURB). The new board's members—gubernatorial appointees subject to senate confirmation—will have expertise in "land use and related fields," and "the time and qualifications to properly supervise and train Act 250 district staff."[134] This change aims to improve the administration of Act 250 regulations and produce clearer, more consistent decisions by the various district commissions.[135]

Both Act 47 and Act 181 seek to preserve Vermont's traditional land-use pattern of densely developed town centers surrounded by countryside, while also addressing the current housing shortage. The following section will assess Vermont's prospects for achieving those goals.

The Housing Crisis and the Challenge Ahead

In a June 2024 report, the Vermont Housing Finance Agency (VHFA) explained that the low availability of homes in Vermont and their high prices have left "thousands of jobs unfilled in numerous industries, including those essential to addressing the housing crisis, such as construction, home repairs, and social services."[136] Other disturbing consequences of this housing shortage include the following: half of all Vermont renters are cost-burdened, spending more than 30 percent of their gross monthly incomes on housing costs; one in four renters spend more than half their monthly incomes on housing costs; and Vermont's statewide rental-vacancy rate is 3 percent, and Chittenden County's rate is just 1 percent. To take one local example, in Rutland County, the monthly cost of renting a one-bedroom apartment climbed from $780 in 2019 to $911 in 2023, and the median home price jumped from $150,000 in 2018 to $229,000 in 2022, according to the VHFA's 2023 housing needs assessment.[137]

Considering these data, it is not surprising that the per-capita rate of homelessness in Vermont, according to the US Department of Housing and Urban Development, is fifty-three for every ten thousand people, the fourth highest in the United States.[138] Therefore, the VHFA estimates that Vermont will need between 24,000 and 36,000 additional homes from 2025 through 2029 to meet the demand, normalize vacancy rates to approximately 5 percent, house the homeless, and replace homes lost to flooding and other causes.[139]

The current conditions result from several causes. First, homebuilding has lagged in Vermont. During the Great Recession of 2008–2012, only 1,500 new homes received building permits in the Green Mountain State. The tally of permits has increased since then, but as of June 2024, it had not returned to prerecession levels; hence, the housing supply has failed to keep pace with the demand in Vermont.[140]

Second, demographics are partly responsible for the current housing shortage. Although the number of households living year-round in Vermont was steady from 2010 until 2017, it began to increase thereafter and jumped considerably beginning in 2020 because of the coronavirus pandemic.[141] The average annual rate of increase in year-round households in Vermont rose from 1 percent before the pandemic to 1.8 percent during the pandemic.[142] Vermont experienced a net population gain of 4,387 residents between 2020 and 2023, resulting entirely from net migration, because deaths exceeded births in the state by 5,191 persons during that period.[143] Another demographic contributor to the housing crunch is the shrinking size of Vermont households, most of which now have just one or two members. Indeed, one- or two-person households comprised 70 percent of all Vermont households in 2022, while households of four or more individuals comprised only 16 percent of the total.[144] As Vermonters increasingly live alone or with one other person, the demand for housing naturally exceeds what it would be if people lived together in larger households.

Third, housing is expensive to build in Vermont because of a shortage of labor, the high cost of materials, and, when Act 250 applies, the costs associated with obtaining an Act 250 permit. As noted earlier, Act 47 and Act 181 aim to lower these regulatory costs, at least temporarily, to spur the development of new housing.[145]

Finally, the short-term-rental industry has boomed in Vermont in recent years, as property owners seek to profit from renting houses and apartments to vacationers for a weekend, a week, or even longer periods of time. Such rentals are not the largest contributor to the current housing squeeze because they account for only about 3.6 percent of Vermont's housing stock. Nevertheless, as the VHFA notes, they remove units from long-term use, placing further stress on an already tight housing market.[146] That scenario is especially prevalent in ski-resort towns. For example, as of September 2023, Stowe, a town with slightly more than five thousand residents, had just over one thousand short-term rentals, the highest number of any Vermont town.[147]

Meanwhile, since Act 47 and Act 181 have taken effect, developers have been willing to increase the number of units in their pending projects, thanks to the temporary exemptions from Act 250 requirements applicable to downtown and village-center locations. When Act 250 does not apply, developers save thousands of dollars on the permitting, design, and engineering fees that would otherwise be required just to prepare an application for the requisite permit; they also can construct more housing units than would otherwise be possible. A few of the projects taking advantage of the temporary exemptions include the conversion of a former nursing home into forty apartments in the town of Hartford, construction of a new subsidized senior housing project in downtown St. Johnsbury, and a hotel-plus-apartments development in the city of Rutland. In Fairlee, home to fewer than one thousand residents, a developer plans to renovate an existing ten-unit apartment complex and build two new fourplexes on the same property, taking advantage of the temporary Act 250 exemption that permits construction of up to fifty housing units in village centers. Several units will be reserved for people exiting homelessness and will be coupled with supportive services.[148]

Act 47 also created a $10 million revolving loan fund that is being used to build affordable housing in several communities. The fund loans money to developers to build affordable housing; it is "revolving" because during the next decade, as developers repay the loans, which have an interest rate of between 0 and 2 percent, the repaid money will be loaned out for new construction projects. The fund is financing projects in Bennington, Bolton, Rutland, Springfield, St. Albans, Vergennes, Windsor, and Winooski. The Springfield and Windsor projects will offer some units to refugees. To ensure that the units in the projects supported by the loan fund remain affordable, developers must maintain the starting rent levels until three years after repaying the money they borrowed.[149]

Sometimes, though, local initiatives are sufficient to make housing affordable. For example, in January 2024, the Woodstock Community Trust created

Local Deeds, a program that assists homebuyers to make down payments in exchange for a deed restriction stipulating that a local worker must live in the home. The Woodstock program is modeled on a similar arrangement called Vail INDEED, begun in Vail, Colorado, which like Woodstock, is an affluent resort town with high housing prices. In 2023, the median sale price for a primary residence in Woodstock reached $550,000, according to the VHFA.[150] About one-quarter of the housing stock consists of second homes.

A household can qualify for Local Deeds if one of its members works an average of twenty-five hours or more per week within a sixteen-mile radius of Woodstock and uses the home as a primary residence. Local Deeds furnishes a one-time cash payment, and in return, the local worker agrees to live in the house or condominium in Woodstock or one of four surrounding towns. As of September 2024, nine months after the program began, it had contributed funds for fourteen housing units, which housed twenty-one local workers and eight school-age children. By then, five teachers in the Woodstock School District had used Local Deeds to purchase homes, and the program had contributed a total of $700,000 in down payment assistance. It is funded with the proceeds from grants and private donations; many of the latter come from local property owners.[151]

Like New Hampshire, Vermont faces a formidable task in addressing its housing crisis. The estimated need for 24,000 to 36,000 new units before 2030 looms large, and the high number of unhoused Vermonters is a black eye for a state that has long trumpeted its quality of life. And if Vermont cannot house younger workers, who are necessary to replenish an aging workforce, it faces the prospect of losing out economically to other states. Indeed, Alex Farrell, Commissioner of Housing and Community Development, told Vermont Public in late 2024 that the availability of housing is a key to maintaining a vibrant economy in Vermont. He added, though, that "we're getting there, we're making progress," noting that he expected the state to build between 3,000 and 3,500 new housing units per year in 2025 and 2026.[152]

State leaders addressed the crisis in 2023 and 2024, passing legislation that has made local zoning rules and Act 250 regulations more flexible to spur housing construction. Both laws make their Act 250 exemptions temporary, though, and apply them only downtown and in village centers, following smart-growth principles. State leaders revisited the crisis in 2025, when they enacted S. 127 (now Act 69), creating the Community and Housing Infrastructure Program (CHIP), which helps municipalities to cover the high cost of infrastructure upgrades necessary for residential development. CHIP enables municipalities and developers to borrow funds needed to build roads, sidewalks, and sewers, for example, and then to use the increased property tax revenue that accrues from new development to pay back the debt incurred. It has the potential to spur $2 billion in infrastructure spending by 2035, a noteworthy contribution to resolving Vermont's housing shortage.[153] Community initiatives, such as the Local Deeds program in Woodstock, have also addressed the state's housing crunch. Thus, cautious optimism seems warranted, despite the challenge ahead, because of the boldness and flexibility of Vermont's response to its housing need.

Conclusion

The darkest cloud on the horizon for both New Hampshire and Vermont may be their chronic shortage of workforce housing, which threatens their economic vitality. Many similarities exist between the two states in their responses to this problem, largely because the impact of political culture on land-use policy is muted. In both states, zoning is a municipal choice, not a constitutionally mandated state responsibility like public education. Consequently, most land-use decisions are left to local volunteer boards and private developers, not elected state officials.

Under these circumstances, it is understandable that both states have responded to the housing shortage with more nudges than shoves, more incentives than mandates. They have passed laws to encourage the building of affordable housing, including ADUs and multifamily housing. Similarly, they have modified density requirements and promoted cluster development to preserve open space. And they have committed public funds to spur the development of workforce housing.

Still, the implications of political culture are evident here. Vermont, in keeping with its tendency toward bolder, more state-centric solutions, has adopted somewhat broader measures for addressing its housing shortage. For example, Act 47 ended the long-standing preference for single-family homes in residential areas, encouraging the construction of affordable housing there. Similarly, Act 181 replaced size-based jurisdiction under Act 250 with location-based jurisdiction, hastening housing construction in downtown areas and village centers while retaining such controls in more rural settings. In other words, Vermont's response to the housing shortage is more ambitious than New Hampshire's in seeking not only to add housing, but also to preserve the natural landscape that shapes its public image and will help to ensure its future prosperity. Only time will tell whether both approaches—or perhaps one more than the other—will resolve the housing crunch the Twin States share.

CHAPTER SEVEN

Policy Consequences of Political Culture

The Case of Public School Finance

Introduction: Contrasting Responses to a Shared Challenge

UNLIKE THE HOUSING SHORTAGE, the perennial dilemma of funding public schools fairly and adequately has drawn contrasting responses from New Hampshire and Vermont. New Hampshire's response has featured litigation, as the state supreme court has held repeatedly that reliance on local property taxes to fund education violates the state constitution. Elected officials have not established a funding mechanism that meets constitutional requirements because they refuse to create a broad-based tax that could yield the funds needed to satisfy those requirements. In contrast, Vermont's response to this issue has included minimal litigation, but several legislative efforts to revamp the funding formula to make it fairer for students and taxpayers, as befits its political culture. The following discussion will highlight the alternative means by which the Twin States have responded to the school funding challenge.

New Hampshire

Historical Patterns

Funding public schools is a long-standing issue in New Hampshire, dating back at least to 1984, when the state commissioned the first of what would become a shelf full of reports on the matter. A 2023 comment in the *New Hampshire Business Review* on this subject noted that school funding "has been so intractable because of the state's political culture, its identity as the only state besides Alaska without broad-based taxes and . . . a lack of consensus on how to raise the money otherwise."[1]

The 1984 Augenblick Report, recognizing New Hampshire's political culture, proposed a funding plan that "could be implemented without new taxes."[2] It offered a formula whereby New Hampshire could make spending somewhat more equitable between school districts, while still providing a modest level of state funding compared to other states. It recommended that school districts with an average capacity to raise revenue should have 8 percent of their "foundation" costs (the basic grant each district receives) covered by the state, whereas districts with less-than-average capacity should have more than 8 percent covered by the state, and districts with higher-than-average capacity should receive less than 8 percent from state funds.[3] To raise the revenue necessary to assist the poorer districts, the report recommended consolidating lottery revenue, a share of Business Profits Tax proceeds, special education support funds, existing foundation aid, and additional money from the General Fund into a new foundation aid program.[4] The report also recommended a funding formula that, when determining a school district's fiscal capacity, included not only its property wealth, but also its median family income.[5] The state legislature failed to fund the formula sufficiently, though, so the continuing frustration of poorer school districts with inadequate state aid prompted a spate of lawsuits in the 1990s and beyond.[6]

Before discussing the lawsuits, it is worth noting that political culture continues to shape public school finance in New Hampshire. A National Education Association (NEA) report published in April 2025 ranked New Hampshire fiftieth with respect to state funding for public education. Specifically, New Hampshire has the lowest contribution of state money and the highest contribution of local money to funding public education of all fifty states, according to the report. In the 2023–24 school year, for example, 28.8 percent of the revenue obtained by public schools in New Hampshire came from the state, whereas 68.6 percent came from local taxpayers and the remainder from federal money. The national average in that year was 48.1 percent for state contributions.[7] Accordingly, the familiar claim that New Hampshire is the fifth-highest-spending state regarding public education is misleading because it counts both state and local spending, whereas the state constitution assigns responsibility for funding schools to the state, not localities.[8] Because New Hampshire provides such a modest level of financial support to its public schools, districts with lower-than-average property wealth must impose relatively high tax rates on their residents to raise the funds necessary to educate their children.[9]

That precise problem—and the failure of elected officials to resolve it—led disadvantaged school districts and their students to seek relief in the New Hampshire courts, beginning in the early 1990s. Five property-poor school districts, five children, and five taxpayers from each of the districts objected to a trial court's conclusion that the state constitution does not require the state to support public schools; hence, they appealed to the state supreme court. In *Claremont School District et al. v. Governor et al.*, decided in 1993, the supreme court reversed the trial court's decision, holding that the state constitution "imposes a duty on the State to provide a constitutionally adequate education to every educable child in the public schools in New Hampshire and to guarantee adequate funding."[10] The appellate court noted that Part II, Article 83 of the state constitution requires legislators and other state officials to "cherish the interest of literature and the sciences, and all seminaries and public schools" and to "encourage private and public institutions, rewards, and immunities for the promotion of agriculture, arts, sciences, commerce, trade, manufactures and natural history of the country," among other things.[11] In the court's view, that language was not just aspirational; instead, it directed the state to educate all its citizens and support all public schools.

In support of that conclusion, the court noted that between 1641 and 1679, New Hampshire was part of Massachusetts and that in 1647, an act of the Massachusetts Legislature established public schools in what is now New Hampshire. The law said that private property was subject to public taxation for the support of public schools, schooling was to be provided to all children, and the state (then a colony) would control education.[12] In 1680, when New Hampshire separated from Massachusetts, it reenacted the latter's education laws then in force. In 1693, New Hampshire enacted a law that required selectmen in the various towns to raise funds by "an equal rate and assessment" on the townspeople for the construction and maintenance of schools and to pay the schoolmaster's salary. The law included a penalty for noncompliance.[13]

Because education has been compulsory in New Hampshire since 1647 and because the state constitution "expressly recognizes education as a cornerstone of our democratic system," the court continued, "in New Hampshire, a free public education is at the very least an important, substantive right."[14] Besides, under current conditions, the state's constitutional duty extends beyond "mere reading, writing, and arithmetic" to "broad educational opportunities needed . . . to prepare citizens for their role as participants and as potential competitors in today's marketplace of ideas."[15] The court then left to the governor and the legislators the task of determining how to fulfill the state's duty to ensure an appropriate education for its children.

The first *Claremont* decision (*Claremont I*) answered the question whether New Hampshire was duty-bound to support its public schools, but it did not determine whether the state's existing system of school funding was constitutional. But in a 1997 case by the same name, commonly known as *Claremont II*,[16] the state supreme court held that "the present system of financing elementary and secondary education in New Hampshire is unconstitutional."[17] Under that system, state financial assistance to schools amounted to an average of 8 percent of the total funds spent on public elementary and secondary education, which meant New Hampshire ranked "last in the United States in percentage of direct support to public education."[18]

To reach its constitutional conclusion, the court first needed to decide whether property taxes imposed to fund public schools were local or state taxes; if they were state taxes, they had to be, under Part II, Article 5 of the state constitution, "proportional and reasonable," meaning equal in valuation and uniform in rate.[19] The court held that the purpose of the property tax—funding schools—was "overwhelmingly a State purpose"; hence, that tax was a state tax.[20] The court acknowledged that the property tax was levied on property located within individual school districts. Nevertheless, it was a state tax because the tax was "authorized by the legislature to fulfill the requirements of the New Hampshire Constitution."[21]

Because the school property tax was a state tax, Part II, Article 5 required it to be proportional and reasonable throughout the state. But the court observed that the tax was disproportionate, citing data from the 1994–95 school year as evidence. In that year, the tax rate in Pittsfield, a property-poor town, was $25.26 per $1000 of property value, whereas in Moultonborough, a property-rich town, the rate was just $5.56 per $1000, which is a disparity of more than 400 percent. Similarly, in the same year, the tax rate in property-poor Allenstown was $26.47 per $1000, whereas in property-rich Rye it was just $6.86, a nearly 400 percent difference.[22]

In the court's view, the system that produced such results was plainly unconstitutional. The court reasoned that the framers of the state constitution could not possibly have intended to create a funding mechanism featuring such wide disparities, which was "presumably why they assigned the duty to support schools to the State, not the towns."[23] Therefore, if New Hampshire continued to use the property tax to fund public education, "the tax must be administered in a manner that is equal in valuation and uniform in rate throughout the State."[24]

Despite invalidating the existing funding mechanism, the court did not fashion an alternative. Instead, in *Claremont II*, as it had done in *Claremont I*, the court left that responsibility to the elected branches of state government. Responding to *Claremont II*, Governor Jeanne Shaheen, a Democrat, proposed a new school funding mechanism early in 1998, called Advancing Better Classrooms, better known as the ABC Plan. She promised that it would provide millions of additional dollars to poorer school districts without impinging on local control, harming property-rich districts, or enacting a broad-based tax.[25] To fund the plan, Shaheen asked the legislature to increase the cigarette tax, allow and tax video gambling machines at the state's racetracks, and extract more money from the nuclear power plant located at Seabrook. The key feature of the plan was a uniform local educational property tax rate, to be applied to every municipality. The plan would place a limit on what municipalities were required to raise for education, but any community could choose to spend more than the required amount, thereby preserving local control. For poorer towns, where the uniform tax rate would likely not yield enough money to pay for an "adequate" education (e.g., $4,500 per student), the state would fill the gap with supplemental funds. For wealthier towns, presumably, the uniform tax rate would yield enough money to fund an adequate education without state assistance.[26]

Predictably, some Granite Staters approved of the ABC Plan's lack of revenue sharing between richer and poorer towns and its avoidance of a broad-based tax. But others disagreed, acknowledging that the plan was politically savvy, but charging that it failed to satisfy the mandate of *Claremont II*. For example, one newspaper editorial board observed that the plan had "an unmistakable New Hampshire flavor; it attempts to do as little as possible and would be financed substantially by people indulging their vices."[27]

The New Hampshire Supreme Court also disapproved of the ABC Plan. New Hampshire permits its highest court to issue advisory opinions about the constitutionality of pending legislation. In one such opinion, the court found the plan unconstitutional for allowing property-rich towns to retain tax revenues beyond what they needed to fund an adequate education. That arrangement made the effective tax rate in these towns less than the rate paid by taxpayers in towns that could not raise enough money to pay for an adequate education.[28]

The court noted that under the ABC Plan, the tax rate for any town that could raise more money than it needed received a "special abatement," that is, fell below the uniform statewide tax rate because the town could raise sufficient sums to achieve adequacy without imposing the statewide rate. Viewed from another angle, such towns could raise an excess amount of money, above the "adequacy" amount, by taxing at the statewide rate. In short, the ABC Plan preserved the problem identified in *Claremont II*: wealthier towns could meet the adequacy standard via a lower property tax rate than poorer towns needed to raise the same amount.[29] Although the poorer towns would receive a state grant to cover the unfunded costs of an adequate education, the court reasoned that property owners in those towns would still pay taxes at a higher rate than residents of towns with surplus revenue. Therefore, because *Claremont II* required that a property tax for education be proportional across the state, the ABC Plan was unconstitutional for lack of a proportional property tax.[30]

Following *Claremont II*, the most ambitious legislative attempt to revamp education funding in New Hampshire proposed (in 1998) a 4 percent personal income tax and a statewide property tax on business properties and second homes, designed to raise more than $700 million annually. Although it passed both houses of the legislature, disparities between the house and senate versions of the bill necessitated a second vote in the house, where it lost by a narrow margin.[31]

In 1999, legislators again attempted to meet the constitutional requirements of *Claremont II*, this time by enacting a statewide education property tax (SWEPT), set initially at $6.60 per $1000 of property value, but reset in 2001 at $5.80 per $1000 and accompanied by increased rates for some existing taxes and property tax rebates for low-income residents.[32] Under SWEPT, each municipality was responsible for raising an amount of money for education that was determined by multiplying the statewide property tax rate by the town's equalized property value. If the total was less than the necessary amount for an adequate education, the state would supply a grant to help defray the municipality's adequate education cost. Municipalities whose property tax revenue exceeded the cost of educational adequacy received no grants and were required to submit their excess funds to the state for redistribution to poorer municipalities. The wealthier municipalities became known as "donor towns."[33] The 1999 law remained in effect until 2003, when a new plan was adopted. Meanwhile, Governor Shaheen appointed a commission to consider various taxation alternatives, and legislators proposed a wide array of funding mechanisms.[34]

The 2003 plan tweaked the funding formula, dropping the property tax rate from $5.80 to $4.92 per $1000 and later to $3.24, and fixing the annual amount of state aid at $363 million, meaning that the tax rate would be set annually to raise that amount. Property-poor municipalities would receive targeted state assistance for transportation costs and for special education students, students eligible for free or reduced-price meals, and English language learners, all of whom cost more to educate than other students.[35] Still, the post-*Claremont* years saw New Hampshire continue to struggle to resolve educational inequities between school districts and financial inequities between taxpayers in those districts. Meanwhile, the donor towns resented having to subsidize the schooling of children in other communities. Without the donor towns, though, New Hampshire's funding system would violate the constitutional requirement of a tax system that is equal in valuation and uniform in rate throughout the state.[36] Political pressure by donor towns to end redistribution finally succeeded in 2011, when a change in the law permitted wealthier municipalities to keep all the money they collected in property taxes and use any excess amount for their own purposes. Because of this change, one commentator opined, "the rich got richer, and the poor got poorer."[37]

Therefore, the litigation continued; in 2006 came another decision of the New Hampshire Supreme Court: *Londonderry School District SAU 12 et al. v. State of New Hampshire*.[38] In *Londonderry*, the state appealed a trial court's decision holding that the state had shirked its duty to define a constitutionally adequate education. The appellate court affirmed the trial court's finding in that regard. It reasoned that any definition of adequacy the governor and the legislature agree to must be clear enough to be understood and to allow for its costs to be objectively determined. Furthermore, the state must "pay for" whatever it identifies as a constitutionally adequate education.[39] Showing frustration with elected officials' grudging responses to *Claremont II*, the court noted that for thirteen years it had avoided usurping the legislature's role in this matter and would continue to do so. Nevertheless, it stated that "the judiciary has a responsibility to ensure that constitutional rights not be hollowed out and, in the absence of action by other branches, a judicial remedy is not only appropriate but essential. . . . We urge the legislature to act."[40]

In response to the *Londonderry* decision, a joint legislative committee was established in 2007 to "study the cost of providing the opportunity for an adequate education and the educational needs and resources necessary to ensure its delivery to the public-school children of the state."[41] The committee set the universal cost of providing the opportunity for an adequate education as defined by New Hampshire law at $3,456 per pupil, but the committee's work reignited the school funding debate instead of extinguishing it.[42] For a decade and a half after *Londonderry*, a bevy of commissions and studies, both public and private, aimed to make New Hampshire's school funding mechanism more generous and equitable.

One such entity, created by the legislature, reported in the fall of 2018 that for FY 2019, New Hampshire provided base adequacy funding of $3,636.05 per student. That amount was supplemented by "differentiated aid" of $1,818.02 for each child eligible for free or reduced-price meals (FRPL, a measure of poverty); $1,956.09 for each child who required special education; and $711.40 for each child who was learning English. Another $711.40 was provided for each third grader whose reading score on the state assessment or a comparable local assessment was below "proficient."[43] This committee concluded that increasing the base adequacy figure to more accurately reflect current costs and implementing a targeted grant program to provide additional funds to the neediest municipalities was "the best option to address the cost of an opportunity for all children for an adequate education."[44] Specifically, the group recommended that base adequacy be raised to $3,897 and that differentiated aid for each FRPL student be boosted to $2,500.[45] Finally, it recommended that legislators provide additional funds to school districts in municipalities whose property values were below average when measured on a per-pupil basis.[46]

Another independent commission—the Commission to Study School Funding—was formed during the 2019 legislative session.[47] In the spring of 2020 the commission received help from the American Institutes for Research (AIR), a private research organization. AIR assessed the equity of the existing funding system for both students and taxpayers by examining relationships between property wealth, tax rates, and education spending.

It also estimated the combined local, state, and federal funding levels that would increase equity across New Hampshire.[48]

Predictably, considering the evidence presented in the *Claremont* and *Londonderry* cases, AIR's August 2020 draft report concluded that New Hampshire's system of school funding was inequitable for both students and taxpayers. Equally unsurprising was the related finding that school districts with higher numbers of low-income students, special education students, and English language learners performed worse on various standardized measures than districts with fewer high-need students. Small districts also required higher per-student spending to achieve favorable student outcomes. Finally, AIR concluded that New Hampshire could generate educational revenue more equitably by means of a revamped statewide property tax that collected funds centrally instead of locally and distributed them according to a weighted funding formula created by AIR.[49]

Using that formula, the authors of the AIR report estimated that in 2018–19, the base adequacy spending level for a school district—which assumed no low-income students, special education students, or English language learners—was $5,868 per pupil (including transportation). The base amount climbed to $8,751 for a low-income student; $12,898 for an English language learner; and $25,183 for a special education student. Dividing the per-pupil cost of educating a low-income student ($8,751) by the per-pupil cost of educating a typical student ($5,868), the authors reached the number 1.49, indicating that a school district spends nearly 1.5 times more money to educate the low-income student than the typical student.[50] Therein lies the need for greater funding equity, which is heightened by the prevalence of low-income students, special education students, and English language learners in property-poor districts.

AIR's partner, the Commission to Study School Funding, also wrote a report, which was released in December 2020. Its recommendations largely mirrored those in the AIR draft report, but the commission's report is still noteworthy. The commission concluded that New Hampshire should prohibit municipalities that can raise funds above and beyond their SWEPT grants from keeping those funds, even if they are used for educational purposes. Instead, the commission recommended that excess funds be used, under a new distribution formula, to "improve student and taxpayer equity." The commission also advised elected officials to bolster taxpayer equity by means of targeted tax relief to low- and moderate-income homeowners and renters.[51]

In 2022, the New Hampshire Fiscal Policy Institute (NFPI) produced an issue brief that examined the recommendations made by the commission and AIR. The issue brief noted that the commission's recommendation would have increased the base per-pupil state grant from $3,636 to $5,868 for the 2018–19 school year in addition to substantially boosting state funding levels for low-income students, special education students, and English language learners. The commission's funding formula, devised by AIR, would have increased the amount of state assistance by nearly $2 billion in the 2018–19 school year, an approximately 209 percent increase over actual state funding during that year.[52] Although the recommended funding increase was considerable, the issue brief noted that the increase appeared less significant when examined in light of New Hampshire providing among the lowest percentages of state funding for public education of any state as a portion of all elementary and secondary school revenue. And New Hampshire ranked forty-eighth among the states in the dollar amount of state per-pupil funding after adjusting for statewide personal income.[53] Thus, even though the commission's recommendation was generous, adopting it would likely not have changed New Hampshire's ranking much. In the school-funding realm, the Granite State has almost nowhere to go but up.

Still, the issue brief concluded that the commission's recommendations, if implemented, would have raised "significantly more resources for local public education at the state level" and would have distributed them to municipalities "in a manner designed to enhance the opportunity for equitable outcomes."[54] But New Hampshire did not adopt the commission's recommendations.

Finally, two reports by the Education Law Center in 2022 and 2024 gave New Hampshire a grade of A for its level of spending on public schools (the cost-adjusted per-pupil revenue from state and local sources combined); a C for its funding effort (the amount of public education funding as a percentage of the state's total economic activity); and an F for its funding distribution (the extent to which additional funds are directed to school districts with high levels of child poverty).[55] The gist of these grades is that New Hampshire spends a comparatively large amount of money on schools, despite a mediocre fundraising effort by state legislators, because municipalities raise hefty sums through property taxes, but the distribution of funds raised via state taxes is highly inequitable. Indeed, the 2022 report stated that in New Hampshire, low-poverty districts received 27 percent more per-pupil aid than high-poverty districts.[56]

Under these circumstances, it was predictable that some New Hampshire school districts and taxpayers, particularly those in communities with low property values, would lose patience with seemingly endless legislative debates and study commissions about school finance, and would return to court instead. The resulting litigation, which continued into 2025, is the focus of the following section.

Current Practices and Problems

Any discussion of current circumstances regarding the funding of public schools in New Hampshire must highlight the two legal challenges to the existing system that the state supreme court decided in 2025. The first one, *Contoocook Valley School District v. New Hampshire*, better known as *ConVal*, which sixteen other school districts joined, was filed in 2019. The second one, *Rand v. New Hampshire*, in which the plaintiffs were taxpayers instead of school districts, was filed in 2022.

The New Hampshire Supreme Court has decided *ConVal* twice, having first done so in 2021.[57] In the earlier litigation, the state appealed a trial court's summary judgment (final judgment issued without a trial) for the plaintiffs, claiming that the trial court had erred in deciding the case without benefit of discovery, the fact-finding process inherent to trials.[58] The appellate court agreed with the state; therefore, it reversed the trial court's decision and sent the case back to the trial court for a trial. Thus, the appellate court's 2021 *ConVal* decision rested entirely on the procedural matter of the trial court's failure to conduct a trial; it did not address the plaintiffs' claim that the state had failed to meet its constitutional duty to give all New Hampshire students the opportunity for an adequate education. That issue had to await a trial in the lower court.[59]

A three-week bench trial (judge but no jury) followed in the Rockingham County Superior Court in April 2023.[60] Six months later, the trial court issued its decision, agreeing with the plaintiffs that the base adequacy amount of money they received from the state—which then stood at $4,100 per pupil per year, failed to provide the adequate education that Part II, Article 83 of the state constitution required. "Thus," the court concluded, "the current allocation of $4,100 per pupil is unconstitutional."[61]

In analyzing the case, the court explained that to provide for a constitutionally adequate education, the state must "define an adequate education, determine the cost, fund it with constitutional taxes, and ensure its delivery through accountability."[62] Effective July 1, 2023, the legislature amended the pertinent law to provide for the base adequacy amount of $4,100 per pupil per year. The plaintiffs argued that the amount was inadequate under Part II, Article 83; hence, the sole issue before the trial court was whether the base amount of state aid met the constitutional standard.[63] The court concluded that it did not because "the evidence at trial overwhelmingly established that no school could provide the opportunity for an adequate education if it had to rely solely on the base adequacy aid from the state."[64]

Based on that evidence, the court determined that the following cost drivers (and their associated costs) must be included in any per-pupil calculation of a constitutionally adequate education:

1. Teachers ($3,981.01)
2. Nonteaching employees ($901)
3. Instructional materials, technology, professional development ($430)
4. Facilities operation and maintenance ($1,000)
5. Transportation ($750)
6. Nurse services ($294)

These amounts total $7,356.01, which the court acknowledged was "quite conservative" as an estimate of likely school costs.[65] It also acknowledged that when applied statewide, the $3,256.01 difference between that amount and the existing state minimum would translate to an increase of at least $537,550,970.95 annually in the state's contribution to its schools.[66]

Nevertheless, the court expressed confidence that "the guidance offered here will empower the legislature to meaningfully consider and appropriately respond to the relevant issues."[67] The court said it trusted the legislature to "set a base adequacy aid figure meaningfully higher than the $7,356.01 threshold," which, after all, is a floor, not a ceiling, for state aid.[68] For some context, the New Hampshire Department of Education put the average annual cost of educating a New Hampshire student in 2023–24 at $21,545.17.[69]

In any event, New Hampshire appealed the trial court's order to the state supreme court, which froze the order pending the outcome of the appeal. The parties argued the case in the supreme court in December 2024, and the justices issued their decision in July 2025. They upheld the trial court's conclusion that the state's school-funding mechanism violates the constitutional requirement of adequacy, but nevertheless reversed the trial court's order to legislators and the governor to boost funding to at least

$7,356.01 per pupil. In other words, the justices affirmed the trial court's decision to the extent that it established the $7,356.01 figure as the minimum constitutional threshold of adequacy, but rejected the order for immediate payment. They reasoned that the order failed to give enough weight to the separation-of-powers principle, which makes elected officials responsible for funding public education. In closing their opinion, the justices wrote: "We urge the legislative and executive branches to act expeditiously to ensure that all the children in public schools in New Hampshire receive a state funded constitutionally adequate education."[70]

The *Rand* case was also litigated in 2025. It focuses on the consequences for property taxpayers of the school funding system's constitutional inadequacy. In the trial court, the plaintiffs, who reside in several property-poor municipalities, alleged that the state improperly relies on local taxpayers to raise the funds needed to pay for the adequate education required by Part II, Article 83 of the state constitution.[71] They argued further that property-poor municipalities do not generate excess educational funds from their property taxes, so they use all the revenues they generate from SWEPT to meet the adequacy standard. Therefore, because SWEPT allows property-rich municipalities to retain their excess funds, they enjoy an effectively lower tax rate to meet the adequacy standard. Thus, SWEPT fosters disproportional tax rates, violating Part II, Article 5 of the state constitution. On this issue, then, the trial court granted summary judgment for the plaintiffs.[72]

The trial court also granted the plaintiffs' request for an injunction, thereby barring municipalities from retaining excess SWEPT funds. It ordered that any SWEPT funds a municipality raises beyond what it needs for educational adequacy should be sent to the state's Department of Revenue Administration for redistribution to municipalities whose SWEPT proceeds do not satisfy the adequacy standard.[73] New Hampshire appealed, and the parties debated the constitutionality of SWEPT at the state supreme court in November 2024. That court decided *Rand* during the summer of 2025, upholding SWEPT and reasoning that the legislature's choice to let wealthy communities retain their excess SWEPT revenues complied with Part II, Article 5 of the state constitution. After all, the justices noted, the taxes collected under SWEPT were assessed at a uniform rate, so they satisfied the constitutional requirements of proportionality and reasonableness. The "effective rates" the plaintiffs challenged were, at most, an indirect consequence of some municipalities raising excess revenue, which SWEPT permitted. Therefore, SWEPT did not violate Part II, Article 5 of the state constitution.[74]

The Challenge Ahead

Regardless of the conclusion in *ConVal* that New Hampshire's school funding system is unconstitutional, the major responsibility for creating a more robust and equitable system will rest with the governor and the legislature. A potential option would be to enact into law the $7,356 per-pupil annual figure identified by the trial court in *ConVal* as meeting the base advocacy standard. A bill to do just that was introduced in the New Hampshire House of Representatives in 2025 but did not get out of committee. It would have replaced the existing $4,100 per pupil base-adequacy amount with the trial court's higher substitute.[75] Testimony before the Education Committee noted that, if enacted, this legislation would have reduced the share of school costs covered by municipalities from the 63 percent in 2022–23 cited in the NEA's 2024 report to about 45 percent.[76] Recall from *Rand* though, that adopting the trial court's adequacy figure would increase the state's financial contribution to education by more than $537 million annually. That would likely be excruciating for notoriously frugal, tax-averse New Hampshire.

Not surprisingly, opposition to expanded state funding of education is also evident in the legislature. During the 2025 session, another house bill, HCR 11, was introduced; it would declare that the *Claremont* decisions are not binding on the legislative or executive branches, thereby ending the duty of those entities to ensure that the state meets a constitutional standard of educational adequacy.[77] In the same vein, when the *Rand* case went to the state supreme court, thirty Republican lawmakers filed an amicus curiae (friend of the court) brief arguing that the *Claremont* cases were decided incorrectly and should be overruled.[78] The bill and the brief recall an unsuccessful attempt in 2005 by then-Governor John Lynch, a Democrat, to evade the *Claremont* mandate by amending the state constitution, ending the state's duty to ensure educational adequacy and freeing it up to distribute "targeted aid" to needy communities.[79] Evidently, that option still has supporters but, as Natalie LaFlamme, one of the plaintiffs' attorneys in *Rand*, observed, it leaves poorer school districts vulnerable to the shifting winds of budgetary priorities and partisan preferences in the legislature.[80]

Budgetary priorities and partisan preferences also affect Education Freedom Accounts (EFAs), which place another demand on New Hampshire's limited education funds. EFAs are grants of public money, generally between $4,000 and $8,000 per student, to parents for home schooling or education at a private school, including a religious school. Begun in 2021, EFAs are a favorite of Republican legislators, who in 2023 expanded income eligibility for them from 300 percent of the federal poverty level ($96,450 for a family of four in 2025 dollars) to 350 percent ($112,525 in 2025 dollars). The program expanded from 1,635 students, at a cost of $8.1 million, in 2021–22 to 5,321 students and a $27.7 million price tag in 2024–25. In June 2025, Governor Kelly Ayotte signed legislation that removed the income cap on eligibility for EFAs, so a family can qualify for state assistance to pay for private school tuition regardless of its income. To encourage families to apply promptly, though, the state capped the number of children to be served for the 2025–26 school year at ten thousand.[81]

Amidst all this political and legal intrigue, one thing is certain: to understand the intractability of the debate about public school finance in New Hampshire, one must appreciate the extent to which the state's political culture is reflected in and influences that debate. If proponents of more robust state funding are to prevail, they will have to overcome long-standing views that government should be small, taxes should be low, and property taxes should support only one's hometown schools.

Vermont

From the eighteenth century, when property taxes first funded public schools, until deep into the twentieth century, Vermont relied largely on local property taxes to support its schools, supplemented by state "foundation aid."[82] Under this system, the state set the per-student cost of a minimally adequate education and sent funds to municipalities whose own property tax proceeds could not generate the requisite amount at a reasonable tax rate. This formula established a financial "floor" under poorer towns, but it allowed wealthy towns to spend much more, and legislators tended to reduce even the minimal aid during tough economic times.[83] Between 1964 and 1997, for example, the state's share of education expenses varied from 20 percent to 37 percent. Periodically, it dipped to the 20 percent range, until "general dissatisfaction and political pressures" spurred a change in the formula, along with additional state dollars."[84] This scenario repeated itself in 1969, 1982, and 1987; by 1997, the state share was just 25.3 percent.[85]

The local property tax was fairer and more effective at raising school funds in Vermont when residents predominantly lived, worked, and shopped in the same town, which they did until the early 1960s, when automobile travel increased considerably. In the days before interstate highways, the tax base in a typical town reflected economic diversity, as mills, factories, farms, and stores were taxed alongside private homes to cover most of the cost of educating local children.[86] But as roads improved and automobiles became prevalent, more Vermonters commuted from home to workplace, and many towns became "bedroom communities," where people lived but did not work.

These social changes had tax consequences because the bedroom communities tended to have a small tax base, for lack of commercial or industrial properties, but many children to educate. Consequently, their schools were often poorly funded, despite high tax rates. In contrast, municipalities with ski areas, large industrial plants, shopping malls, or numerous second homes were well funded, thanks to a large tax base and, sometimes, a small school-age population. These municipalities could fund their schools generously despite low tax rates. In 1993, for example, tax rates in Vermont ranged from a low of $.12 per $100 of property value to fund spending of $12,300 per pupil to a high of $2.28 per $100 of property value to fund spending of $7,850 per pupil.[87]

Four years later, in *Brigham v. State*,[88] the Vermont Supreme Court responded to such concerns by holding that the state's existing school-funding mechanism "deprive[d] children of an equal educational opportunity in violation of the Vermont Constitution."[89] A trial court had rejected the claim by the plaintiffs—two students, two school districts, and several taxpayers—that Chapter II, Section 68 of the state constitution guaranteed a fundamental right to an education and, by extension, a right to equal educational opportunity, which Vermont's school-funding mechanism violated.[90] Section 68 stated that "a competent number of schools ought to be maintained in each town unless the general assembly permits other provisions for the convenient instruction of youth."[91]

On appeal, the state supreme court noted that under the existing funding system, some school districts spent twice as much or more money per student as others, owing to the disparities in property wealth. The state's foundation aid only equalized funds across districts to a level of minimal adequacy; anything above that was the responsibility of local taxpayers.[92] In the appellate court's view, the state had not provided "a persuasive rationale" for the funding disparity between municipalities; therefore, the current funding system was "constitutionally deficient," having violated Chapter II, Section 68.[93]

The court also found that the funding system violated Chapter I, Section 7 of the state constitution, the "common benefits" clause, which ensures equal treatment under the law to all Vermonters.[94] In light of that guarantee, the court concluded, no "legitimate governmental purpose" warranted "the gross inequities in educational opportunities" indicated by the evidence. "The distribution of a resource as precious as educational opportunity may not have as its determining force the mere *fortuity* of a child's residence."[95] Despite holding that the state was constitutionally required to ensure "substantial equality of educational opportunity" statewide,[96] the Vermont Supreme Court—like its New Hampshire counterpart in the *Claremont* decisions, left the choice of a remedy to the state legislature.[97]

The legislative upshot of the *Brigham* decision was the Equal Educational Opportunity Act of 1997, better known as Act 60, which became law in June of that year. Act 60 was unique because it honored the tradition of local control over school spending while establishing a statewide mechanism to pay for the choices made by individual towns and cities. Local school districts establish their own budgets, whereas the state sets tax rates, collects revenue through a statewide property tax, and distributes it to school districts to satisfy their budgets.[98] In other words, Act 60 transformed tax revenue raised to pay for education, which previously had been local, into state tax revenue to cover not only line items in district budgets, but also "categorical grants" of supplementary funding for transportation, special education, and small schools.[99] State and local responsibilities under Act 60 are described in the following chart.

SCHOOL FUNDING RESPONSIBILITIES UNDER ACT 60

State	*School Districts*	*Voters*
1. Set tax rates and state policy, 2. Collect education taxes, including statewide property tax, 3. Transfer money from General Fund to Education Fund 4. Distribute money to districts.[100]	1. Decide how much money to spend, set school policies, pay school expenses.	1. Approve local school budgets, pay education taxes

Thus, under Act 60, the voters of each town or city choose the level of spending for their schools annually, but the revenue to cover that spending comes from several state sources, predominantly residential and nonresidential (business or second home) property taxes.[101] The system ensures that taxpayers who adopt the same spending level in different municipalities will pay the same tax rate regardless of where they live.[102]

Act 60 established a statewide property tax, at a rate of $1.10 per $100 of property value to equalize the highly unequal local property tax system. When revenue from the new tax was combined with revenue from other sources, the total funded a new basic $5,200-per-pupil grant to all Vermont schools.[103] Therefore, public education funds come principally from two taxes on property: the "state-share" property tax established by Act 60 and the "local-share" property tax, which long predated Act 60.[104] A municipality can spend more than the basic grant to support its schools by using local property taxes, but for any per-pupil expenditures above the grant, the voters have to tax themselves at the same rate as any other community, thereby negating the previous tax-rate advantage of wealthy municipalities.[105] An equalized yield formula was adopted to ensure that every school district received the same additional amount in per-pupil expenditures for the same additional increment in tax effort.[106] Vermont's statewide property tax differs from its New Hampshire counterpart in that the revenue raised by the Vermont tax does not remain local; instead, it is transferred to the state's Education Fund for distribution to all schools. Thus, Vermont's Education Fund operates like its Transportation Fund, which receives contributions from all taxpayers to improve infrastructure statewide.[107]

The bulk of the Education Fund's revenue derives from the taxes on "homestead" and nonresidential property. The homestead property tax applies to a primary residence and up to two acres of land and the nonresidential property tax pertains to commercial or rental property and second homes. The Education Fund also includes revenue from the sales tax, the rooms and meals tax, the state lottery, and Medicaid reimbursements. In the wake of Act 60, when these revenue sources were combined and applied to school funding, the state's share of total education spending jumped to 84 percent, a dramatic increase from its previous 25.3 percent contribution.[108]

Two other features of Act 60 are also noteworthy. First, when property-rich municipalities raised funds beyond the amount of the basic state grant, they were required to do so through local property taxes only and to divert some of those dollars to a sharing pool for redistribution to property-poor municipalities. All municipalities that planned to raise an identical amount of additional funds had to pay the identical rate of local property tax, regardless of their property wealth.[109] Second, although Act 60 ostensibly levied a property tax, it was income-sensitive; for households that earned $75,000 or less annually, the property tax burden was capped at 2 percent of household income unless a taxpayer's town or city voted to tax itself at a higher rate. In FY 2000, households that earned more than $75,000 also received a property tax break when the state extended the 2 percent rate cap to homesteads valued at less than $160,000.[110]

The consequences of Act 60 were dramatic. Within the first year after its enactment, 89 percent of Vermont residents saw reductions in their net state and local property tax bills. Local property tax bills declined in 32 percent of municipalities, remained constant in 51 percent, and increased in just 17 percent. Most significantly, 229 school districts received more funding than before, and only 23 received less, partly because they could not retain the amount of local tax revenue they had previously.[111]

Not all Vermonters welcomed Act 60, though. Indeed, a backlash developed against it, as residents of property-wealthy ski resort towns faced sharp hikes in their tax bills and realized that their local schools could no longer benefit from raising ample funds despite low property tax rates.[112] Other unhappy constituencies included owners of second homes and farmers whose land sat close to property-rich towns; the former, in particular, were often affected by local spending decisions on which they, as nonresidents, lacked a vote. These groups banded together to evade the sharing pool by creating private education foundations for raising extra school funds or by withholding excess local revenue from the state.[113] Being subject to the sharing pool was as unpopular in Vermont as being a donor town was in New Hampshire.

Instead of eliminating the sharing pool, though, Vermont legislators reconfigured it in new legislation—Act 68—which they enacted in 2003. Act 68 increased the per-pupil base spending amount from $5,200 to $6,800 as of FY 2005, thereby giving all municipalities a larger funding base.[114] It also established a separate statewide tax rate for owners of second homes and commercial property, which eliminated any connection between their property taxes and local school spending decisions in which they could not participate. To increase funding equity between school districts, Act

68 imposed a surtax on municipalities that spent more than 125 percent above the statewide per-pupil average for the previous school year.[115] For homestead (residential) property owners, it set two tax rates: (1) a uniform statewide property tax rate and (2) a town-specific tax rate that depended on the amount above the state-designated spending figure that the town voted to approve at its annual meeting. These provisions ensured that the amounts spent on education did not vary according to local property wealth.[116] After Act 68 took effect, private fundraising by wealthy towns through foundations declined significantly.[117]

The components of Act 68 are outlined in the following table.

ACT 68 TAX REGIME

Nonhomestead Property	Homestead Property
1. Statewide non-homestead property tax rate	1. Statewide homestead property tax rate + 2. Town-specific homestead property tax rate (based on local spending decisions) + 3. Town-specific surtax (levied only if town's per-pupil spending is a certain percentage above last year's state average)[118]

Thanks to Acts 60 and 68, Vermont's school funding system has largely achieved taxpayer equity. It has not achieved spending equity across school districts, though.[119] In FY 2023, for example, per-pupil spending across districts ranged from a low of $13,314 to a high of $25,738.[120] Still, despite persistent disparities, because of Acts 60 and 68 property-poor municipalities no longer need to levy high taxes to fund low levels of school spending. Act 68, especially, has made each municipality's tax rate more proportionate to its school spending than before.[121]

More recently, Vermont legislators have continued to address school funding, albeit sometimes indirectly. For example, Act 153 (2010), Act 156 (2012), and most notably, Act 46 (2015) have all encouraged mergers and consolidations among school districts to reduce costs and enhance educational opportunities. The Vermont Supreme Court rejected a state constitutional challenge to Act 46, which used tax breaks to encourage school districts to merge voluntarily and authorized the state's Board of Education to reorganize districts that resisted mergers.[122] These laws spurred 206 school districts in 185 towns to condense into 50 union school districts, a reduction of 156 districts statewide between 2010 and 2023.[123]

Act 173, passed in 2018, changed the formula for distributing special education funds to schools. The previous funding model was based on the number of children for whom a district provided special education services. The new model is based instead on a school district's share of the state's total school population.[124] Finally, Act 127, passed in 2022, responded to a task force report that found Vermont was underfunding low-income students, special education students, English language learners, and students at small, rural schools.[125] It became wildly unpopular with taxpayers, though, after many school districts interpreted it to permit higher spending, which triggered the prospect of large property tax increases in 2024. But that story is best told in the following section, which discusses current school finance in Vermont.

Current Practices and Problems

A process and a timeline exist for determining school budgets in Vermont. By December 1, the state's tax commissioner recommends education tax rates for the next fiscal year. Meanwhile, in the fall and early winter, local school boards—with advice from their school superintendents and business managers—develop budgets, which they submit to voters for their approval at Town Meeting in March.[126] Voters in each school district then review the proposed budget and either approve or reject it by means of a school budget vote. If voters approve the budget, the school district is entitled to receive the approved amount from the state minus any offsetting revenues, such as expected federal aid.[127] Before adjournment, which usually occurs in May, the legislature sets base educational tax rates at the level necessary to fund the school budgets the voters have approved. Before June 30, the Vermont Department of Taxes sets a spending-adjusted homestead tax rate for each town.[128] In late summer and early fall, towns send individual tax bills to property owners. School districts receive three equal payments from the state, on September 10, December 10, and April 30.[129]

For example, assume that a school district creates a budget of $19.8 million, to which the school board adds $200,000 to avoid cutting any staff members. The board then votes to approve the revised budget of $20 million, after which the voters approve it. Consequently, the state will provide $20 million to the school district minus other income sources, such as federal grants.[130]

The state pays school districts from its Education Fund, which is not a preexisting pot of money, but rather, the annual sum of all the approved budgets from each school district across the state and of their program costs, such as transportation and school meals.[131] Before paying out money from the Education Fund, the state must adjust for differences between districts, which it does by means of categorical aid and pupil weighting. Categorical aid adjusts for differences in educational costs across districts by providing additional state funds that help to cover the costs of special education and transportation, along with operating small schools. The state reimburses a school district for part of the costs of services provided. The categorical aid is not included in the district's budget for purposes of calculating its school tax rate.[132] Similarly, pupil weighting counts a weighted pupil as more than just one pupil because a weighted pupil is more expensive to educate than a typical pupil. Weights are assigned to high school students, economically disadvantaged students, and English-language learners. Therefore, if two districts (A and B) have an identical number of actual pupils, but District A has more weighted pupils, the state will treat District A as if it has more actual pupils and will fund it accordingly without increasing the district's tax rate.[133] After the weighting adjustments are made, each district is credited with having a specific number of equalized pupils.[134]

The key determinant of any school district's tax rate, then, is the total voter-approved budget minus federal aid, categorical aid, and any tuition receipts the district receives by admitting nonresident students. The resulting figure is the district's education spending. On average, it is about 85 percent of the voter-approved budget. Dividing the amount of education spending by the number of equalized pupils yields the district's per-pupil spending number, which is an important factor in calculating the homestead tax rate that school district residents will pay.[135]

The homestead property tax is levied on property, but it includes an adjustment for household income. In FY 2024, 90 percent of the households that earned less than $47,000 paid the tax based solely on income. Eighty percent of households with incomes between $47,001 and $90,000 also paid based on income, unless the value of their homestead exceeded $400,000, in which case they paid based on both income and the amount of the homestead value above $400,000. Two-thirds of households with incomes between $90,001 and $115,000 paid based on household income plus the homestead value above $225,000. And households that earned more than $115,000 paid solely on assessed homestead value.[136] The income adjustment seeks to protect homeowners against high property taxes if what they would pay based on income is less than what they would pay based on the value of their property.[137]

A final adjustment to the funding formula, made annually by the state tax department, is to set the Common Level of Appraisal (CLA) for each municipality. It tweaks local property tax rates to account for rate differences that exist between municipalities. The differences result from towns and cities reappraising property on varying schedules, causing a gap between the fair market value and the assessed value of the same property. Assessed property values are typically lower than fair market values. Therefore, if no adjustment device existed, cities and towns would send more or less than their fair share of property tax revenue to the Education Fund.[138]

The CLA fills the gap between fair market value and assessed value because it is the ratio between them. In other words, in a municipality with a CLA of .90, the total assessed value of property is 90 percent of the state-calculated fair market value of the municipality's property. The CLA is part of the calculation that determines the tax rates to be applied when collecting education property taxes from Vermont communities.[139] The CLA does not affect students directly, but like categorical aid and pupil weighting, it aims to equalize burdens and benefits in Vermont's school funding system.

In recent years, Vermont's system for funding public education has been the subject of numerous critiques for its complexity, high cost, and lack of a clear connection between local budgets, statewide spending, and individual tax bills.[140] Statewide factors affect local districts because Vermont pools education costs across districts, meaning that costs in each town are paid by property taxes collected from many towns under the funding formula.[141]

One critique recommends exempting from property taxes all primary residences plus two acres of land, while taxing all other property at the uniform, nonresidential rate. Residents would pay school taxes based on their adjusted gross incomes. The author of this critique argues that the income-based plan is fairer than the existing system, under which low- and middle-income Vermonters pay higher school taxes, as a percentage of their incomes, than their wealthy neighbors.[142] Similarly, a 2021 legislative task force recommended that the tax-writing committees consider basing the education tax entirely on income to simplify matters and ensure that all Vermonters pay their "fair share."[143] And a 2023 report by the legislature's Joint Fiscal Office proposed several options for cost containment, such as (1) adjusting staffing ratios (Vermont has the lowest ratio in the country of pupils [4.4] per staff member), (2) encouraging or mandating more district mergers, and (3) transferring the responsibility for education-spending decisions to the state level.[144]

The loudest calls for education funding reform, though, came from taxpayers in late 2023 and early 2024, upon learning that their forthcoming education tax bills would likely increase by 15 percent or more because of the passage in 2022 of Act 127, which encouraged many districts to increase their spending. The taxpayers' protest, the dramatic reform proposal that it prompted from the governor, and the future of education funding in Vermont are the subjects of the following section.

The Challenge Ahead

Act 127 set new pupil weights to steer more money to school districts with many low-income students and English language learners, and to small schools in rural districts. It included a transition provision that capped at 5 percent per year for five years the rate at which a school district's homestead property tax could rise, even if the district's spending exceeded that rate.[145] Evidently, nobody informed school leaders that the 5 percent cap was intended to apply only to districts slated to lose substantial pupil weight under the new law, meaning they would have to raise more tax money just to maintain existing budgets. Consequently, many other districts, mistakenly thinking that the cap applied to them—and faced with rising costs for employee health care and mental health services for students, plus the loss of pandemic-era federal funds—proposed FY 2025 budgets that increased spending by an average of almost 15 percent over FY 2024. News of the impending increases triggered howls of protest from politicians and taxpayers alike.[146] Governor Scott and legislators heard the howls and responded in February 2024 by repealing the 5 percent cap, substituting a new tax benefit, and applying it only to residents of districts that had lost weighted pupils under Act 127.[147]

Repeal of the transition provision did not erase the projected double-digit increase in property taxes, though, so voters in one-third of Vermont's municipalities rejected proposed school budgets in the spring of 2024. Usually, only a handful of school budgets fail in any given year.[148] Seeing an opportunity in the grim results, Governor Scott hinted that the time was right to overhaul Vermont's education system, which suffered from rising costs, extraordinary complexity, too many small schools, and a failure to get sufficient resources to needy students.[149] Buoyed by Republican legislative gains in the 2024 elections, Scott introduced his sweeping reform plan in February 2025.[150]

The plan, which legislators debated extensively during the 2025 legislative session, addressed not only school funding but school governance and educational quality too. It proposed, as its funding mechanism, a foundation formula: a base per-pupil amount that represents the resources required to educate a student with no special needs in a school district with no special circumstances. The funding process would begin with the Agency of Education determining this base amount instead of school districts telling the agency what spending levels their voters have approved. The foundation formula, then, is a major change from the funding arrangement it would replace, effectively turning the latter on its head.[151] The original Scott proposal projected a base funding amount of $13,200 per pupil.[152]

After the base amount were determined, pupil weights would be added to adjust for student needs, including for economically disadvantaged students (0.75), English language learners (1.5), career and technical education students (1.3), and preschool students (1.0). Weights would also be added for students attending small schools in sparsely populated districts.[153] The final component of the proposed funding formula would be categorical aid, chiefly for special education ($20 million) and transportation ($50 million). Displayed graphically, the proposed funding formula appears as follows:

Base Funding	x	Weighted Pupils	=	Foundation Funding	+	Categorical Aid
($13,200)				(Total base funding and pupil weights)		(Special education transportation)[154]

The proposal anticipates that, if adopted, the new funding system would reduce overall annual spending by $183.6 million dollars.[155]

Governor Scott's proposal reshapes the governance structure for public education in Vermont, which in 2025 included 52 supervisory unions and 119 school districts.[156] Supervisory unions are collections of multiple school districts that share some centralized services but retain individual boards and responsibilities for budgeting, employment, contracting, and facilities. They are rare nationwide but common in Vermont, having developed as a means of achieving some efficiencies through their size while preserving many small school districts. Governor Scott's plan would eliminate supervisory unions.[157]

They would be replaced by five regional school districts, each with one central office and one board, the latter comprised of elected, part-time members. Supporters claim that the new structure would reduce inequities in per-pupil spending, eliminate costly inefficiencies, and facilitate salary increases for teachers by reducing administrative overhead.[158] Each district would include local elementary schools, centrally located middle schools, and comprehensive high schools, and would serve at least 3,900 students from kindergarten through high school.[159]

Another important feature of the governor's proposal is an expanded system of school choice for students. In Vermont, school choice exists for high school students statewide and for students whose local communities lack a high school or, sometimes, any school. They can attend a public or private school elsewhere, and their hometowns pay the tuition at the receiving school.[160] Under the Scott proposal, each student would be assigned to a public elementary, middle, and high school in the student's home district, but could potentially choose another K–8 school within the home district or another district, depending on school board policy. And the school board must designate at least one public or private high school other than the assigned high school, as a School Choice School to receive incoming students. If the number of interested students exceeds that school's capacity, a lottery system would determine which students could enroll. State money would follow the student to the chosen school, which would receive tuition payments from the state.[161]

After a long debate and much compromise, the governor's education reform bill became law in June 2025, as Act 73. Its principal feature is a foundation formula whereby the state will provide school districts with $15,030 per pupil, adjusted for student weighting. This formula amends the weighting system that Act 127 created, to provide additional funds for pre-K students, economically disadvantaged students, English language learners, and special education students. Schools with small enrollments and schools located in sparsely populated areas will also receive additional funds. But the foundation formula will not take effect unless the legislature approves the creation of consolidated school districts in 2026. If created, those larger districts, which are slated to serve at least four thousand students each, will become operational on July 1, 2028. Before that can happen, though, legislators must propose, consider, and vote on potential plans for large consolidated districts during the 2026 legislative session.[162]

Besides the foundation formula and larger school districts, Act 73 contemplates higher minimum class sizes, more stringent criteria for independent schools to receive state money for educating students, and new rules for giving property tax relief to homeowners. Unless legislators can agree on the new school districts, though, Act 73 will not achieve the educational transformation that Governor Scott envisioned in the spring of 2025.[163] Still, Vermont deserves credit for a bold attempt to make its public education system less costly, more manageable, and easier to understand.

Conclusion

In New Hampshire and Vermont, political culture affects school finance more profoundly than it affects land-use regulation. Each state's constitution makes education a state responsibility, so courts have directed elected officials to fund public education adequately and equitably. New Hampshire's localism and distaste for broad-based taxes cause it to rely on local property taxes to fund its public schools. But districts with lower-than-average property wealth cannot raise enough money to educate their children adequately. That problem, which existed in the 1990s, when the *Claremont* litigation began, continues today, despite a 2025 ruling for the plaintiffs in *ConVal*. Thus far, the state supreme court has not imposed a particular funding mechanism on the state, instead inviting elected officials to create one that is constitutional. To date, those officials have failed in that endeavor because they oppose broad-based taxes and cannot identify a suitable alternative. Their response to the *ConVal* decision remains to be seen. Litigation has not been futile because it has likely nudged the state's contribution from the 8 percent figure of the early 1990s to the 28 percent share noted by the National Education Association for 2023–24. Still, that contribution remains the lowest of the fifty states.[164]

Vermont's response to this issue has been almost directly opposite of New Hampshire's, featuring limited judicial action, but aggressive legislative action. Just months after the state supreme court invalidated Vermont's funding mechanism, the legislature enacted Act 60, authorizing the state to set tax rates, collect revenue through a statewide property tax, and distribute the proceeds to local school districts. Later, it increased state aid, encouraged school mergers and consolidations, and boosted funding for special education, low-income and rural students, and English language learners. In FY 2025, rising school costs spurred Vermont to pursue more reform, this time to revamp not only the funding but also the organization and governance of Vermont's public schools. The prospects for this "transformation," embodied in Act 73, are unclear at this writing, although the new law is bold in vision and broad in scope.

Thus, in both states, an observer of school finance awaits action by state government. In New Hampshire, one waits for a response by elected officials to another court decision necessitated by the failure of previous officials to identify a constitutionally and politically satisfactory funding source. In Vermont, one waits for the implementation of new legislation designed to produce fewer school districts, larger schools, and a simpler but more state-controlled funding system. In each state, current conditions reflect political culture.

CHAPTER EIGHT

Conclusion

New Hampshire and Vermont are Fraternal Twins

A Tale of Two Senators

A USEFUL DEVICE FOR comparing the political cultures of New Hampshire and Vermont is to highlight the careers of two politicians who served those states as governor and later United States senator for several decades. Like their respective states, Styles Bridges of New Hampshire and George Aiken of Vermont had much in common, but they also had important ideological differences that became evident over time in their policy choices. Examining their lives and careers helps to show how New Hampshire and Vermont are fraternal, not identical, twins.

Styles Bridges

Henry Styles Bridges was born in West Pembroke, in rural northeast Maine, in 1898. He was the first child of a store owner and a teacher turned homemaker. When Styles graduated from high school in 1916, the family's financial circumstances were difficult, but his by-then-widowed mother insisted that he pursue higher education, so he completed a two-year agricultural program at the University of Maine in Orono. After college, he spent two years teaching agriculture at a high school in Massachusetts. He then returned to Maine, where he became a county agricultural agent, organizing soil-conservation programs and editing a farmer's bulletin, while also serving on the school board and the board of a local bank.[1]

Near the end of 1921, Bridges moved to New Hampshire to join the Agricultural Extension staff of New Hampshire College, which later became the University of New Hampshire. He assisted county extension agents in mapping demonstration plots and showing farmers new methods of increasing their yields. Just six months later, he was elected secretary of the

New Hampshire Farm Bureau Federation. During this period, he became acquainted with Robert Bass, a progressive Republican and former New Hampshire governor, with whom Bridges shared an interest in scientific agriculture. But Bass was interested in far more than agriculture, so when Bass hired him as an aide in 1924, worlds beyond farming suddenly became accessible to young Styles Bridges. For the rest of the 1920s, in Bass's employ, Bridges exhibited his versatility by editing a magazine Bass owned, managing both the successful 1924 gubernatorial campaign of progressive Republican Gil Winant and Bass's unsuccessful 1926 campaign for the US Senate, and later running Bass's business affairs, including his New Hampshire Investment Company.[2]

In 1929 Governor Charles Tobey appointed Bridges to New Hampshire's Public Service Commission, his first governmental post. That position became a foothold for him after the stock market crash in 1929, when he lost his job managing the Bass family investments.[3] He used the public service post to advocate for rural electrification, later telling a reporter, "When you've gone to bed by candle light and done your morning milking by lantern, you appreciate what power means to common people."[4]

Thanks to his association with Robert Bass and his advocacy for rural electrification, Bridges could count on the support of the New Hampshire Republican Party's progressive wing when, in September 1933, he announced his intention to run for governor the following year. He won a narrow victory over his Democratic opponent, becoming one of only seven Republicans elected governor in the United States in 1934 and, at age thirty-six, the youngest person ever elected to that office in New Hampshire.[5] When he took office, New Hampshire was in the throes of the Depression; one of every eleven citizens in the state depended on public assistance. Farm prices fell by 53 percent between 1932 and 1939, and by the winter of 1935, the textile industry was on its knees.[6]

As governor, Styles Bridges was mostly conservative, but occasionally progressive. His conservatism was reflected in support for "local control," a belief that state government should play only an indirect, supervisory role in many policy areas, including public assistance to needy individuals, and opposition to the Roosevelt administration's practice of spending public funds to stimulate the economy and combat the Depression.[7] Nevertheless, he appointed the first woman municipal judge, director of a new Division of State Employment, and administrator of a Minimum Wage Division, respectively; the latter two posts were the highest ever held by women in New Hampshire. Reflecting his preference for local solutions, he championed an unemployment compensation law, sponsored a Milk Control Act and an Agricultural Standards Act to ensure the quality of farm products, reorganized the state Fish and Game Department, and created the position of Special Veterans' Officer in the Welfare Department. He even redesigned New Hampshire's old-age assistance program so that the state could qualify early on for participation in the new federal Social Security Program.[8]

Styles Bridges did not remain governor for long, though; in June 1936, he announced his plan to run for an open US Senate seat in the fall. He won sizable victories in both the primary and general elections, including the largest vote total in the history of the New Hampshire primary.[9]

Bridges went on to serve as a senator from January 1937 until his death in November 1961. He was elected five times, winning a higher percentage of votes in each succeeding election, ranging from 52.2 percent in 1936 to 60.3 percent in 1960.[10] Ever ambitious, he ran unsuccessfully for the Republican presidential nomination in 1940. In 1944, despite receiving encouragement to run for president again, he opted out, apparently recognizing, according to his biographer, that "his limited financial resources and New Hampshire's small electoral vote total eliminated him as a serious presidential candidate."[11] Thereafter, he confined his ambitions to the Senate.

As a senator, Bridges was more conservative than he had been as governor, having continued a rightward drift that had already soured his friendship with Robert Bass. By and large, his vote was reliably conservative, as were his public comments. He opposed FDR's New Deal and urged Republicans to devise constructive alternatives to centralization of power in the federal government.[12] He also opposed President Harry Truman's National Health Insurance Program and rallied the medical profession in New Hampshire to do likewise.[13] In a speech in Nashua in 1950, he warned, "We are entering a decade of decision, and our greatest problem is that of socialism creeping into our way of life."[14] Also in 1950, he stated, "Atomic weapons should be used, if necessary, to end the Korean war."[15] Four years later, he voted (in the minority) against censuring Senator Joseph McCarthy of Wisconsin despite the latter's by-then-discredited pursuit of alleged Communists inside and outside of government.[16]

Bridges was a fierce partisan and sometime "attack dog," too, for which he was rewarded, such as with the chairmanship of the Appropriations Committee, when his party held a majority of seats in the Senate. That reward may also have reflected Bridges's negotiating skills; according to a staff member, he was not inclined to speak on the Senate floor but was instead "a committee tactician" who "wanted to get things done."[17] And he could be bipartisan when necessary, as evidenced by his appointment to a committee that monitored wartime weapons production to ensure that military contractors did not overcharge the government for their products and his status as one of four senators entrusted with the secret of the Manhattan Project, which produced the atomic bomb.[18] Bridges also deviated from his usual conservatism on occasion, such as when he pushed the Army to investigate whether its Air Corps had a "whites only" policy for pilot training and, later, urged it to begin training Black pilots at the Tuskegee Air Base in Alabama.[19]

Bridges won his fifth Senate term in 1960 by his largest vote total ever, but that term, which began in January 1961, ended less than a year later, when he died in his sleep while recovering at home from a heart attack.[20] His death ended an unlikely journey from a small town in rural Maine and a modest professional start as a high school agriculture teacher to the halls of power in Washington, DC, and the duty of keeping the Manhattan Project a secret.

George Aiken

George Aiken, born in 1892, grew up on a fifty-acre hill farm in Putney, Vermont, where his family raised vegetables and berries, which George's father peddled from a one-horse wagon in nearby Brattleboro.[21] Young George completed primary school in Putney, followed by three years of high school, which was all that the town offered; therefore, he had to travel to Brattleboro, nine miles away, for his senior year. That experience gave him an inspiring story to tell many years later in an oral history interview. He recalled, "I had to walk down to the depot, about four miles, every morning to take the nine o'clock train to Brattleboro and then walk about three-quarters of a mile up to the high school."[22] Despite that daunting commute, he had enough energy to compete on the track team before graduating in 1909, at age sixteen, the youngest member of his class.[23]

After high school, Aiken could not afford college, so he worked for his father for several years until, at age twenty, he and a business partner entered the nursery business. They bought a forty-acre field near the Aiken homestead, planted apples and wildflowers in the summer and in the winter cut blocks of ice from a small pond, storing the ice in sawdust until neighbors needed it for their iceboxes.[24] The younger Aiken showed a penchant for community service too, helping to organize the Windham County Farm Bureau in 1912, and later, at age twenty-five, being elected president of the Vermont Horticulturist Society.[25]

In 1922, at age thirty, progressive Republican George Aiken lost his first race for the Vermont House, then withdrew from politics for eight years to focus on his nursery business, after which he ran for office again in 1930 and won.[26] He used the eight-year hiatus well, expanding his customer list to about ten thousand in Vermont alone and writing two books on horticulture, one of which, *Pioneering with Wildflowers*, published in 1935, remains in print today.[27]

In the legislature, Aiken's colleagues were considering a flood-control bill that would have authorized private power companies to construct dams throughout the state and to generate hydroelectric power from them. Support for the dams came not only from the power companies themselves, but from other pillars of the Republican Party's "Old Guard," including the granite, marble, and insurance industries. Had the bill been enacted, approximately eighty rivers and streams would have been dammed, and the power would have gone out of state.[28] Representative Aiken quickly became the Old Guard's nemesis; backed by several allies on the House Conservation Committee, he moved to bring the flood-control bill to a vote when some of its supporters were absent, defeating it in committee and causing the speaker to withdraw the bill. Having taken the legislature by storm in his first term, Aiken was not only reelected in 1932, but when the new session began, his house colleagues elected him as speaker.[29] Despite opposition from the Old Guard, he won because the Democratic legislators from Bennington and Essex Counties joined progressive Republicans in voting for him.[30]

Two years later, using his statewide customer list and his frequent flower talks throughout Vermont to good effect, George Aiken was elected lieutenant governor. At that time, private power companies served only those electricity customers who lived close to the main roads; households located on back roads—mostly farm families—were denied electricity. Lieutenant Governor Aiken championed the passage of Rural Electrification Act legislation in the Vermont Senate that made it possible, after the federal law took effect, for electric cooperatives to form, enabling Vermonters who lived on hillsides to have electricity.[31] After serving two years as lieutenant governor, Aiken was elected governor in 1936 and was reelected in 1938.[32]

As governor, he opposed a New Deal program (later abandoned) that sought to construct hydropower dams in the Connecticut River Valley, fearing that Vermonters would not benefit from the power the project generated. He opposed even more intensely a companion project that would have resettled two groups of residents: those living in the areas to be flooded because of the dams and those living on marginal hill farms in the valley, including his own farm in Putney.[33] Yet he favored New Deal programs that furthered health, education, and the public welfare, notably the Civilian Conservation Corps (CCC), which benefited Vermont considerably by laying the groundwork for a state park system.[34] Indeed, his two gubernatorial terms were devoted to protecting Vermont's natural resources, fostering an expansion of electrical service to rural areas, and supporting agriculture, especially the dairy industry.[35] In 1939, he threw the switch for the Washington Electric Coop, bringing the first electric power to Vermont under FDR's Rural Electrification Act.[36]

Thus, George Aiken's progressive Republicanism shared some goals and methods with the New Deal. It differed, though, because Aiken rejected deficit spending and insisted that state and local governments play major roles in addressing the problems of their citizens. In his view, instead of looking to the federal government to rescue them, Americans should try to solve problems for themselves, aided by cooperatives and interstate compacts.[37] Earlier in life, he had seen how cooperation among farmers could reduce the cost of marketing, secure for them a fair share of the price the consumer paid for agricultural products, facilitate the standardization of grading and testing, and create savings in the purchase of supplies, along with sharing risks through insurance and providing capital and credit for agricultural production. Later, he applied that lesson to other subjects, including relations between labor, management, and government, preferring cooperation to government regulation.[38]

Governor Aiken's unorthodox brand of Republicanism attracted national attention among Republicans seeking an alternative to FDR's New Deal, and he was invited to be the main speaker at the National Republican

Club's Lincoln Day Dinner at the Waldorf Astoria Hotel in New York City in February 1938.[39] After the speech, in which Aiken chastised the party for being beholden to wealth and unwelcoming to young people, he began to be mentioned as a potential GOP presidential nominee in 1940. Later in 1938, though, he decided not to run for president. In an oral history interview many years later, he explained that he had not wished to submit to the control of fundraisers and handlers.[40] Therefore, instead of running for president in 1940, George Aiken ran for an open seat in the United States Senate. After winning a close race in the Republican primary, he won the general election easily, taking office in January 1941. He was reelected five times, always garnering more than 60 percent of the vote; in 1968, his last Senate race, he won the endorsement of both the Democratic and Republican Parties.[41]

Aiken's independence from the Republican establishment continued in Washington and prevented him from holding leadership positions in the Senate or in his party. Consequently, he attended only two Republican National Conventions, one in 1940, when the state party initially denied him a delegate's seat, and another in 1964, when he nominated for president Senator Margaret Chase Smith of Maine, a fellow moderate, as an alternative to conservative Senator Barry Goldwater of Arizona.[42] Ten years earlier, he had voted to censure fellow Republican Senator Joseph McCarthy for "violating the dignity of the Senate" in an unprincipled pursuit of alleged Communists.[43]

But Aiken's independence enabled him to negotiate numerous compromises that produced legislation. The mediator role suited Aiken well; he was fond of saying, "You can catch more flies with honey than vinegar,"[44] and if you could not get all you wanted in legislation, "take ninety percent, eighty, or sixty."[45] Those values enabled him to play an important role in the crafting of landmark legislation during his Senate years.

Several examples illustrate this point. In 1954 he cosponsored, along with Senator Hubert Humphrey (D-MN) Public Law 480, better known as the Food for Peace program. It enabled developing countries to feed their hungry citizens by purchasing, in their own currency, surplus American farm products, thereby improving nutrition, shrinking farm surpluses, and building goodwill toward the United States around the world.[46] In 1969 he persuaded the Department of Agriculture to establish in Vermont one of five national pilot programs for feeding low-income expectant mothers and infants; five years later that program, known as Women, Infants, and

Children (WIC) became permanent.[47] In 1973 Senators Aiken and Humphrey sponsored Public Law 93–189, the Foreign Assistance Act, which directed federal foreign aid programs to focus on improving health, education, and agricultural development in poor countries.[48] And in January 1975, three days after Aiken retired, the Eastern Wilderness Areas Act, which he had begun pushing for two years earlier, became law, establishing sixteen wilderness areas in the eastern half of the United States.[49]

Perhaps the clearest example, though, of George Aiken's mediating role in the Senate occurred during the lengthy debate about America's involvement in the Vietnam war. Aiken's close friend, Senate Majority Leader Mike Mansfield (D-MT) characterized the Vermont senator as neither a pro-war "hawk" nor an antiwar "dove," but instead a "wise old owl" who generally supported American policy in Vietnam, but with serious reservations. Those reservations were evident on October 19, 1966, when he argued in a speech on the Senate floor that American troops had stabilized South Vietnam sufficiently that they could now claim a "victory" of sorts and begin a "gradual redeployment" around "strategic centers," and substitute "intensive reconnaissance" of the enemy for continued bombing.[50] The redeployment and a cessation of the bombing, he contended, would facilitate the emergence of a political solution to the war.[51]

Although President Johnson rejected Aiken's position, President Nixon ultimately adopted it by signing the Paris Peace Accords in 1973, whereby the United States claimed victory and ended combat operations in Vietnam.[52] One cannot help but wonder how many lives, on both sides, could have been spared if Aiken's advice had been taken when offered.

In January 1975, George Aiken retired from the Senate after thirty-five years of service. He returned to Vermont, where he died in 1984 at age ninety-two.

The Senators as Reflections of Their States

The careers of Senators Bridges and Aiken invite comparison because both men grew up in the same era in the same region of this country under similar economic circumstances and served together in the Senate, as members of the same political party, from 1941 until 1961. Even their early professional experiences, as an agricultural extension agent and a horticulturist, respectively, were comparable. Their two states also have much in common, being of similar geographic size, still reasonably rural, and home to majorities of residents who were born elsewhere. Both states are blessed with mountains, lakes, and forests that offer stunning landscapes and abundant three-season outdoor recreational opportunities. An autumn hike in a New Hampshire forest, a winter ski outing on a snowy Vermont trail, or a summertime paddle on a quiet lake in either state is a magic elixir for the human spirit.

The Twin States share some noteworthy political characteristics too, such as a distrust of concentrated power, which has resulted in two-year gubernatorial terms and part-time "citizen" legislatures in which the members receive minimal compensation and lack both offices and personal staffs. Both states also show a healthy respect for judicial independence by selecting most of their judges by appointment instead of by election. Nevertheless, the two states have political cultures that make them fraternal—not identical—twins.

Even during the more than one hundred years that both states were solidly Republican, New Hampshire was more wedded to local control, small government, and minimal taxation than Vermont was. Beginning in the late nineteenth century, state government was more active in Vermont than in New Hampshire, assuming responsibility for public services that small, rural towns could not provide for themselves. In the twentieth century, Vermont enacted a personal income tax and a sales tax, whereas New Hampshire resisted both and still does. George Aiken noted in an oral history interview after he retired from public life that Vermont has also typically been willing to be a "guinea pig" in new federal programs, such as the Women, Infants, and Children (WIC) nutrition program and Head Start, which provides early education to children from low-income families. He observed, "Vermont has been willing to try things first."[53]

In recent decades, New Hampshire has become less Republican and less conservative than it was in Senator Bridges's day, electing a succession of Democratic governors between 2004 and 2016 and an entirely Democratic congressional delegation since 2016. Yet localism and an aversion to taxation still attract small-government libertarians, such as the Free Staters, to New Hampshire, and broad-based taxes remain anathema to many residents. A 2020 study of why people migrate to and remain in the Granite State found that 20 percent of migrants cited "taxes" and 10 percent cited "the economy" as a major reason for moving there, suggesting that the state's free-market ethos induces at least some of the migration the state experiences. The same percentages of established residents cited those factors as major reasons for remaining in New Hampshire.[54] Although other factors (e.g., family, employment, the natural environment, and quality of life) are more powerful influences on migration to New Hampshire and continued residency there, the Live Free or Die ethos surely spurs some of both.

Differences in political culture produce different policy choices. Sometimes, as Chapter Six shows, those differences are subtle, as in the case of land-use regulation, where state government shares the field with local volunteer boards and private land developers and homebuilders. Both New Hampshire and Vermont have enacted laws to encourage the building of affordable housing, have modified density rules and promoted cluster development to preserve open space, and have spent public money to facilitate the construction of workforce housing. Still, differences are evident in the two states' responses to the current housing shortage.

For example, New Hampshire's attachment to local control is reflected in its Workforce Housing Law, which features incentives instead of requirements, such as permitting developers to build more dense housing if they agree to set aside a fixed portion of the units for affordable housing. To be sure, this law requires municipalities to enact regulations that provide "reasonable and realistic opportunities" to develop such housing, including "rental and multi-family housing." But municipalities must only allow workforce housing to exist on "most, but not necessarily all" of the land within their boundaries that is zoned for residential use.[55]

In contrast, Vermont's tradition of somewhat bolder, state-directed solutions is reflected in the more comprehensive policies it has devised to address its housing shortage. For example, Act 47 (2023) eliminated the traditional zoning preference for single-family homes in residential areas, meaning that ADUs and multifamily housing are eligible to be built in residential areas. This change gives a big boost to the construction of affordable housing in residential zones. A second law, Act 181 (2024), revamped preexisting land use law by replacing the prior trigger for state regulation of a development project—its size—with a new one, the project's location. "Location-based jurisdiction" applies different degrees of regulation within three major locational tiers throughout Vermont, with the aim of promoting housing within well-planned smart growth areas, while reducing harm to critical natural resource areas and wetlands.[56]

Thus, New Hampshire and Vermont have responded to the housing crisis with some similar tools, yet Vermont's approach has been more dramatic and comprehensive, eliminating the historical preference for single-family zoning and seeking, in Act 181, to preserve the natural landscape that makes possible its tourism and recreation industry.

An even larger difference between the two states is reflected in their funding of public education, as Chapter Seven illustrates. Because of divergent political cultures, elected officials in New Hampshire and Vermont have responded in profoundly different ways to state supreme court decisions in 1997 holding that each state's property-tax-based mechanism for funding public schools was unconstitutional. Those decisions flowed from a provision in each state's constitution that makes education (unlike land-use regulation) a state responsibility.

Nevertheless, because New Hampshire remains committed to local control and hostile to broad-based taxes, it continues to rely heavily on local property taxes to fund public schools. That is why, even though more state aid is directed to poor school districts nowadays, the fundamental problem of inequitable funding across districts that existed in 1997 still exists in New Hampshire, and a mechanism to conform school funding to state constitutional requirements remains elusive.

In contrast, after the Vermont Supreme Court issued its 1997 decision, the state legislature quickly enacted legislation that authorized the state to set tax rates, collect revenue through a statewide property tax, and distribute the proceeds to local school districts. Later, it increased per-pupil state aid, promoted school mergers and consolidations to lower operating costs, and increased funding for special education students, low-income and rural students, and English language learners. Vermont's funding system still falls short of its goals because it is expensive, complex, and less equitable than it could be. At this writing, legislation designed to revamp both the organizational structure and the funding of public education in Vermont is in place and awaiting implementation.

Under these circumstances, the most descriptive metaphor to use in explaining New Hampshire and Vermont as political entities is fraternal twins. The factors that account for their differences are the subjects of the next section.

Accounting for Differences

No single cause explains why the political cultures of New Hampshire and Vermont present contrasting profiles. Therefore, to posit a single-cause explanation is to overlook or understate the interlocking relationships between the various causes that shape a political culture. Contributing causes can range from the natural environment at the time of settlement to the course of economic and industrial development thereafter to socioeconomic tensions among the early inhabitants to the self-portrait each state has displayed to the outside world to the demographic patterns that portrait has prompted. Chapter One introduced these factors but did not explain the important links between them that have produced the unique political cultures of these two states. The factors and links are discussed below.

1. Geology

As used here, "geology" refers to the physical structure and substance of the earth. It is one causal factor underlying the respective political cultures of New Hampshire and Vermont. Recall that although both states have granite in their subsoil, granite is more prominent in New Hampshire, whereas Vermont's soil is predominantly soft, worn-down limestone common to the Appalachian Mountain chain. When the ice sheet retreated a million years ago, it removed more soil from New Hampshire than from Vermont. Later, when it melted, it deposited more stone in New Hampshire than in Vermont. For that reason, and because of how the mountains in the two states were formed, Vermont's settlers were able to farm successfully, whereas New Hampshire's settlers frequently abandoned their farms when alternative means of earning a living became available.[57] As a result, Vermont was still heavily agrarian in the mid-nineteenth century, when young men and women from New Hampshire began exiting the farms for the mills and factories of Manchester and other locales in southern New England. Thus, New Hampshire's early industrialization resulted directly from its geological inheritance: the same rocky soil that made it the Granite State.

2. Geography

In this context, "geography" means the ways in which people adapt and relate to the physical features of the earth. It is another factor in the causal chain that produced the respective political cultures of the Twin States. Nature saddled New Hampshire with rocky soil but blessed it with abundant waterways and waterfalls. The latter were the best sources of mechanical power in 1800, aside from horses and oxen. Indeed, the ten best hydropower sites in New Hampshire and Vermont were in New Hampshire.

If the Granite State's soil was unproductive, its waterways and waterfalls were spectacularly productive, spawning the founding and growth of numerous wool and cotton mills in the Merrimack River Valley. Therefore, geology and geography drove economic activity in the state during the eighteenth and early nineteenth centuries, making New Hampshire, by 1900, one of the nation's most "urban" states, as measured by the percentage of people living in towns and cities with populations of more than 2,500 people. Measured by the same metric, Vermont remained one of the most rural states.[58] Meanwhile, in northern New Hampshire, where nature had bequeathed mountains and forests, two economic beneficiaries of that bequest—the timber and tourist industries—clashed over the loggers' land-use practices, spawning, in turn, a fledgling conservation movement.

New Hampshire also has a seacoast, which aided the state's mills because of their relative proximity to a port at Portsmouth. The seacoast was a mixed blessing, though. It enabled some coastal residents to accumulate great wealth as merchants and ship captains, as evidenced by their opulent homes and lifestyles, and by the political power they wielded, especially during the colonial era. But it also bred class distinctions and regional resentments between the coastal elites and the subsistence farmers of the Merrimack and Connecticut River Valleys. In this environment, delegates to the 1784 convention that drafted New Hampshire's first constitution tried to mitigate the distinctions and resentments by limiting the power of state government as much as possible. This tradition took hold and remains a cornerstone of New Hampshire's political culture today. It is reflected in a two-year gubernatorial term, a five-member elected Executive Council designed to check the governor's power, a 424-member legislature whose members earn $200 every two years for their service, an aversion to broad-based taxes, and a commitment to local control.[59] Thus, the diversity of New Hampshire's geography and the socioeconomic distinctions it produced exerted lasting influences on the state's political culture.

Geography also shaped Vermont's political culture, although differently than it affected the political culture of New Hampshire. Lacking a seacoast and a merchant class, Vermont was an agrarian society in the eighteenth and nineteenth centuries, which inspired a fierce egalitarianism that was reflected in its 1777 constitution. That document, which governed the independent Republic of Vermont from 1777 until 1791, when statehood was achieved, outlawed slavery and abolished property qualifications for voting.[60]

Because Vermont remained largely agrarian in the late nineteenth and early twentieth centuries, its small rural towns could not afford many of the public services that residents increasingly expected, such as road maintenance, public utilities, and education. Consequently, they began to look to the state government to assist them and to safeguard public health and safety through business regulation. One illustration of Vermont's increased governmental activity early in the twentieth century was its adoption of a personal income tax in 1931.[61] Thus, the state's contemporary progressivism—its willingness, for example, to use government to make housing more affordable and education more equitable—is rooted in the expansion of state services that occurred in the late nineteenth and early twentieth centuries. That expansion, in turn, is traceable to the financial limitations of Vermont's predominantly agrarian economy during those years.

3. Advertising and Place Reputation

Geology, geography, and the economic choices they promote are powerful influences on political culture, but they do not operate in a vacuum. Just as advertising has long affected public attitudes toward everything from household cleaning products to clothing to political candidates, so has it created distinct place reputations for New Hampshire and Vermont.[62] As Chapter One noted, during the twentieth century, when both states began marketing themselves beyond their borders, they courted different audiences. New Hampshire's advertising stressed the state's proximity to Boston, its many golf courses, modern amenities, low property taxes, and horseracing track. Today, although a wish to be closer to family members is the most important reason motivating migration to New Hampshire, the influence of "taxes" and "the economy" increase in importance with higher-income survey respondents. Meanwhile, radio and television commercials still invite nonresidents to shop in "tax free New Hampshire," thereby avoiding a sales tax, and the state's license plates, which proclaim "Live Free or Die," are ubiquitous mobile billboards for a libertarian ethic. Under these circumstances, it is no secret why members of the Free State Movement chose to move to New Hampshire rather than Vermont.

Vermont is a persistent marketer of its self-image too, but instead of emphasizing economic freedom and small government, as New Hampshire does, it promotes what one historian has termed "Vermont as a Way of Life."[63] Vermont's advertising has long highlighted the state's small, close-knit communities, featuring church suppers and town meetings, intact village centers surrounded by farms and forests, and tolerance for the eccentricities of one's neighbors, both long-standing and recently arrived. Historically, that image has brought to the Green Mountains a bevy of writers, artists, academics, and other expatriates from the crowds and consumerism of urban America. Just as it was predictable, then, that the individualistic Free Staters of recent years would migrate to New Hampshire, it is equally unsurprising that the communally-oriented hippies of the Vietnam war generation left the cities and suburbs for Vermont.

Thus, the political cultures of New Hampshire and Vermont are rooted in their respective geological and geographical inheritances, which burdened and benefited them with natural limitations and gifts. Based on those burdens and benefits, the two states made economic choices that, in turn, helped to shape their political personalities. Later, both states advertised themselves to the outside world, drawing enthusiastic migrants who often reinforced the existing political culture in both places. Migration (like generational change) does not always reinforce the prevailing political culture, as evidenced by increased inter-party competition in New Hampshire nowadays, but it may do so, as indicated by Vermont's steady leftward shift since the 1950s.

4. Parting Thoughts

This book has sought to answer a persistent question among observers of New Hampshire and Vermont politics: Why are the two states so different from one another politically? The answer lies in the multiple factors from which each state's political culture derives and the important consequences of those factors. Political culture deserves our close attention because it can telegraph the policy options that elected officials will consider carefully or reject summarily when faced with a major issue. For example, political culture enables one to understand why New Hampshire and Vermont have responded so differently to judicial decisions concerning their respective school funding mechanisms. Political cultures can change, though, so continued attention will be necessary to see whether the Twin States remain fraternal or become more alike as they face the demographic and economic challenges ahead.

AFTERWORD

Political culture continued to influence political events in the Twin States in 2026. In New Hampshire, school funding sparked drama and garnered headlines, while in Vermont, school funding shared the limelight with land-use regulation.

In July 2025, when the New Hampshire Supreme Court decided the *ConVal* case, it urged legislators and the governor "to act expeditiously" to ensure that the state's schoolchildren receive a constitutionally adequate education. Instead, the elected officials not only declined to increase school funding, but also enacted a law designed to effectively overturn the court's prior decisions holding the state constitutionally responsible for funding public education adequately. The new law divides that responsibility between the state and its municipalities, assigning instructional costs to the state and nonacademic costs (buses, nurses, etc.) to the municipalities. Consequently, the new law appears to conflict with the *Claremont* decisions and *ConVal*.[1] If the legislators thought this law would end school-funding litigation, they probably miscalculated because the law seems likely to ignite litigation, not quash it.

Regarding litigation, the state attorney general's office entered the school-funding fray early in 2026 by appealing an outstanding issue in the trial court's 2025 *Rand* decision to the state supreme court. The state argues that the funding of an adequate education is a "non-justiciable political question" that elected officials (not courts) must decide. This appeal is pending. Taken together, recent legislative and executive actions in New Hampshire seek to end court involvement in the school-funding debate.

School funding also commanded attention in Vermont in 2026. After insisting on mandatory school district mergers for much of the legislative session, Governor Phil Scott relented at the eleventh hour, settling instead for a bill that encourages and facilitates voluntary mergers. It also enables school districts to share resources, such as special education, information technology, and administrative services.[2] The legislature has passed the bill, which awaits the governor's signature. Governor Scott signed the bill (H. 955) into law on June 18, 2026.

Land-use legislation was also front-and-center in Vermont in 2026. A key bill sought to partially repeal Act 181, a 2024 law that modified Act 250, the state's historic land-use-planning statute. The partial repeal followed vociferous opposition by rural landowners, who saw Act 181's "road rule," requiring a permit to construct a private road longer than 800 feet, as intrusive. The landowners also objected to the amount of rural land included in "Tier III," to which Act 250 permit requirements applied. The new law repeals the road rule and eliminates Tier III.[3] Governor Scott signed the bill (H. 955) into law on June 18, 2026.

Judging by these events, "Live Free or Die" still rules the day in New Hampshire, while "Freedom and Unity" requires an ongoing give-and-take in Vermont.

NOTES

Chapter One

1 Edward Connery Latham, ed., *The Poetry of Robert Frost* (Holt, Rinehart and Winston, 1969), 164.
2 Holly Ramer, "Twin States' Demographics Diversifying, Census Data Says," *Valley News*, August 13, 2021, A1; Wilson Ring, "Census: Minority Population Growing in VT, 2nd Whitest State," Associated Press, August 12, 2021, https://apnews.com/article/race-and-ethnicity-census-2020-vermont-721d8201122a857b4565b4a37bd77d24.
3 Ralph Nading Hill, "Yankee Kingdom," in *New Hampshire vs. Vermont: Sibling Rivalry Between the Twin States*, ed. Lisa Shaw (Williams Hill Publishing, 1997), 106.
4 Barbara Radcliffe Rogers, "A Good Friend," in *New Hampshire vs. Vermont*, 21.
5 David R. Holmes, *On Being a Vermonter and the Rise and Fall of the Holmes Farm, 1822–1923* (White River Press, 2021), 229.
6 Judson Hale, "Why I live in New Hampshire," in *New Hampshire vs. Vermont*, 23.
7 Howard Dean, "The Politicos Speak," in *New Hampshire vs. Vermont*, 47.
8 Mary Soderstrom, *Frenemy Nations: Love and Hate Between Neighboring States* (University of Regina Press, 2019), 136.
9 Soderstrom, *Frenemy Nations*, 136.
10 Donna Dubuc, "What New Hampshire and Vermont Have in Common: A Dislike of Massachusetts," in *New Hampshire vs. Vermont*, 61.
11 Gabriel A. Almond and Sidney Verba, *The Civic Culture: Political Attitudes and Democracy in Five Nations* (Sage Publications, 1989), 62.
12 Daniel J. Elazar, *American Federalism: A View from the States*, 3rd ed. (Harper & Row, 1984), 117.
13 Elazar, *American Federalism*, 115–16.
14 Elazar, *American Federalism*, 118–19.
15 Elazar, *American Federalism*, 135.
16 Brian L. Porto, "Town Meetings, Tight Budgets, and Frugal Yankees: Explaining the Campaign-Finance Jurisprudence of Justice David Souter," *Vermont Law Review* 37, no. 2 (2012): 346.
17 Elizabeth H. Thompson, Eric R. Sorenson, and Robert Zaino, *Wetland, Woodland, Wildland: A Guide to the Natural Communities of Vermont*, 2nd ed. (Vermont Fish and Wildlife Department, The Nature Conservancy, and Vermont Land Trust, 2019), 14.
18 Frank M. Bryan, *Real Democracy: The New England Town Meeting and How It Works* (University of Chicago Press, 2004), 109.
19 Ralph Nading Hill, *Yankee Kingdom: Vermont and New Hampshire* (Countryman Press, 1984), 253.
20 Chuck Wooster, "Vermont—New Hampshire: The Hydropower Difference," *Northern Woodlands*, April 14, 2002, https://northernwoodlands.org/outside_story/article/vermont-new-hampshire-the-hydropower-difference.

21 Wooster, "The Hydropower Difference."

22 Nancy Coffey Heffernan and Ann Page Stecker, *New Hampshire: Crosscurrents in its Development*, 3rd ed. (University Press of New England, 2004), 191.

23 Heffernan and Stecker, *New Hampshire: Crosscurrents*, 170–71.

24 Heffernan and Stecker, *New Hampshire: Crosscurrents*, 171.

25 Charles T. Morrissey, *Vermont: A History* (W. W. Norton & Company, 1981), 166.

26 Corydon Ireland, "Vermont and New Hampshire, Geographic Twins, Cultural Aliens," *The Harvard Gazette*, November 1, 2007, http://news.harvard.edu/gazette/story/2007/11/vermont-and-new-hampshire-geographic-twins-cultural-aliens/.

27 Dorothy Canfield Fisher, *Vermont Tradition: The Biography of an Outlook on Life* (Little, Brown and Company, 1953), 8.

28 Fisher, *Vermont Tradition*, 395.

29 Jason Kaufman and Matthew E. Kaliner, "The Re-Accomplishment of Place in Twentieth Century Vermont and New Hampshire: History Repeats Itself, Until It Doesn't," *Theory and Society* 40, no. 2 (2011): 121–24.

30 Kenneth M. Johnson and Kristine Bundshuh, *Why People Move to and Stay in New Hampshire* (Carsey School of Public Policy, UNH, 2020), 3, carsey.unh.edu/publication/why-people-move-to-stay-in-NH.

31 Johnson and Bundschuh, *Why People Move*.

32 Kaufman and Kaliner, "The Re-Accomplishment of Place," 146.

33 Ireland, "Geographic Twins, Cultural Aliens."

34 Ireland, "Geographic Twins, Cultural Aliens."

35 Tom W. Rice and Alexander F. Sumberg, "Civic Culture and Government Performance in the American States," *Publius* 27, no. 1 (1997): 108–12.

36 Nora Doyle-Burr, "Health Care Experts Urge New Hampshire to Be More Like Vermont with COVID-19 Prevention," *Valley News*, December 19, 2020, https://www.vnews.com/Dartmouth-researchers-is-new-hampshire-doing-enough-to-prevent-COVID-19-spread-37826931.

37 Doyle-Burr, "Health Care Experts Urge."

38 Ethan DeWitt, "After Uvalde Shooting, Little Chance for New Gun Laws in New Hampshire," *New Hampshire Bulletin*, June 3, 2022, newhampshirebulletin.com/2022/06/03/after-uvalde-shooting-little-chance-of-new-gun-laws-in-new-hampshire/.

39 Everytown Research & Policy, "2025 Everytown Gun Law Rankings," https://everytownresearch.org/rankings/compare.

40 Paul Heintz, "Red Flags in the Green Mountains: How VT's 'Extreme Risk' Gun Law is Working," *Seven Days*, August 14, 2019, sevendaysvt.com/news/red-flags-in-the-green-mountains-how-vts-extreme-risk-gun-law-has-worked-28220723/.

41 Act 45 was previously referred to as H.230. Sarah Mearhoff, "Phil Scott Allows Gun Control Bill to Go into Law Without His Signature," *VTDigger*, June 1, 2023, vtdigger.org/2023/06/01/phil-scott-allows-gun-control-bill-to-go-into-law-without-his-signature/. The safe storage provision is codified in Title 13 of the Vermont Statutes Annotated at Section 4024, the red flag provisions are at Title 13, Sections 4053 and 4054, and the waiting period provision can be found at Title 13, Section 4019a.

42 142 S. Ct. 2111, 2126 (2022). Vermont satisfied the *Bruin* standard in *Vermont Federation of Sportsmen's Clubs v. Birmingham*, 741 F. Supp. 3d 172 (D. Vt. 2024), in which a federal district court denied the plaintiffs' request for a preliminary injunction to prevent enforcement of state laws restricting large capacity magazines and requiring

waiting periods for gun transfers. The court held that such laws are consistent with the United States' tradition of firearms regulation. The plaintiffs' appeal is pending in the US Court of Appeals for the Second Circuit.

43 *Contoocook Valley School District v. New Hampshire*, 2025 N.H. 29, 347 A.3d 541 (2025).

Chapter Two

1 John Lewis Gaddis, *The Landscape of History* (Oxford University Press, 2002), 65.

2 Gaddis, *The Landscape of History*, 114.

3 Mary Coffey Heffernan and Ann Paige Stecker, *New Hampshire: Crosscurrents in its Development*, 3rd ed. (University Press of New England, 2004), 13–17.

4 Jere R. Daniell, *Colonial New Hampshire: A History* (University Press of New England, 1981, 2015), 20.

5 Heffernan and Stecker, *New Hampshire: Crosscurrents*, 20.; Theodore B. Lewis, "Royal Government in New Hampshire and the Revocation of the Charter of the Massachusetts Bay Company, 1679–1683," *Historical New Hampshire* 25 (1970): 4.

6 Heffernan and Stecker, *New Hampshire: Crosscurrents*, 23.

7 Heffernan and Stecker, *New Hampshire: Crosscurrents*, 26–27.

8 Heffernan and Stecker, *New Hampshire: Crosscurrents*, 28.

9 Michael J. Caduto, *A Time Before New Hampshire: The Story of a Land and Native Peoples* (University Press of New England, 2003), x.

10 Daniell, *Colonial New Hampshire*, 3. Today, "Penacook" (spelled with one "n") is a section of Concord, which is New Hampshire's capital.

11 William Cronon, *Changes in the Land: Indians, Colonists, and the Ecology of New England* (Hill and Wang, 1983, 2003), 40.

12 Cronon, *Changes in the Land*, 65.

13 Cronon, *Changes in the Land*, 75.

14 Cronon, *Changes in the Land*, 56.

15 Daniell, *Colonial New Hampshire*, 9–10; Elizabeth Forbes Morrison and Elting E. Morrison, *New Hampshire: A Bicentennial History* (W. W. Norton & Company, 1976), 30.

16 Jill Lepore, *The Name of War: King Philip's War and the Origins of American Identity* (Alfred A. Knopf, 2009), 95.

17 Daniell, *Colonial New Hampshire*, 9.

18 Daniell, *Colonial New Hampshire*, 16.

19 Daniell, *Colonial New Hampshire*, 3.

20 Cronon, *Changes in the Land*, 89–90.

21 Lepore, *The Name of War*, 8

22 Laurel Thatcher Ulrich, *Good Wives: Image and Reality in the Lives of Women in Northern New England 1650–1750* (Alfred A. Knopf, 1982), 173–77.

23 Daniell, *Colonial New Hampshire*, 107.

24 Daniell, *Colonial New Hampshire*, 143.

25 Heffernan and Stecker, *New Hampshire: Crosscurrents*, 29.

26 Heffernan and Stecker, *New Hampshire: Crosscurrents*, 29.

27 Charles E. Clark, *The Eastern Frontier: The Settlement of Northern New England, 1610–1763* (University Press of New England, 1983), 3.

28 Heffernan and Stecker, *New Hampshire: Crosscurrents*, 30.
29 Clark, *The Eastern Frontier*, 98.
30 Clark, *The Eastern Frontier*, 100.
31 Heffernan and Stecker, *New Hampshire: Crosscurrents*, 32.
32 Clark., *The Eastern Frontier*, 114.
33 Morrison and Morrison, *New Hampshire: A Bicentennial History*, 26.
34 Daniell, *Colonial New Hampshire*, 43–44.
35 Daniell, *Colonial New Hampshire*, 143.
36 Daniell, *Colonial New Hampshire*, 57.
37 Daniell, *Colonial New Hampshire*, 119–20.
38 Daniell, *Colonial New Hampshire*, 135.
39 Clark, *The Eastern Frontier*, 105.
40 Clark, *The Eastern Frontier*, 358.
41 Daniell, *Colonial New Hampshire*, 137.
42 Heffernan and Stecker, *New Hampshire: Crosscurrents*, 50.
43 Daniell, *Colonial New Hampshire*, 209.
44 Heffernan and Stecker, *New Hampshire: Crosscurrents*, 50, citing Jeremy Belknap, *The History of New Hampshire*, vol. I (Robert Aitken, 1784), 324.
45 Clark, *The Eastern Frontier*, 358.
46 Heffernan and Stecker, *New Hampshire: Crosscurrents*, 55; Paul W. Wilderson, *Governor John Wentworth and the American Revolution: The English Connection* (University Press of New England, 1994), 97, 114.
47 Heffernan and Stecker, *New Hampshire: Crosscurrents*, 59–60.
48 Daniell, *Colonial New Hampshire*, 237.
49 Heffernan and Stecker, *New Hampshire: Crosscurrents*, 61–64.
50 Lynn Warren Turner, *The Ninth State: New Hampshire's Formative Years* (University of North Carolina Press, 1983), 14–15.
51 Jere R. Daniell, *Experiment in Republicanism: New Hampshire Politics and the American Revolution* (Harvard University Press, 1970), 114.
52 Jere R. Daniell, "Ideology and Hardball: Ratification of the Federal Constitution in New Hampshire," in *The Constitution and the States: The Role of the Original Thirteen in the Framing and Adoption of the Federal Constitution*, eds. Patrick T. Conley and John P. Kaminski (Madison House, 1988), 185. The 1784 New Hampshire Constitution was amended in 1792 to (1) adopt the name "governor" for the chief executive and give that officer veto power over legislation; (2) choose senators from districts instead of counties; (3) popularly elect council members from counties; and (4) prohibit council members from serving as legislators simultaneously.
53 Heffernan and Stecker, *New Hampshire: Crosscurrents*, 74–77; Wilderson, *Governor John Wentworth*, 223.
54 Daniell, *Colonial New Hampshire*, 245.
55 Heffernan and Stecker, *New Hampshire: Crosscurrents*, 66.
56 Daniell, *Colonial New Hampshire*, 245.
57 Heffernan and Stecker, *New Hampshire: Crosscurrents*, 67–68.
58 Jeremy Belknap, *History of New Hampshire*, 2nd ed., vol. II (Bradford and Read, 1813), 323–24.
59 Daniell, *Experiment in Republicanism*, 160–62; Michael Sherman, Gene Sessions, and P. Jeffrey Potash, *Freedom and Unity: A History of Vermont* (Vermont Historical

Society, 2004), 111; Morrison and Morrison, *New Hampshire: A Bicentennial History*, 81.

60 Sherman et al., *Freedom and Unity*, 115.

61 Daniell, *Experiment in Republicanism*, 162.

62 Jere R. Daniell, "Counting Noses: Delegate Sentiment in New Hampshire's Ratifying Convention," *Historical New Hampshire* 43, no. 2 (1988): 136; Daniell, "Ideology and Hardball," in *The Constitution and the States*, 181.

63 Turner, *The Ninth State*, 155.

64 Turner, *The Ninth State*, 81.

65 Heffernan and Stecker, *New Hampshire: Crosscurrents*, 103.

66 Turner, *The Ninth State*, 234.

67 Turner, *The Ninth State*, 329.

68 Heffernan and Stecker, *New Hampshire: Crosscurrents*, 89.

69 Heffernan and Stecker, *New Hampshire: Crosscurrents*, 88.

70 Heffernan and Stecker, *New Hampshire: Crosscurrents*, 93.

71 Heffernan and Stecker, *New Hampshire: Crosscurrents*, 131.

72 Donald B. Cole, *Jacksonian Democracy in New Hampshire 1800–1851* (Harvard University Press, 1970), 100.

73 Cole, *Jacksonian Democracy*, 125.

74 Gordon B. McKinney, "The Politics of Protest: The Labor Reform and Greenback Parties in New Hampshire," *Historical New Hampshire*, 36, nos. 2 and 3 (1981): 151.

75 Lex Renda, *Running on the Record: Civil War-Era Politics in New Hampshire* (University Press of Virginia, 1997), 5; Peter A. Wallner, *Franklin Pierce: New Hampshire's Favorite Son* (Plaidswede Publishing, 2004), 201–3, 230.

76 Renda, *Running on the Record*, 14.

77 Donald B. Cole, "The Presidential Election of 1832 in New Hampshire," *Historical New Hampshire* 21, no. 4 (1966): 44.

78 Cole, *Jacksonian Democracy in New Hampshire*, 155–56.

79 Richard P. Sewell, *John P. Hale and the Politics of Abolition* (Harvard University Press, 1965), 57; Wallner, *Franklin Pierce*, 257.

80 Sewell, *John P. Hale*, 108.

81 Sewell, *John P. Hale*, 172, 179.

82 Sewell, *John P. Hale*, 231.

83 Renda, *Running on the Record*, 69.

84 Renda, *Running on the Record*, 130.

85 Mike Pride and Mark Travis, *My Brave Boys: To War with Colonel Cross and the Fighting Fifth* (University Press of New England, 2001), 1–2.

86 McKinney, "The Politics of Protest," *Historical New Hampshire* 36 (1981): 152.

87 James Wright, *The Progressive Yankees: Republican Reformers in New Hampshire, 1906–1916* (University Press of New England, 1987), 7.

88 Ronald Jager and Grace Jager, *Portrait of a Hill Town: A History of Washington, New Hampshire 1876–1976* (Washington History Committee, 1977), 13–14.

89 Jager and Jager, *Portrait of a Hill Town*, 208.

90 Renda, *Running on the Record*, 174.

91 Wright, *The Progressive Yankees*, 33.

92 Renda, *Running on the Record*, 173.

93 Renda, *Running on the Record*, 173–74.

94 Jager and Jager, *Portrait of a Hill Town*, 97.
95 Wright, *The Progressive Yankees*, 24.
96 Jager and Jager, *Portrait of a Hill Town*, 293.
97 Heffernan and Stecker, *New Hampshire: Crosscurrents*, 151–52.
98 Heffernan and Stecker, *New Hampshire: Crosscurrents*, 155–56.
99 Wright, *The Progressive Yankees*, 7.
100 Heffernan and Stecker, *New Hampshire: Crosscurrents*, 157–58.
101 Wright, *The Progressive Yankees*, 8.
102 Heffernan and Stecker, *New Hampshire: Crosscurrents*, 158–59.
103 Heffernan and Stecker, *New Hampshire: Crosscurrents*, 180–81.
104 Heffernan and Stecker, *New Hampshire: Crosscurrents*, 163.
105 Leon Burr Richardson, *William E. Chandler: Republican* (Dodd, Mead & Company, 1940), 636.
106 Wright, *The Progressive Yankees*, xxii.
107 Wright, *The Progressive Yankees*, 121.
108 Heffernan and Stecker, *New Hampshire: Crosscurrents*, 165.
109 Heffernan and Stecker, *New Hampshire: Crosscurrents*, 168–70.
110 Heffernan and Stecker, *New Hampshire: Crosscurrents*, 171; Bernard Bellush, *He Walked Alone: A Biography of John Gilbert Winant* (Mouton Publishing, 1968), 100.
111 Wright, *The Progressive Yankees*, 33.
112 Tamara K. Hareven and Randolph Langenbach, *Amoskeag: Life and Work in an American Factory City* (University Press of New England), 10.
113 Hareven and Langenbach, *Amoskeag*, 18–20.
114 Hareven and Langenbach, *Amoskeag*, 22.
115 Hareven and Langenbach, *Amoskeag*, 116–18.
116 Hareven and Langenbach., *Amoskeag*, 26.
117 Hareven and Langenbach, *Amoskeag*, 26.
118 Heffernan and Stecker, *New Hampshire: Crosscurrents*, 150.
119 Heffernan and Stecker, *New Hampshire: Crosscurrents*, 174; Philip N. Guyol, *Democracy Fights: A History of New Hampshire in World War II* (Dartmouth Publishing, 1951), 139, 160–61.
120 Heffernan and Stecker, *New Hampshire: Crosscurrents*, 171–72.
121 Eric P. Veblen, *The Manchester Union Leader in New Hampshire Elections* (University Press of New England, 1975), 9.
122 Veblen, *The Manchester Union Leader*, 12, 22.
123 Veblen, *The Manchester Union Leader*, 64.
124 Veblen, *The Manchester Union Leader*, 10.
125 Veblen, *The Manchester Union Leader*, 171.
126 Morrison and Morrison, *New Hampshire: A Bicentennial History*, 193.
127 Morrison and Morrison, *New Hampshire: A Bicentennial History*, 193–94.
128 Heffernan and Stecker, *New Hampshire: Crosscurrents*, 176.
129 Morrison and Morrison, *New Hampshire: A Bicentennial History*, 163–64.
130 Donald Hall, *String Too Short to be Saved: Recollections of Summers on a New England Farm* (David R. Godine Publishers, 1960, 1979).
131 Heffernan and Stecker, *New Hampshire: Crosscurrents*, 182–83.
132 David W. Moore and Andrew E. Smith, *The First Primary: New Hampshire's Outsize Role in Presidential Nominations* (University of New Hampshire Press, 2015), 202.

According to Moore and Smith, "the notion that the primary is an enormous money maker for New Hampshire is a myth," but it "gives visibility to New Hampshire's mountains, beaches, and lakes, even two annual NASCAR races."

133 Michael J. Birkner, "Bringing Out the Vote: New Hampshire and the Presidential Vote of 1952," *Historical New Hampshire*, 75, nos. 1 and 2 (2022): 29.

134 Morrison and Morrison, *New Hampshire: A Bicentennial History*, 196.

135 Robert E. Craig and Richard F. Winters, "Party Politics in New Hampshire," in *New England Political Parties*, eds. Josephine F. Milburn and William Doyle (Schenkman Publishing Company, 1983), 141–42.

136 Veblen, *The Manchester Union Leader*, 13.

137 Thomas J. McIntyre, *The Fear Brokers* (The Pilgrim Press, 1979), 208.

138 Heffernan and Stecker, *New Hampshire: Crosscurrents*, 190. For an excellent account of the lengthy political battle surrounding the power station, see Henry F. Bedford, *Seabrook Station: Citizen Politics and Nuclear Power* (University of Massachusetts Press, 1990). For an equally compelling account of the unsuccessful efforts by Governor Thomsen and Mr. Loeb to attract an oil refinery to the New Hampshire coast, see David Moore, *Small Town, Big Oil: The Untold Story of the Women Who Took on the Richest Man in the World—and Won* (Diversion Books, 2018).

139 Niall Palmer, *The New Hampshire Primary and the American Electoral Process* (Westview Press, 1997), 41–42.

140 Moore and Smith, *The First Primary*, 154.

141 Christopher J. Galdieri, *Donald Trump and New Hampshire Politics* (Palgrave MacMillan, 2020), 79–80.

142 Moore and Smith, *The First Primary*, 156.

143 Daniell, *Colonial New Hampshire*, 248–49.

144 In 2009 New Hampshire became the first state to legalize same-sex marriage by an act of the legislature that the governor signed. Moore and Smith, *The First Primary*, 172. New Hampshire abolished capital punishment in 2019 for murders committed as of May 30, 2019, but the penalty remains in effect for the one offender who was convicted of capital murder before that date. In other words, the 2019 law does not apply retroactively.

Chapter Three

1 John Lewis Gaddis, *The Landscape of History* (Oxford University Press, 2002), 65.

2 Charles T. Morrissey, *Vermont: A History* (W. W. Norton & Company, 1981), 75.

3 Allan R. Raymond, "Benning Wentworth's Claims in the New Hampshire-New York Border Controversy: A Case of Twenty-Twenty Hindsight?" *Vermont History* 43, no. 1 (1975): 28.

4 John H. Duffy, H. Nicholas Muller III, and Gary G. Shattuck, *The Rebel and the Tory: Ethan Allen, Phillip Skene, and the Dawn of Vermont* (Vermont Historical Society, 2020), 1.

5 William A. Haviland and Marjory W. Power, *The Original Vermonters: Native Inhabitants Past and Present* (University Press of New England, 1981), 197.

6 Michael Sherman, Gene Sessions, and P. Jeffrey Potash, *Freedom and Unity: A History of Vermont* (Vermont Historical Society, 2004), 27–28.

7 Haviland and Power, *The Original Vermonters*, 239.

8 Neil Goodwin, *We Go as Captives: The Royalton Raid and the Shadow War on the Revolutionary Frontier* (Vermont Historical Society, 2010), 12.; Colin G. Calloway, *Western Abenakis of Vermont, 1600–1800* (University of Oklahoma Press, 1990), 223.
9 Goodwin, *We Go as Captives*, 37, 68.
10 Goodwin, *We Go as Captives*, 8.
11 Morrissey, *Vermont: A History*, 77.
12 Willard Stearne Randall, *Ethan Allen: His Life and Times* (W. W. Norton & Company, 2011), 191.
13 Sherman et al., *Freedom and Unity*, 74.
14 Duffy et. al, *The Rebel and the Tory*, 157. A quitrent was a sum paid by a tenant of property that another person owned. Paying the quitrent freed the tenant from having to pay any other rent during the rental period.
15 Raymond, "Benning Wentworth's Claims," 30.
16 Randall, *Ethan Allen*, 196.
17 Frank M. Bryan, *Yankee Politics in Rural Vermont* (University Press of New England, 1974), 7.
18 Randall, *Ethan Allen*, 202.
19 Randall, *Ethan Allen*, 98. Although most famous for his physical exploits, Allen never lost his youthful interest in the life of the mind. In adulthood he published three books, *A Brief Narrative of the Proceedings of the Government of New York* (1774), *Narrative of Col. Ethan Allen's Captivity* (1779), and *Reason: The Only Oracle of Man* (1785).
20 Randall, *Ethan Allen*, 112–13; Roger Allbee, *Turning the Soil: 250 Years of Vermont Agriculture* (Center for Research on Vermont, 2025), 4.
21 Randall, *Ethan Allen*, 183.
22 Morrissey, *Vermont: A History*, 81–82.
23 J. Kevin Graffagnino, "The Country My Soul Delighted In: The Onion River Land Company and the Vermont Frontier," in *Vermont Heritage: Essays on Green Mountain History 1770–1920*, H. Nicholas Muller III and J. Kevin Graffagnino (Center for Research on Vermont, 2020), 238.
24 Duffy et al., *The Rebel and the Tory*, 97.
25 Duffy et al., *The Rebel and the Tory*, 45–46.
26 Duffy et al., *The Rebel and the Tory*, 99–100.
27 Randall, *Ethan Allen*, 248.
28 Randall, *Ethan Allen*, 255.
29 Randall, *Ethan Allen*, 291.
30 Randall, *Ethan Allen*, 299–301.
31 Robert E. Shalhope, *Bennington and the Green Mountain Boys: The Emergence of Liberal Democracy in Vermont, 1760–1850* (Johns Hopkins University Press, 1996), 163. Benedict Arnold became infamous to Americans later in the war, when he defected to the British side.
32 Randall, *Ethan Allen*, 336.
33 Randall, *Ethan Allen*, 434.
34 Frank Smallwood, *Thomas Chittenden: Vermont's First Statesman* (New England Press, 1997), 56.
35 Smallwood, *Thomas Chittenden*, 57–59.
36 Sherman et al., *Freedom and Unity*, 102–3.

37 Shalhope, *Bennington and the Green Mountain Boys*, 171.
38 Randall, *Ethan Allen*, 444. The Vermont Constitution did not end slavery in the Green Mountain State, though. Instead, it "made steps toward abolition." Specifically, it prohibited holding by law, as a servant, slave, or apprentice, males over age 21 and females over age 18, "unless with their consent or if bound by law for payment of debts, damages, fines, etc." Thus, slavery persisted in Vermont for more than thirty years after adoption of the state constitution when masters defied the law by purchasing and selling slaves and white Vermonters referred to African Americans as "servants," even when the latter were held in bondage. Harvey Amani Whitfield, *The Problem of Slavery in Early Vermont, 1777–1810* (Vermont Historical Society, 2014), 3, 19.
39 John N. Shaeffer, "A Comparison of the First Constitutions of Vermont and Pennsylvania," *Vermont History* 43, no. 1 (1975): 36.
40 Shaffer, "A Comparison of the First Constitutions," 39, 43.
41 Smallwood, *Thomas Chittenden*, 59.
42 Sherman et al., *Freedom and Unity*, 109–10.
43 Smallwood, *Thomas Chittenden*, 62.
44 Smallwood, *Thomas Chittenden*, 106; Sherman et al., *Freedom and Unity*, 115.
45 Peter S. Onuf, "State-Making in Revolutionary America: Independent Vermont as a Case Study," *The Journal of American History* 67, no. 4 (1981): 798.
46 Randall, *Ethan Allen*, 491–92.
47 Smallwood, *Thomas Chittenden*, 114–17.
48 Randall, *Ethan Allen*, 492.
49 Morrissey, *Vermont: A History*, 93–94.
50 Morrissey, *Vermont: A History*, 100.
51 Sherman et al., *Freedom and Unity*, 126.
52 Onuf, "State-Making in Revolutionary America," 815.
53 Haviland and Power, *The Original Vermonters*, 245–46.
54 Morrissey, *Vermont: A History*, 56.
55 Morrissey, *Vermont: A History*, 167–70.
56 Randolph A. Roth, *The Democratic Dilemma: Religion, Reform, and the Social Order in the Connecticut River Valley of Vermont, 1791–1850* (Cambridge University Press, 1987), 5.
57 Smallwood, *Thomas Chittenden*, 165.
58 Morrissey, *Vermont: A History*, 106.
59 Morrissey, *Vermont: A History*, 106–7.
60 Shalhope, *Bennington and the Green Mountain Boys*, 264.
61 Sherman et al., *Freedom and Unity*, 169.
62 Smallwood, *Thomas Chittenden*, 182–83; Roth, *The Democratic Dilemma*, 14.
63 Aleine Austin, "Vermont Politics in the 1780s: Emergence of Rival Leadership," *Vermont History*, 42, no. 2 (1974): 146.
64 Edward Brynne, "Patterns of Dissent: Vermont's Opposition to the War of 1812," *Vermont History*, 40, no. 1 (1972): 20–21.
65 Roth, *The Democratic Dilemma*, 5.
66 Sherman et al., *Freedom and Unity*, 145–46.
67 Sherman et al., *Freedom and Unity*, 152–55.
68 Brynne, "Patterns of Dissent: Vermont's Opposition to the War of 1812," 13–14.

69 H. Nicholas Muller III, "From Ferment to Fatigue? 1870–1900: A New Look at the Neglected Winter of Vermont" in *Vermont Heritage: Essays on Green Mountain History 1770–1920* eds. H. Nicholas Muller III and J. Kevin Graffagnino (Center for Research on Vermont, 2020), 296.
70 Sherman et al., *Freedom and Unity*, 163; Morrissey, *Vermont: A History*, 110.
71 Brynne, "Patterns of Dissent," 21.
72 Sherman et al., *Freedom and Unity*, 164.
73 Roth, *The Democratic Dilemma*, 173.
74 Sherman et al., *Freedom and Unity*, 170.
75 Sherman et al., *Freedom and Unity*, 172.
76 Sherman et al., *Freedom and Unity*, 175.
77 Sherman et al., *Freedom and Unity*, 194.
78 Sherman et al., *Freedom and Unity*, 200.
79 Sherman et al., *Freedom and Unity*, 210.
80 Sherman et al., *Freedom and Unity*, 196; Paul M. Searls, *Two Vermonts: Geography and Identity, 1865–1910* (University of New Hampshire Press, 2006), 53.
81 Sherman et al., *Freedom and Unity*, 220–21; Allen F. Davis, *Postcards from Vermont: A Social History, 1905–1945* (University Press of New England, 2002), 129–30.
82 Shalhope, *Bennington and the Green Mountain Boys*, 267–68.
83 Roth, *The Democratic Dilemma*, 257.
84 Roth, *The Democratic Dilemma*, 176.
85 Sherman et al., *Freedom and Unity*, 185.
86 David Ludlum, *Social Ferment in Vermont, 1791–1850* (AMS Press, 1966), 129.
87 William Doyle, "Political Parties in Vermont," in *New England Political Parties*, eds. Josephine F. Milburn and William Doyle (Schenkman Publishing Company, 1983), 118.
88 Roth, *The Democratic Dilemma*, 259.
89 Sherman et al., *Freedom and Unity*, 242.
90 Sherman et al., *Freedom and Unity*, 242–43.
91 Sherman et al., *Freedom and Unity*, 248–49.
92 Samuel B. Hand, *The Star That Set: The Vermont Republican Party, 1854–1974* (Lexington Books, 2002), 5.
93 Sherman et al., *Freedom and Unity*, 249.
94 Sherman et al., *Freedom and Unity*, 252.
95 Sherman et al., *Freedom and Unity*, 253; Howard Coffin, *Full Duty: Vermonters in the Civil War* (Countryman Press, 1993).
96 Sherman et. al., *Freedom and Unity*, 253.
97 Sherman et al., *Freedom and Unity*, 259.
98 Sherman et al., *Freedom and Unity*, 269.
99 Coffin, *Full Duty*, 356.
100 Sherman et al., *Freedom and Unity*, 270.
101 For those who had served in the military during the war, the federal government credited their service when they applied for quarter-section homesteads in the West. Morrissey, *Vermont: A History*, 123.
102 Sherman et al., *Freedom and Unity*, 284.
103 Morrissey, *Vermont: A History*, 125.
104 Morrissey, *Vermont: A History*, 126–27.

105 Ernest L. Bogart, *Peacham: The Story of a Vermont Hill Town* (Vermont Historical Society, 1948), 312, 336.
106 Sherman et al., *Freedom and Unity*, 232.
107 Sherman et al., *Freedom and Unity*, 298–99.
108 Sherman et al., *Freedom and Unity*, 301–3.
109 J. Kevin Graffagnino, "Arcadia in New England: Divergent Views of a Changing Vermont," in *Vermont Heritage*, 373.
110 Muller, "From Ferment to Fatigue," 342–43.
111 Searls, *Two Vermonts*, 28.
112 Sherman et al., *Freedom and Unity*, 322–23.
113 Sherman et al., *Freedom and Unity*, 319.
114 Searls, *Two Vermonts*, 89.
115 Peter A. Gilbert, "Vermont's World of Letters and Learning: Libraries, Lyceums, Literacy, and Lifelong Learning," in *The Vermont Difference: Perspectives on Vermont*, eds. J. Kevin Graffagnino, H. Nicholas Muller III, David A. Donath, and Kristin Peterson-Ishaq (Woodstock Foundation and Vermont Historical Society, 2014), 206–7.
116 Hand, *The Star That Set*, 59.
117 Samuel B. Hand, "It Won't Be in the Book, Or Why the Fluid Milk Market Curdled Our Hopes," in *Green Mountain Scholar: Samuel B. Hand, Dean of Vermont Historians*, eds. H. Nicholas Muller III, Kristin Peterson-Ishaq, J. Kevin Graffagnino, and Richard Watts (Center for Research on Vermont, 2017), 33.
118 Samuel B. Hand, Jeffrey D. Marshall, and D. Gregory Sanford, "Little Republics?: The Structure of State Politics in Vermont, 1854–1920, in *Green Mountain Scholar*, 51.
119 Hand et al., "Little Republics: The Structure of State Politics in Vermont, 1854–1920, in *Green Mountain Scholar*, 50–51.
120 Sherman et al., *Freedom and Unity*, 323.
121 Joe Sherman, *Fast Lane on a Dirt Road: A Contemporary History of Vermont* (Chelsea Green Publishing Company, 2000), 125.
122 Sherman et al., *Freedom and Unity*, 363–64.
123 Sherman et al., *Freedom and Unity*, 371–72.
124 Sherman et al., *Freedom and Unity*, 374–75.
125 Sherman et al., *Freedom and Unity*, 380.
126 Morrissey, *Vermont: A History*, 120.
127 Sherman et al., *Freedom and Unity*, 421–23.
128 Sherman et al., *Freedom and Unity*, 425–27.
129 Hand, *The Star That Set*, 128.
130 Sherman et al., *Freedom and Unity*, 427.
131 Sherman et al., *Freedom and Unity*, 323–24.
132 Sherman et al., *Freedom and Unity*, 432.
133 Richard Munson Judd, *The New Deal in Vermont: Its Impact and Aftermath* (Garland Publishing, 1979), 24.
134 Sherman et al., *Freedom and Unity*, 449.
135 Judd, *The New Deal in Vermont*, 33.
136 Sherman et al., *Freedom and Unity*, 467.
137 Judd, *The New Deal in Vermont*, 115.

138 Judd, *The New Deal in Vermont*, 215.
139 Hannah Silverstein, "No Parking: Vermont Rejects the Green Mountain Parkway," *Vermont History* 63, no. 3 (1995): 141.
140 Silverstein, "No Parking," 143.
141 Silverstein, "No Parking," 153.
142 Sherman et al., *Freedom and Unity*, 489.
143 Sherman et al., *Freedom and Unity*, 493–96.
144 Sherman et al., *Freedom and Unity*, 499.
145 Sherman et al., *Freedom and Unity*, 499.
146 Sherman et al., *Freedom and Unity*, 500.
147 Sherman et al., *Freedom and Unity*, 522–23
148 Sherman et al., *Freedom and Unity*, 523.
149 Sherman, *Fast Lane on a Dirt Road*, 71.
150 Sherman et al., *Freedom and Unity*, 503. Many of those disaffected Republicans were unwilling to cast their votes for the Democratic line on the ballot, so two makeshift third parties were created, the Vermont Independent Party and the Independent Democrats, which were loyal to Hoff. He won 56,196 votes on the Democratic line; 3,200 votes on the Vermont Independent Party line; and just under 1,900 votes on the Independent Democrat line, giving him 50.6 percent of the vote, a 1,348-vote edge over Republican incumbent F. Ray Keyser. See Samuel B. Hand, Anthony Marro, and Stephen C. Terry, *Philip Hoff: How Red Turned Blue in the Green Mountain State* (University Press of New England, 2011), 40.
151 Readers should not confuse the reference here to "progressivism" as a synonym for Vermont's Progressive Party. To be sure, the Progressive Party regularly advocates bold government actions to produce social and economic change, but it is distinct from progressivism, our focus here, which Democrats regularly and Republicans occasionally demonstrate too.
152 Sherman et al., *Freedom and Unity*, 512–13
153 Sherman et al., *Freedom and Unity*, 511.
154 Hand, *The Star That Set*, 257.
155 Hand, *The Star That Set*, 261.
156 Jim Jeffords was a moderate Republican during his fourteen years in the House and his first twelve years in the Senate. Early in his third term, though, he became frustrated by the efforts of his conservative Republican colleagues to undermine his authority, often by removing money at the last minute from bills he had moved through the chamber. Fed up, he left the Republican Party in May 2001 and became an Independent who caucused with the Democrats, a historic move because it converted a 50–50 numerical split between the two parties in the Senate into a 51–49 advantage for the Democrats. Jeffords served out his final Senate term as an Independent, retiring in January 2007.

Chapter Four

1 Mary Soderstrom, *Frenemy Nations: Love and Hate Between Neighboring States* (University of Regina Press, 2019), 136.
2 Jason Kaufman and Matthew E. Kaliner, "The Re-Accomplishment of Place in Twentieth Century Vermont and New Hampshire: History Repeats Itself, Until It Doesn't," *Theory and Society* 40, no. 2 (2011): 146.

3 Matthew Hongoltz-Hetling, *A Libertarian Walks into a Bear: The Utopian Plan to Liberate an American Town (and Some Bears)* (Public Affairs Press, 2020), 221.
4 Hongoltz-Hetling, *A Libertarian Walks into a Bear*, 282–83.
5 Hongoltz-Hetling, *A Libertarian Walks into a Bear*, 70.
6 Hongottz-Hetling, *A Libertarian Walks into a Bear*, 91–94.
7 Dan Barry, "A New Hampshire Town's Lesson in Democracy," *The New York Times*, July 10, 2022, https://www.nytimes.com/2022/07/10/us/croydon-free-state-politics.html.
8 Barry, "A New Hampshire Town's Lesson in Democracy."
9 Hongoltz-Hetling, *A Libertarian Walks into a Bear*, 140.
10 Nora Doyle-Burr, "Health Care Experts Urge New Hampshire to Be More Like Vermont with COVID-19 Prevention," *Valley News*, December 19, 2020, https://www.vnews.com/Dartmouth-researchers-is-New-Hampshire-doing-enough-to-prevent-COVID-19-spread-37826931.
11 Ethan DeWitt, "Little Chance for New Gun Laws in New Hampshire. Sununu, Republicans Say None are Needed," *Seacoastonline*, June 3, 2022, seacoastonline.com/story/news/state/2022/001/03/new-hampshire-gun-laws-nh-sununu-republican-opposition/7495602001/.
12 Miriam Israel, Joe Field, and Roger Stephenson, *New England State Climate Assessment Using the UCS Resilience Gap Framework* (University of New Hampshire Sustainability Institute and the Union of Concerned Scientists, 2022), 23, ucs.org/sites/default/files/2022-10/new-england-state-climate-action-assessment-full-report.pdf.
13 Israel et al., *New England Climate Assessment*, 24–25; Claire Sullivan, "How New Hampshire's Candidates for Governor Would Lead on Energy, Climate Change," *New Hampshire Bulletin*, August 21, 2024, newhampshirebulletin.com/2024/08/21/how-new-hampshires-candidates-for-governor-would-lead-on-energy-climate-change/.
14 Jennifer Weiner, *How Does New Hampshire Do It? An Analysis of Spending and Revenues in the Absence of a Broad-Based Income or Sales Tax* (Federal Reserve Bank of Boston New England Public Policy Center, 2011).
15 Weiner, *How Does New Hampshire Do It*, 5.
16 Weiner, *How Does New Hampshire Do It*, 9.
17 Weiner, *How Does New Hampshire Do It*, 17.
18 Weiner, *How Does New Hampshire Do It*, 18.
19 Weiner, *How Does New Hampshire Do It*, 18.
20 Weiner, *How Does New Hampshire Do It*, 23.
21 Weiner, *How Does New Hampshire Do It*, 37.
22 United States Department of Commerce, Census Bureau, *Annual Survey of State Government Finances Summary: 2021* (Department of Commerce, 2023), 1, census.gov/library/publications/2023/econ/g21-asfin-summary.html.
23 Department of Commerce, *Annual Survey*, 2.
24 Phil Sletten, *Funding Public Services in New Hampshire and the State Budget Process: Presentation to the Kent Street Coalition* (New Hampshire Fiscal Policy Institute, July 25, 2024), 3–4, nhfpi.org/assets/2024/07/NHFPI-Funding-Public-Services-in-New-Hampshire-and-the-State-Budget-Process-7.25.24.pdf.
25 Sletten, *Funding Public Services in New Hampshire*, 31–32.
26 Sletten, *Funding Public Services in New Hampshire*, 33.

27 Sletten, *Funding Public Services in New Hampshire*, 35.
28 Carsey School of Public Policy, *What is New Hampshire? Where We Are, Where We Have Been, and What Challenges We May Face*," (University of New Hampshire, 2019), B-1, carsey.unh.edu/what-new-hampshire/what-new-hampshire-budget.
29 Carsey School, *What is New Hampshire*, B-2.
30 Carsey School, *What is New Hampshire*, B-1.
31 Carsey School, *What is New Hampshire*, B-2.
32 Kevin Landrigan, "New Hampshire's GOP Governor Extends Medicaid Expansion but Adds Work Requirement," *Governing*, July 2, 2018, governing.com/archive/tns-medicaid-expansion-sununu.html.
33 Carsey School, *What is New Hampshire*, B-9.
34 Phil Sletten, *How Public Services are Funded in New Hampshire at the State and Local Levels: A Presentation to the New Hampshire Government Finance Officers Association* (New Hampshire Fiscal Policy Institute, August 10, 2022), 38–39, https://nhfpi.org/resource/how-public-services-are-funded-in-new-hampshire-at-the-state-and-local-levels-2/.
35 New Hampshire Fiscal Policy Institute, *Revenue in Review: An Overview of New Hampshire's Tax System and Major Revenue Sources* (New Hampshire Fiscal Policy Institute, May 2017), 10, nhfpi.org/resource/revenue-in-review-an-overview-of-new-hampshires-tax-system-and-major-revenue-sources/. See also New Hampshire Fiscal Policy Institute, *Issue Brief: Business Tax Rate Reductions Led to Between $795 Million and $1.17 Billion in Foregone Revenues for Public Services Since 2015* (New Hampshire Fiscal Policy Institute, April 1, 2025), nhfpi.org.
36 New Hampshire Fiscal Policy Institute, *Revenue in Review*, 12; New Hampshire Fiscal Policy Institute, *Issue Brief: Business Tax Rate Reductions*, nhfpi.org/.
37 New Hampshire Fiscal Policy Institute, *Revenue in Review*, 16.
38 New Hampshire Fiscal Policy Institute, *Revenue in Review*, 18.
39 New Hampshire Fiscal Policy Institute, *Revenue in Review*, 20.
40 New Hampshire Fiscal Policy Institute, *Revenue in Review*, 22.
41 New Hampshire Fiscal Policy Institute, *Revenue in Review*, 24.
42 New Hampshire Fiscal Policy Institute, *Revenue in Review*, 26.
43 New Hampshire Fiscal Policy Institute, *Revenue in Review*, 27.
44 New Hampshire Fiscal Policy Institute, *Revenue in Review*, 27.
45 New Hampshire Fiscal Policy Institute, *Revenue in Review*, 27.
46 New Hampshire Fiscal Policy Institute, *Revenue in Review*, 25. This list includes most, but not all, of New Hampshire's taxes. The full list includes a beer tax, excavations ("gravel") tax, railroad tax, timber tax, and a Nursing Home Quality Assessment. They have been excluded from the list of major taxes because their proceeds go to certain dedicated purposes instead of to the General Fund and because, except for the Nursing Home Quality Assessment, they do not raise significant revenue. More detailed descriptions of these taxes are available at revenue.nh.gov/assistance/tax-overview.htm.
47 Sletten, *Funding Public Services in New Hampshire*, 51.
48 New Hampshire Fiscal Policy Institute, *Revenue in Review*, 6.
49 New Hampshire Fiscal Policy Institute, *Revenue in Review*, 5.
50 Weiner, *How Does New Hampshire Do It*, 23, 37.
51 New Hampshire Fiscal Policy Institute, *Limited State Funding for Public Higher Education Adds to Workforce Constraints* (New Hampshire Fiscal Policy Institute, November 16, 2023), 6, nhfpi.org.

52 New Hampshire Fiscal Policy Institute, *Limited State Funding for Public Higher Education*, 6.

53 New Hampshire Fiscal Policy Institute, *Limited State Funding for Public Higher Education*, 7.

54 New Hampshire Fiscal Policy Institute, *Limited State Funding for Public Higher Education*, 10. The TICAS study—*Student Debt and the Class of 2020: 16th Annual Report*—is available at ticas.org/wp-content/uploads/2021/11/classof2020.pdf. It was published in November 2021.

55 New Hampshire Fiscal Policy Institute, *Limited State Funding for Public Higher Education*, 10.

56 Kenneth M. Johnson, Dante J. Scala, and Andrew E. Smith, *First in the Nation: New Hampshire's Changing Electorate in Changing Times*, Regional Issue Brief #60 (Carsey School of Public Policy, UNH, Winter 2019), 1, scholars.unh.edu/cgi/viewcontent.cgi?article=1383&context=carsey/.

57 Johnson et al., *First in the Nation*, 1.

58 Kenneth M. Johnson, *Migration Sustains New Hampshire's Population Gain: Examining the Origins of Recent Migrants*, Regional Issue Brief #174 (Carsey School of Public Policy, UNH, Fall, 2023), 3, carsey.unh.edu/publication/migration-sustains-new-hampshires-population-gain.

59 Carsey School, *What is New Hampshire*, D1–D3.

60 Carsey School, *What is New Hampshire*, 3.

61 Carsey School, *What is New Hampshire*, 4.

62 Carsey School, *What is New Hampshire*, 5.

63 Carsey School, *What is New Hampshire*, 6.

64 Kenneth M. Johnson, *New Census Data Reveal Modest Population Growth in New Hampshire Over the Past Decade* (Carsey School of Public Policy, UNH, Summer 2021), 1, scholars.unh.edu/cgi/viewcontent.cgi?article=1438&context=carsey.

65 Johnson, *New Census Data*, 2.

66 Kenneth M. Johnson, *Population Gains Continue in New Hampshire, But the Pace Varies*, Issue Brief #180, (Carsey School of Public Policy, UNH, 2024), 1, scholars.unh.educgi/viewcontent.cgi?article=1483&context=carsey.

67 Johnson, *Population Gains Continue*, 2.

68 As of July 1, 2023, the median age in New Hampshire was 43.4 years, meaning the Granite State was tied with Vermont as the second oldest state in the United States, behind only Maine. New Hampshire also ranks as the third whitest state, behind Maine and Vermont. See New Hampshire Fiscal Policy Institute, *Issue Brief: New Hampshire's Growing Population and Changing Demographics Before and Since the COVID-19 Pandemic* (New Hampshire Fiscal Policy Institute, August 16, 2024), nhfpi.org.

69 Kenneth Johnson and Kristine Bundschuh, *Why People Move to and Stay in New Hampshire* (Carsey School of Public Policy, UNH, Summer 2020, 1–2, carsey.unh.edu/publication/why-people-move-to-stay-in-NH.

70 Carsey School, *What is New Hampshire*, 2.

71 Carsey School, *What is New Hampshire*, 9.

72 Kenneth M. Johnson, *New Hampshire Demographic Trends in an Era of Economic Turbulence* (Carsey School of Public Policy, UNH, Fall 2019), 9, scholars.unh.edu/carsey/380/.

73 Johnson and Bundschuh, *Why People Move to and Stay in New Hampshire*, 3.

74 Johnson, *Migration Sustains New Hampshire's Population Gain*, 1.

75 Kenneth M. Johnson, *Modest Population Gain, but Growing Diversity in New Hampshire With Children in the Vanguard*, Regional Issue Brief # 66 (Carsey School of Public Policy, UNH, Summer 2021), 1, carsey.unh.edu/publication/modest-population-gains-growing-diversity-new-hampshire-children-vanguard.

76 Johnson, *Modest Population Gain*, 1–2.

77 David W. Moore and Andrew E. Smith, *The First Primary: New Hampshire's Outsize Role in Presidential Nominations* (University of New Hampshire Press, 2015), 153.

78 Moore and Smith, *The First Primary*, 154.

79 Moore and Smith, *The First Primary*, 155.

80 Moore and Smith, *The First Primary*, 156.

81 Johnson et al., *First in the Nation*, 2

82 Johnson et al., *First in the Nation*, 2–3.

83 Johnson et al., *First in the Nation*, 3.

84 Christopher J. Galdieri, *Donald Trump and New Hampshire Politics* (Palgrave Macmillan, 2020), 54.

85 Galdieri, *Donald Trump*, 26.

86 Moore and Smith, *The First Primary*, 170.

87 Johnson et al., *First in the Nation*, 5.

88 Dante J. Scala, "Politics in New Hampshire," *New England Journal of Political Science*, 7, no. 1 (2013): 143, https://digitalcommons.library.umaine.edu/nejps/vol7/iss1/8/.

89 Dante J. Scala, *Stormy Weather: The New Hampshire Primary and Presidential Politics* (Palgrave Macmillan, 2003), 42.

90 Scala, *Stormy Weather*, 43.

91 Carol Shea-Porter was elected to Congress in 2006, 2008, 2012, and 2016. Frank Guinta defeated Shea-Porter in 2010 and 2014. Thus, one or the other represented New Hampshire's First Congressional District during a twelve-year span from January 2007 until January 2019.

92 Jennifer Lucas, Tauna S. Sisco, and Christopher J. Galdieri, "New Hampshire Senate Race: Closest in the Nation," in *The Roads to Congress 2016: American Elections in a Divided Landscape*, eds. Jennifer Lucas and Marcia L. Godwin (Palgrave Macmillan, 2018), 322.

93 Lucas et al, "New Hampshire Senate Race," 324; Molly Ball, "How She Does It," *The Atlantic*, April 11, 2014, https://www.theatlantic.com/politics/archive/2024/04/how-she-does-it/360471/.

94 Lucas et al., "New Hampshire Senate Race," 328–29.

95 Lucas et al., "New Hampshire Senate Race," 328.

96 Christopher J. Galdieri, "New Hampshire Politics in 2023: Aftermath and Anticipation," *New England Journal of Political Science* 14, no. 1 (2023): 1, https://digitalcommons.library.umaine.edu/nejps/vol14/iss1/8.

97 Galdieri, "New Hampshire Politics in 2023," 1.

98 The 2016 presidential election was a squeaker in New Hampshire, as Hillary Clinton won by just 2,736 votes, or 0.37 percent. The Democrats prevailed more easily in 2020, as Joe Biden beat Donald Trump by 52,267 votes, or more than 7 percent. See Louis Jacobson, "A Left Turn for Democrats in New Hampshire?" *U.S. News and World Report*, November 22, 2023, https://www.usnews.com/news/politics/articles/2023-11-22/a-left-turn-for-democrats-in-new-hampshire. In 2024 Democrat Kamala Harris beat Donald Trump by 22,918 votes, or 2.8 percent.

99 Dante J. Scala, "New Hampshire's 2018 Midterms," *New England Journal of Political Science* 11, no. 2 (2019): 117–18.

100 Galdieri, *Donald Trump*, 84. Predictably, the Democratic legislature passed many bills that the Republican governor opposed. Governor Sununu issued fifty-seven vetoes during the 2018–20 biennium, nearly all of which were sustained. Still, the Democrats prevailed on their bill to outlaw the death penalty in New Hampshire; Sununu vetoed it, but the legislators overrode his veto. Galdieri, "New Hampshire Politics on the Cusp of the 2020 Election," *New England Journal of Political Science* 12, no. 1 (2020): 122.

101 Galdieri, "New Hampshire Politics in 2023," 1.

102 Local 8027, AFT-NH, AFL-CIO v. Edelblut, 2024 WL 2722254 (May 28, 2024), 1. As of February 2026, the education commissioner's appeal in this case was pending in the United States Court of Appeals for the First Circuit.

103 Local 8027, AFT-NH, AFL-CIO v. Edelblut, 2024 WL 2722254 (May 8, 2024), 13.

104 *Tirrell v. Edelblut*, 748 F. Supp. 3d 19, 41 (D.N.H. 2024). Transgender issues continued to be prominent in New Hampshire in 2025, when Governor Kelly Ayotte signed two bills concerning transgender medical care. One (HB 577) prohibits performing a medical procedure on, or prescribing medication for, a minor that is intended to alter the child's gender assigned at birth. The other (HB 712) limits breast surgeries for minors to procedures necessary for treating cancer, injury, infection, malformation, or a related reconstruction. Both bills subject violators to professional disciplinary penalties.

105 New Hampshire Fiscal Policy Institute, Issue Brief: *The Fragile Economics of the Child Care Sector* (New Hampshire Fiscal Policy Institute, May 17, 2024) 2–3, nhfpi.org/resource/the-fragile-economics-of-the-child-care-sector/.

106 New Hampshire Fiscal Policy Institute, Issue Brief: *The Fragile Economics*, 3.

107 Nicole Heller, *New Hampshire's Labor Force and the State of the Child Care Industry*: Presentation to the Granite United Way Business Roundtable (New Hampshire Fiscal Policy Institute, June 20, 2024), 7, nhfpi.org/resource/new-hampshirer-labor-force-and-the-state-of-the-child-care-industry. See also New Hampshire Fiscal Policy Institute, *Headwinds Hit the New Hampshire Economy* (New Hampshire Fiscal Policy Institute, August 28, 2025), nhfpi.org/resource/headwinds-hit-the-new-hampshire-economy/.

108 New Hampshire Fiscal Policy Institute, Issue Brief: *The Fragile Economics*, 4.

109 New Hampshire Fiscal Policy Institute, Issue Brief: *The Fragile Economics*, 7.

110 New Hampshire Fiscal Policy Institute: Issue Brief: *The Fragile Economics*, 6.

111 New Hampshire Fiscal Policy Institute, Issue Brief: *The Fragile Economics*, 7.

112 Madeleine Smith et al., *From a Shorter Winter Season to More Storm Damage: New Hampshire Outdoor Recreation Providers Feel Climate Impacts Far More Than Visitors*, Issue Brief # 181 (University of New Hampshire, Carsey School of Public Policy, 2024), 1–2, carsey.unh.edu.

113 Smith et al., *From a Shorter Winter Season*, 2.

114 Smith et al., *From a Shorter Winter Season*, 3–4.

115 Smith et al., *From a Shorter Winter Season*, 4.

116 Smith et al., *From a Shorter Winter Season*, 5.

117 Smith et al., *From a Shorter Winter Season*, 5.

118 Smith, *From a Shorter Winter Season*, 5. See also *New Hampshire Statewide Comprehensive Outdoor Recreation Plan 2024–2028*, 68–71, nhstateparks.org/NHStateParks

/media/NHStateParks/PDFs/Community-Recreation/NH-SCORP-2024-28-Final-3-5-24-(1).pdf.

119 Phil Sletten, *The New Hampshire Economy and State Revenues*: Presentation to the New Hampshire Senate Ways and Means Committee (New Hampshire Fiscal Policy Institute, April 19, 2023), 6, nhfpi.org/assets/2023/04/NHFPI-The-New-Hampshire-Economy-and-State-Revenues-4.19.23.pdf.

120 Ethan DeWitt, "New Hampshire Housing Prices Hit New Record," *New Hampshire Bulletin*, July 7, 2025, https://newhampshirebulletin.com/2025/07/07/new-hampshire-housing-prices-hit-new-record/.

121 New Hampshire Fiscal Policy Institute, Fact Sheet: *Housing in New Hampshire: Shortage Raises Costs*, January 14, 2025, 1, nhfpi.org/resource/housing-in-new-hampshire-shortage-raises-costs-2.

122 New Hampshire Fiscal Policy Institute, *New Hampshire Policy Points 2023: A Guide to Key Issues Facing Granite Staters* (New Hampshire Fiscal Policy Institute, February 2023), 24, nhfpi.org/assets/2023/02/NewHampshirePolicyPoints2023.pdf.

123 See Part II, Section 83 of the New Hampshire Constitution and Chapter II, Section 68 of the Vermont Constitution.

124 New Hampshire Fiscal Policy Institute, *New Hampshire Policy Points 2023*, 33–34.

125 New Hampshire Fiscal Policy Institute, *New Hampshire Policy Points 2023*, 34.

126 New Hampshire Fiscal Policy Institute, *New Hampshire Policy Points 2023*, 34–35.

127 *Contoocook Valley School District v. State of New Hampshire*, 2025 N.H. 29, 347 A.3d 541 (2025).

Chapter Five

1 Michael Sherman, Gene Sessions, and P. Jeffrey Potash, *Freedom and Unity: A History of Vermont* (Vermont Historical Society, 2004), xiii.

2 Paul Searls, "America and the State That 'Stayed Behind,' An Argument for the National Relevance of Vermont History," *Vermont History*, 71 (2003): 81.

3 Frank M. Bryan, *Yankee Politics in Rural Vermont* (University Press of New England, 1974), viii.

4 Bryan, *Yankee Politics*, 19; David J. Plazek, "The Reflections of a First-Year Political Scientist in Vermont: The Relevance of Identity in Sub-National Entities," *New England Journal of Political Science*, 2, no. 2 (2007): 93.

5 Plazek, "Reflections," 93.

6 William Doyle, *The Vermont Political Tradition: And Those Who Helped Make It* (Northlight Studio Press, 1984), 71.

7 Doyle, *The Vermont Political Tradition*, 72.

8 Sherman et al., *Freedom and Unity*, 129.

9 Sherman et al., *Freedom and Unity*, 129; Doyle, *The Vermont Political Tradition*, 73.

10 Doyle, *The Vermont Political Tradition*, 75–76.

11 Doyle, *The Vermont Political Tradition*, 77.

12 Doyle, *The Vermont Political Tradition*, 80; Sherman et al., *Freedom and Unity*, 146

13 Sherman et al., *Freedom and Unity*, 532–34.

14 Chris Graff, *Dateline Vermont: Covering and Uncovering Newsworthy Stories that Shaped a State—and Influenced a Nation* (Thistle Hill Publications, 2006), 101.

15 Graff, *Dateline Vermont*, 103.

16 Graff, *Dateline Vermont*, 109.
17 Graff, *Dateline Vermont*, 112.
18 Graff, *Dateline Vermont*, 112.
19 Daniel Nasaw, "Vermont Legalises Same-Sex Marriage," *The Guardian*, April 7, 2009, guardian.com. See also marriageequality.org/region_vermont.
20 New Hampshire legalized civil unions in 2008 and same-sex marriage in 2010.
21 Russell Berman, "America's Bluest State Loves Its Republican Governor," *The Atlantic*, May 21, 2021, https://www.theatlantic.com/politics/archive/2021/05/phil-scott-vermont-republican/618944/.
22 Sarah Mearhoff, "Vermont Democrats Pushed Through Major Firearms Legislation This Year. Will It Hold Up in Court?" *VTDigger*, May 19, 2023, vtdigger.org/2023/05/19/Vermont-democrats-pushed-through-major-firearms-legislation-this-year-will-it-hold-up-in-court.
23 597 U.S. 1 (2022).
24 Sarah Mearhoff, "Phil Scott Allows Gun Control Bill to Go into Law Without His Signature," *VTDigger*, June 1, 2023, vtdigger.org/2023/06/01/phil-scott-allows-gun-control-bill-to-go-into-law-without-his-signature. As of the spring of 2026, the constitutionality of the restriction on magazine size and of the waiting period is the subject of litigation before the U.S. Court of Appeals for the Second Circuit. See *Vermont Federation of Sportsmen's Clubs v. Birmingham*, 714 F. Supp. 3d 172 (D. Vt. 2024).
25 Plazek, "Reflections," *New England Journal of Political Science*, 93–94.
26 Frank M. Bryan, *Real Democracy: The New England Town Meeting and How It Works* (University of Chicago Press, 2004), 26.
27 Bryan, *Real Democracy*, 26–27.
28 Bryan, *Real Democracy*, 27.
29 Bryan, *Real Democracy*, 57.
30 Bryan, *Real Democracy*, 78.
31 Bryan, *Real Democracy*, 88.
32 Bryan, *Real Democracy*, 99.
33 Bryan, *Real Democracy*, 288.
34 Susan Clark and Frank Bryan, *All Those in Favor: Rediscovering the Secrets of Town Meeting and Community* (RavenMark, 2005), 14.
35 Sally Pollak, "What Makes Vermont What It Is?" *Burlington Free Press*, July 12, 2014, burlingtonfreepress.com/story/life/2014/07/12/makes-vermont/12542015.
36 Pollack, "What Makes Vermont What It Is?"
37 Almanac of American Politics, "Vermont Expected to Retain Its Blue Tint for the Foreseeable Future," August 8, 2021, vtdigger.org/2021/08/08/almanac-american-politics-vermont/.
38 Lola Duffort, "Child Care Law Inches Vt. Ahead," *Valley News*, June 27, 2023, A1.
39 Duffort, "Child Care Law."
40 Public Assets Institute, *The State of Working Vermont 2023* (Public Assets Institute, 2024), public assets.org/wp-content/uploads/2024/02/SWVT23.pdf.
41 Duffort, "Child Care Law."
42 Duffort, "Child Care Law."
43 Duffort, "Child Care Law."
44 Duffort, "Child Care Law." The pertinent statutory language can be found in Title 33, Section 3512(a)(2) of the *Vermont Statutes Annotated*.

45 Sithembiso Muhlauri and Tammie Ab Hazlett, "Act 76 is Transforming Child Care in Vermont," *Valley News*, May 4, 2024, C1.

46 Emma Malinak, "Payroll Tax to Fund Child Care Subsidies Will Take Effect July 1," *Valley News*, July 1, 2024, A1. Under Act 76, an employer could share responsibility for paying the tax with its employees, for example by paying 0.34 percent itself and requiring the employees to pay 0.10 percent, to be deducted from their regular paychecks. The pertinent statutory language can be found in Title 32, Section 10553(b) of the *Vermont Statutes Annotated*.

47 Emma Malinak, "Vermont's Child Care Providers Have New Hope After Act 76, But Worries Remain," *VTDigger*, July 17, 2024, vtdigger.org/2024/07/17/Vermonts-child-care-providers-have-new-hope-after-act-76-but-worries-remain/.

48 Duffort, "Child Care."

49 Vermont Business Roundtable, *Pulse of Vermont: Quality of Life Study 2010* (Center for Social Science Research 2010), 6, vtroundtable.org/wp-content/uploads/2015/08/Pulse-of-Vermont2010.pdf.

50 Vermont Business Roundtable, *Pulse of Vermont*, 16.

51 Vermont Business Roundtable, *Pulse of Vermont*, 9.

52 Vermont Business Roundtable, *Pulse of Vermont*, 21–23.

53 Vermont Business Roundtable, *Pulse of Vermont*, 32.

54 Vermont Business Roundtable, *Pulse of Vermont*, 32.

55 The Urban Institute, *State Fiscal Briefs: Vermont* (The Urban Institute, April 2023), urban.org/policy-centers/cross-center-initiatives/state-and-local-finance-initiative/projects/state-fiscal-briefs/Vermont.

56 Vermont Legislative Joint Fiscal Office, *2023 Fiscal Facts Booklet* (Vermont Legislative Joint Fiscal Office, March 2023), 12, 34, ljfo.vermont.gov/assets/Publications/2023-Fiscal-Facts-Booklet/541265ebf8/Fiscal-Facts-Booklet-2023_FINAL-v3.pdf.

57 Joint Fiscal Office, *2023 Fiscal Facts Booklet*, 9.

58 Joint Fiscal Office, *2023 Fiscal Facts Booklet*, 13–14.

59 Joint Fiscal Office, *2023 Fiscal Facts Booklet*, 26.

60 Joint Fiscal Office, *2023 Fiscal Facts Booklet*, 28.

61 Joint Fiscal Office, *2023 Fiscal Facts Booklet*, 29.

62 Joint Fiscal Office, *2023 Fiscal Facts Booklet*, 31.

63 Joint Fiscal Office, *2023 Fiscal Facts Booklet*, 30.

64 Joint Fiscal Office, *2023 Fiscal Facts Booklet*, 32.

65 Jack Hoffman, *Covid Showed Us the Value of Public Investment* (Public Assets Institute, January 12, 2023), publicassets.org/blog/covid-showed-us-the-value-of-public-investment/.

66 Jim Douglas, *The Vermont Way: A Republican Governor Leads America's Most Liberal State* (Common Ground Communications, 2014), 208.

67 Joyce Manchester, *Vermont's Population Estimates for 2023* (Vermont Legislative Joint Fiscal Office (2024), 1, ljfo.vermont.gov/assets/Publications/Issue-Briefs/Issue_Brief_VT_Demographics_in_2023.pdf.

68 Manchester, *Vermont's Population Estimates*, 4.

69 Manchester, *Vermont's Population Estimates*, 1.

70 Andrew Van Dam, "The Rise and Fall of the Most European State in the Union," *The Washington Post*, March 2, 2019, washingtonpost.com/us-policy/2019/03/02/rise-fall-most-european-state-union/.

71 Manchester, *Vermont's Population Estimates*, 6.

72 Andrew Van Dam, "States with the Worst Brain Drain-and More," *The Washington Post*, September 9, 2022, washingtonpost.com/business/2022/09/09/films-assigned-college/. The author notes that Montana and Wyoming, despite being rural, do not suffer the significant brain drains that Vermont, New Hampshire, and West Virginia experience, although he offers no explanation for this disparity. Montana loses just 27.2 percent of its college graduates annually, and Wyoming loses 40.4 percent.

73 Amanda Van Vranken, *An Unbalanced Equation* (Vermont Futures Project, December 22, 2022), vtfuturesproject.org/an-unbalanced-equation/.

74 Kevin Chu, *Four Key Population Trends Shaping the Vermont Economy—Part 1: Age Composition* (Vermont Futures Project, August 26, 2022), 1, vtfuturesproject.org/four-key-population-trends-shaping-the-vermont-economy-part-1-age-composition.

75 Chu, *Four Key Population Trends*, 3.

76 Kevin Chu, *Four Key Population Trends—Part 2—Labor Force Participation*, (Vermont Futures Project, September 26, 2022) 3.

77 Kevin Chu, *Four Key Population Trends—Part 3—Age Dependency Ratio* (Vermont Futures Project, November 28, 2022), 1.

78 Chu, *Four Key Population Trends—Part 3*, 2.

79 Chu, *Four Key Population Trends—Part 3*, 3.

80 Public Assets Institute, *Vermont's Workforce is Growing but Not Fast Enough* (Public Assets Institute, December 22, 2023), publicassets.org/research-publications/vermonts-workforce-is-growing-but-not-fast-enough.

81 Public Assets Institute, *Vermont's Workforce is Growing.*

82 Public Assets Institute, *Vermont's Workforce is Growing.*

83 Mikaela LeFrak, Tedra Meyer, and Andrea Laurion, "A Think Tank Says Vermont Should Grow to 802,000 by 2035. Here's Why and How," *Vermont Public*, August 17, 2023, vermontpublic.org.

84 Bill McKibben, "What Vermont and its History Might Teach the Nation about Handling the Corona Virus," *The New Yorker*, July 28, 2020, newyorker.com/news/daily-comment/what-vermont-and-its-history-might-teach-the-nation-about-handling-the-coronavirus.

85 See https://ballotpedia.org/Vermont_State_Legislature.

86 See https://ballotpedia.org/Vermont_State_Legislature.

87 See https://ballotpedia.org/Vermont_State_Legislature.

88 The death of Democrat Dick Mazza later temporarily created a vacancy that reduced that number by one.

89 Sarah Mearhoff, "What's Next for Vermont GOP?" *Valley News*, November 21, 2022, A 1.

90 Paul Petterson, "Vermont Politics in 2023–2024: Political Continuity and Changing Realities," *New England Journal of Political Science* 14, no. 1 (2023): 1.

91 Hoffman, *Covid Showed Us the Value of Public Investment*.

92 Peter Hirschfeld and Bob Kinzel, "Scott Chides 'Arrogant' Legislature After Democrats Flex Supermajority in Veto Session," *Vermont Public*, June 18, 2024, vermontpublic.org/local-news/2024-06-18/scott-chides-arrogant-legislature-after-democrats-flex-supermajority-in-veto-session.

93 Hirschfeld and Kinzel, "Scott Chides 'Arrogant' Legislature."

94 Petterson, "Vermont Politics in 2023–2024," 2.

95 Petterson, "Vermont Politics in 2023–2024," 2.

96 Hirschfeld and Kinzel, "Scott Chides 'Arrogant' Legislature."

97 The law at issue is Vermont's Climate Superfund Act, better known as Act 122. As of February 2026, it is being litigated in *United States v. Vermont*, No. 225-cv-00463 (D. Vt. filed May 1, 2025).

98 Richard Snelling died in August of 1991, during his fifth term as governor. Howard Dean, then the lieutenant governor, completed Snelling's term, then won five terms in his own right, from 1993 until 2003.

99 Douglas, *The Vermont Way*, 105; Jeremy A. Hansen, "Ballot-Level Observations About Vermont's 2014 General Election," *New England Journal of Political Science* 8, no. 2 (2015): 2.

100 See Chapter II, Article 47 of the Vermont Constitution.

101 Graff, *Dateline Vermont*, 193–94.

102 Senator Patrick Leahy, *The Road Taken: A Memoir* (Simon & Schuster, 2022), 59.

103 Bob Kinzel, Mitch Wertlieb, and Karen Anderson, "One Last Look Back at Patrick Leahy's 48 Years in the U.S. Senate, *Vermont Public*, January 3, 2023, vermontpublic.org/local-news/2023-01-03/one-last-look-back-at-patrick-leahys-48-years-in-the-u-s-senate.

104 Kinzel et al., "One Last Look."

105 Kinzel et al., "One Last Look."

106 Philip Baruth, *Senator Leahy: A Life in Scenes* (University Press of New England, 2017), 103, 108–10.

107 Kinzel et al., "One Last Look Back."

108 Kevin McCallum, "Leahy's Departure from the U.S. Senate Could Stanch the Flow of Federal Cash to Vermont," *Seven Days*, December 21, 2022, sevendaysvt.com/news/leahys-departure-from-the-us-senate-could-stanch-the-flow-of-federal-cash-to-vermont-37191398.

109 Maury Thompson, "In Vermont, a Season of Political Change," *Hill Country Observer*, July 2022, hillcountryobserver.com/2022news/July2022vt-politics.htm.

110 Paul Petterson, "Vermont Politics in 2022: A Year of Transition—And Continuities," *New England Journal of Political Science* 13, no. 1 (August 1, 2023): 1–2, digitalcommons.library.umaine.edu/cgi/viewcontent.cgi?article=1012&context=nejps.

111 Petterson, "Vermont Politics in 2022,"3–4. The original language of the Vermont Constitution, despite outlawing slavery, included an exception clause that permitted childhood slavery, slavery by consent, and slavery for nonpayment of debts. The amended language strikes the exception clause, replacing it with a blanket prohibition of slavery and indentured servitude. Auditi Guha, "Vermont Voters Pass Constitutional Amendment Explicitly Prohibiting Slavery," *VTDigger*, November 8, 2022, vtdigger.org/2022/11/08/Vermont-voters-remove-slavery-references-from-the-states-constitution/.

112 Neal Gaswami, "Democrats Lose Supermajority—and a Pair of Committee Chairs—in the Vermont House," *VTDigger*, November 5, 2024, vtdigger.org/2024/11/05/Vermont-gop-knocks-off-two-democratic-house-chairs/.

113 Ethan Weinstein, "Republicans Flip Six Seats in the Vermont Senate, Shattering Democratic Supermajority," *VTDigger*, November 5, 2024, vtdigger.org/2024/11/05/republicans-flip-grand-isle-senate-seat/. See also stateside.com/state-resource/legislative-partisan-splits.

114 Lola Duffort, "Vermont Legislature Passes Landmark Education Reform, Despite Fierce Dissent," *Vermont Public*, June 16, 2025, https://www.vermontpublic.org/local

-news/2025-06-16/vermont-legislature-passes-landmark-education-reform-despite-fierce-dissent.

115 Graff, *Dateline Vermont*, 163–67.

116 Scott Detrow, "8 Key Moments that Helped Define Bernie Sanders' Presidential Runs," *National Public Radio*, April 9, 2020, npr.org/2020/04/09/830728501/8-key-moments-that-helped-define-bernie-sanders-presidential-runs.

Chapter Six

1 Richard Ober, ed., *Shaping the Land We Call New Hampshire: A Land Use History* (The New Hampshire Historical Society and the Society for the Protection of New Hampshire Forests, 1992), 17–18.

2 Ober, *Shaping the Land*, 18–19.

3 R. Stuart Wallace, "New Hampshire's Changing Landscape" (lecture, New Hampshire Historical Society, Concord, NH, April 27, 2023).

4 Ober, *Shaping the Land*, 29.

5 Ober, *Shaping the Land*, 29.

6 Ober, *Shaping the Land*, 31.

7 Ober, *Shaping the Land*, 25.

8 Ober, *Shaping the Land*, 32.

9 Ober, *Shaping the Land*, 34.

10 Ober, *Shaping the Land*, 34.

11 William A. Fischel, "An Economic History of Zoning and a Cure for Its Exclusionary Effects," *Urban Studies*, 41 (February 2004): 321.

12 Fischel, "An Economic History of Zoning," 321.

13 Fischel, "An Economic History of Zoning," 318.

14 Fischel, "An Economic History of Zoning," 318.

15 William A. Fischel, *Zoning Rules! The Economics of Land Use Regulation* (Lincoln Institute of Land Policy, 2015), 29.

16 Vanessa Brown Calder, *Zoning, Land Use Planning, and Housing Affordability*: Policy Analysis No. 823 (The Cato Institute, October 18, 2017): 2, cato.org/policy-analysis/zoning-land-use-planning-housing-affordability.

17 Calder, *Zoning, Land Use Planning, and Housing Affordability*, 2.

18 272 U.S. 365 (1926).

19 272 U.S. at 386.

20 Ober, *Shaping the Land*, 34.

21 Fischel, "An Economic History of Zoning," 330.

22 Fischel, "An Economic History of Zoning," 330.

23 Ober, *Shaping the Land*, 44.

24 Fischel, "An Economic History of Zoning," 330.

25 Fischel, *Zoning Rules*, xi.

26 Clayton Robert Mitchell, *The Local Land Use Process in New Hampshire: Does It Contribute to Sprawl?* (PhD diss., University of New Hampshire, 2008), 28.

27 *Sundeen v. Rogers*, 83 N.H. 253 (1928).

28 Johnny Bassett, "Invisible Walls: The Shackles of Zoning," *New Hampshire Public Radio*, February 21, 2022, nhpr.org/nh-news/2022-02-21/invisible-walls-the-shackles-of-zoning.

29 Bassett, "Invisible Walls."
30 Bassett, "Invisible Walls."
31 Bassett, "Invisible Walls."
32 Bassett, "Invisible Walls."
33 *Britton v. Town of Chester*, 134 N.H. 434, 595 A.2d 492.
34 134 N.H. at 445, 595 A.2d at 498.
35 The workforce housing law is located at N.H. Revised Statutes Annotated (N.H.R.S.A.), Chapter 674, Sections 58–61.
36 Anthony Flint, *The State of Local Zoning: Reforming a Century-Old Approach to Land Use* (Lincoln Institute of Land Policy, 2022), 2, lincolninst.edu/publications/articles/2022-12-state-local-zoning-reform/.
37 Fischel, *Zoning Rules*! 170.
38 Peter Francese and Lorraine Stuart Merrill, *Communities and Consequences II: Rebalancing New Hampshire's Human Ecology* (Peter E. Randall Publisher, 2020), 6.
39 This language is located at N.H. R.S.A., Chapter 674, Section 58, IV (a).
40 Dixi Wu, "Inclusionary and Incentive Zoning in the Six New England States" (Harvard University Joint Center for Housing Studies, November 4, 2021, jchs.harvard.edu/blog/inclusionary-and-incentive-zoning-six-new-england-states.
41 Wu, "Inclusionary and Incentive Zoning."
42 N.H. R.S.A. Chapter 674, Section 21, IV(a).
43 N.H. R.S.A. Chapter 674, Section 58, II.
44 N.H. R.S.A. Chapter 674, Section 58, IV.
45 N.H. R.S.A. Chapter 674, Section 59.
46 N.H. R.S.A. Chapter 674, Section 59.
47 N.H. R.S.A. Chapter 674, Section 59.
48 Haewon Ma, "How Nonprofits are Using Accessory Dwelling Units as an Affordable Housing Strategy," *Housing Perspectives* (Harvard Joint Center for Housing Studies, 2024), 2–3, jchs.harvard.edu/blog/how-nonprofits-are-using-accessory-dwelling-units-affordable-housing-strategy.
49 Ellie Shields and David Uberoff, "Learning from State Efforts to Encourage Accessory Dwelling Units," *Housing Perspectives* (Harvard Joint Center for Housing Studies, 2023), 2, jchs.harvard.edu/blog/learning-state-efforts-encourage-accessory-dwelling-units.
50 Emily Hamilton and Abigail Houseal, *A Taxonomy of State Accessory Dwelling Unit Laws* (Mercatus Center, George Mason University, 2023), 1, mercatus.org.
51 Hamilton and Houseal, *A Taxonomy*, 2.
52 Hamilton and Houseal, *A Taxonomy*, 7.
53 Hamilton and Houseal, *A Taxonomy*, 9.
54 Ethan DeWitt, "Ayotte Signs Slate of Bills to Encourage Housing Construction," *New Hampshire Bulletin*, July 23, 2025, https://newhampshirebulletin.com/2025/07/23/ayotte-signs-slate-of-bills-to-encourage-housing-construction-but-not-all-ideas-advance/.
55 See N.H. R.S.A. Chapter 674: 21, which authorizes the use of innovative land use controls, and Chapter 674:22, which empowers municipalities to control the timing of development.
56 N.H. R.S.A. Chapter 679: (1)-(19).

57 Olivia Richardson, "Pandemic Relief Funds Aiding Thousands of Housing Units in NH, State Officials Say," *Valley News*, November 21, 2024, vnews.com/Pandemic-relief-funds-aiding-thousands-of-housing-units-in-NH-state-officials-say-58078826.

58 New Hampshire Housing, *2023 New Hampshire Statewide Housing Needs Assessment* (New Hampshire Housing, March 2023), 1, nhhfa.org/wp-content/uploads/2023/04/2023/NH-Statewide-Housing-Needs-Assessment.pdf.

59 New Hampshire Housing, *2023 Housing Needs Assessment*, 1.

60 New Hampshire Housing, *2023 Housing Needs Assessment*, 1.

61 New Hampshire Housing, *2023 Housing Needs Assessment*, 1.

62 New Hampshire Housing, *2023 Housing Needs Assessment*, 1.

63 New Hampshire Housing, *2023 Housing Needs Assessment*, 76.

64 New Hampshire Housing, *2023 Housing Needs Assessment*, 83.

65 New Hampshire Housing, *2023 Housing Needs Assessment*, 4.

66 New Hampshire Housing, *2023 Residential Rental Cost Survey Report* (New Hampshire Housing, July 2023), 4, nhhfa.org.

67 New Hampshire Housing, *2023 Housing Needs Assessment*, 151.

68 New Hampshire Housing, *2024–2025 Biennial Housing Plan* (New Hampshire Housing, December 2023), 4.

69 New Hampshire Housing, *2024–2025 Biennial Housing Plan*, 14.

70 Ethan DeWitt, "New Hampshire Housing Prices Hit New Record," *New Hampshire Bulletin*, July 7, 2025, https://newhampshirebulletin.com/2025/07/07/new-hampshire-housing-prices-hit-new-record/.

71 Flint, *The State of Local Zoning*, 2.

72 Flint, *The State of Local Zoning*, 2.

73 Ethan DeWitt, "Housing a Top Issue for NH Voters—and Candidates, Too," *New Hampshire Bulletin*, June 21, 2024, newhampshirebulletin.com/2024/06/21/housing-a-top-issue-for-nh-voters-and-candidates-too/.

74 Fischel, *Zoning Rules!* 48.

75 New Hampshire Housing, *New Hampshire's Workforce Housing Law: A 10-Year Retrospective on the Law's Impact on Local Zoning and Creating Workforce Housing* (New Hampshire Housing, December 2021), 53, nhhfa.org/wp-content/uploads/2021/12/Workforce-Housing-Law-Report-12.2021.pdf.

76 David Brooks, "NH Housing Shortage is Hurting Business' Ability to Attract Workers," *Concord Monitor*, February 19, 2022, concordmonitor.com/housing-business-nh-45142680.

77 Alvina Snegach and Noah Hodgetts, *The State of Local Land Use Regulations in New Hampshire—2024 Update* (NH Department of Business and Economic Affairs, August 2025), 2, www.nheconomy.com.

78 Snegach and Hodgetts, *The State of Local Land Use Regulations*, 2.

79 Snegach and Hodgetts, *The State of Local Land Use Regulations*, 2.

80 Snegach and Hodgetts, *The State of Local Land Use Regulations*, 3.

81 Snegach and Hodgetts, *The State of Local Land Use Regulations*, 4.

82 New Hampshire Housing, *New Hampshire's Workforce Housing Law*, 54.

83 New Hampshire Housing, *New Hampshire's Workforce Housing Law*, 56.

84 Mitchell, *The Local Land Use Process in New Hampshire*, 31.

85 Jason Sorens, *Residential Land Use Regulations in New Hampshire: Causes and Consequences* (Josiah Bartlett Center for Public Policy 2021), 3, vapda.org/uploads/1/3/1/8/131894470/essentials_black_white.pdf.

86 In 2022 thirteen New Hampshire municipalities added definitions for short-term rentals or short-term-rental regulations to their zoning ordinances, increasing to forty-one the number of municipalities that regulate such rentals. See Hodgetts and Snegach, *The State of Local Land Use Regulations*, 3 .

87 New Hampshire Housing, *New Hampshire's Workforce Housing Law*, 54–55.

88 New Hampshire Housing, *2023 Housing Needs Assessment*, 176.

89 272 U.S. 365 (1926).

90 Vermont Land Use Education and Training Center, *Essentials of Local Land Use Planning and Regulation* (Vermont Planning Information Center, 2007), vpic.info/Essentials.html.

91 Vermont Land Use Education and Training Collaborative, *Essentials of Local Land Use Planning and Regulation*.

92 Vermont Land Use Education and Training Collaborative, *Essentials of Local Land Use Planning and Regulation*.

93 Vermont Land Use Education and Training Collaborative, *Essentials of Land Use Planning and Regulation*; Margaret DeWeese-Boyd, "Community Versus Development? Land Use and Development Policy in Vermont as a Tool Toward Community Viability," *Community Development Journal* 41, no. 3 (2006): 335.

94 Vermont Land Use Review Board, "What is Act 250?" act250.vermont.gov/act-250program.

95 DeWeese-Boyd, "Community Versus Development? Land Use and Development Policy in Vermont," 336.

96 Vermont Land Use Review Board, Act 250 Program and History: "What is Act 250?" act250.vermont.gov/act250-program.

97 DeWeese-Boyd, "Community Versus Development?" 336.

98 DeWeese-Boyd, "Community Versus Development?" The named criteria include (1) air and water pollution; (2) the future water supply; (3) the existing water supply; (4) soil erosion; (5) traffic; (6) educational services; (7) municipal or governmental services; (8) scenic and natural beauty, aesthetics, natural areas, and historic sites; and (9) conformance with the state's Capability and Development Plan, which concerns the impact of growth on an array of natural and energy resources.

99 DeWeese-Boyd, "Community Versus Development? 337. A detailed presentation of these criteria is available in Title 10 of the Vermont Statutes Annotated (V.S.A.), Section 6086 (a)-(h).

100 DeWeese-Boyd, "Community Versus Development?" 336–37.

101 DeWeese-Boyd, "Community Versus Development?" 339.

102 DeWeese-Boyd, "Community Versus Development?" 343.

103 DeWeese-Boyd, "Community Versus Development?" 343–44.

104 DeWeese-Boyd, "Community Versus Development?" 338.

105 DeWeese-Boyd, "Community Versus Development?" 347.

106 Vermont Land Use Education & Training Collaborative, *Chapter 117 Overview* (Vermont Land Use Education &Training Collaborative, November 2004), vpic.info/Publications/Reports/Bulletins/Overview.pdf.

107 See vhfa.org/documents/developers/ACT%20200%20Plan.pdf.

108 Jack Kraichman, "Vermont's Act 183: Smart Growth Takes Root in the Green Mountain State," *Vermont Law Review* 32 (2008): 587, citing Title 24 of the Vermont Statutes Annotated, Section 4302(c)(1)B).
109 Kraichman, "Vermont's Act 183," 587.
110 Kraichman, "Vermont's Act 183," 583.
111 Kraichman, "Vermont's Act 183," 583.
112 Kraichman, "Vermont's Act 183," 583.
113 Benjamin Harrold, *Affordable Housing: Barriers and Incentives in Vermont Towns* (Vermont Housing Finance Agency, August 2, 2021), 5, vhfa.org/sites/default/files/publications/Affordable_housing_VT_towns_1.pdf.
114 Harrold, *Affordable Housing*, 6.
115 Harrold, *Affordable Housing*, 14–15.
116 Harrold, *Affordable Housing*, 24.
117 Vermont Housing Finance Agency, *2023 Vermont Housing Investment Fund Annual Report* (Vermont Housing Finance Agency, 2023), 2, vhfa.org/sites/default/files/publications/VHIF-Annual-Report-2023.pdf.
118 Chelsea Edgar and Kevin McCallum, "Obstruction Zone: How Vermont's Land-Use Regulations Impede New Development—and Complicate the State's Housing Crisis," *Seven Days*, December 6, 2022, sevendays.com.
119 Vermont Housing Finance Agency, *2023 Vermont Housing Investment Fund Annual Report*, 16.
120 Lola Duffort, "House Passes 'Home' Bill, Which Would End Single-Family Zoning and Tweak Act 250," *VTDigger*, May 8, 2023, vtdigger.org/2023/05/08/house-passes-home-bill-which-would-end-single-family-zoning-and-tweak-act-250/.
121 This provision of the Act is located at Title 24 of the Vermont Statutes Annotated, Section 4412(12).
122 This provision is located at Title 24 of the Vermont Statutes Annotated, Section 4412(1)(D).
123 Lola Duffort, "New Law Goes After Crunch in Housing," *Valley News*, June 7, 2023, A.1.
124 This provision is located at Title 24 of the Vermont Statutes Annotated, Section 4414(4).
125 This provision is located at Title 24 of the Vermont Statutes Annotated, Section 4412(1)(E).
126 This provision is located at Title 24 of the Vermont Statutes Annotated, Section 4412(13).
127 Peter Hirschfeld, "Vermont Housing Bill Becomes Law, Easing Rules for Some New Construction Amid Home Shortage," *Vermont Public*, June 6, 2023, vermontpublic.org/local-news/2023-06-06/Vermont-housing-bill-becomes-law-easing-rules-for-some-new-construction-amid-home-shortage.
128 This provision is located at Title 10 of the Vermont Statutes Annotated, Section 6001(3)(A) and (3)(D).
129 This provision is located at Title 24 of the Vermont Statutes Annotated, Section 4465(b)(4).
130 Carly Berlin, "With Veto Override, Act 250 Reform Bill Becomes Law," *VTDigger*, January 17, 2024, https://vtdigger.org/2024/06/17/with-veto-override-act-250-reform-bill-becomes-law/.

131 Vermont Natural Resources Council, *H.687 Summary: As Passed by the Vermont Legislature*, June 5, 2024 (Vermont Natural Resources Council June 2024), vnrc.org/wp-content/uploads/2024/06/DRAFT-H.687-Overview-As-Passed-By-the-Legislature-6-14-24.pdf.

132 Vermont Natural Resources Council, *H. 687 Summary*.

133 Vermont Natural Resources Council, *H. 687 Summary*.

134 Vermont Natural Resources Council, *H. 687 Summary*.

135 Vermont Natural Resources Council, *H. 687 Summary*.

136 Vermont Housing Finance Agency, *Vermont Housing Needs Assessment: 2025–2029* (Vermont Housing Finance Agency, 2024), 5, vhfa.org/sites/default/files/publications/VT-HNA-2025.pdf.

137 Greta Solsaa, "Rutland Ramps Up Incentives, Cuts Red Tape, in Push for 1,000 New Housing Units by 2028," *VTDigger*, November 18, 2024, vtdigger.org/2024/11/18/rutland-ramps-up-incentives-cuts-red-tape-in-push-for-1000-new-housing-units-by-2028/.

138 Carly Berlin, "Vermont's Rate of Homelessness Now Ranks 4th in Nation," December 31, 2024, vtdigger.org/2024/12/31/vermonts-rate-of-homelessness-now-ranks-4th-in-the-nation/. See also US Department of Housing and Urban Development, Office of Community Planning and Development, *The 2024 Annual Homelessness Assessment Report to Congress*, December 2024, 71–79, huduser.gov/portal/sites/default/files/pdf/2024-AHAR-Part-1.pdf.

139 Vermont Housing Finance Agency, *Vermont Housing Needs Assessment: 2025–2029*, 6.

140 Vermont Housing Finance Agency, *Vermont Housing Needs Assessment: 2025–2029*, 6.

141 Vermont Housing Finance Agency, *Vermont Housing Needs Assessment: 2025–2029*, 10.

142 Vermont Housing Finance Agency, *Vermont Housing Needs Assessment: 2025–2029*, 10.

143 Vermont Housing Finance Agency, *Vermont Housing Needs Assessment: 2025–2029*, 11.

144 Vermont Housing Finance Agency, *Vermont Housing Needs Assessment: 2025–2029*, 12.

145 Carly Berlin, "Vermont Needs at Least 24,000 More Homes in the Next Five Years, Report Says," *Vermont Public*, September 16, 2024, vermontpublic.org/local-news/2024-09-16/Vermont-needs-at-least-24000-more-homes-in-next-five-years-housing-needs-report.

146 Carly Berlin, "Short-Term Rentals Are on the Rise in Vermont. So are Debates Over How to Regulate Them," *VTDigger*, November 15, 2023, vtdigger.org/2023/11/15/short-term-rentals-are-on-the-rise-in-vermont-so-are-debates-over-how-to-regulate-them/.

147 Carly Berlin, "Short-Term Rentals Are on the Rise in Vermont."

148 Carly Berlin, "Vermont Loosened Act 250 Rules for Housing. Here's Where Developers are Responding," *VTDigger*, December 11, 2024, vtdigger.org/2024/12/11/Vermont-loosened-act-250-rules-for-housing-heres-where-developers-are-responding/.

149 Emma Roth-Wells, "Revolving Loan Fund Supports New Housing in Two Upper Valley Towns," *Valley News*, December 4, 2024, vnews.com/windsor-affordable-housing-58102495.

150 Anne Wallace Allen, "Woodstock's Worker Housing Program Finds Many Takers," *Seven Days*, October 9, 2024, sevendaysvt.com/news/woodstocks-worker-housing-program-finds-many-takers-42022175.
151 Allen, "Woodstock's Worker Housing Program."
152 Berlin, "Vermont Needs At Least 24,000 More Homes."
153 Carly Berlin, "Gov. Phil Scott Signs Housing Package into Law, Creating New Infrastructure Program," *VTDigger*, June 12, 2025, https://vtdigger.org/2025/06/12/gov-phil-scott-signs-housing-package-into-law-creating-new-infrastructure-program/?utm_medium=email&utm_campain.

Chapter Seven

1 David Solomon, "Could ConVal Case Solve the State's Malfunctioning School-Funding System?" *New Hampshire Business Review*, May 10, 2023, nhbr.com/could-conval-case-solve-the-states-malfunctioning-school-funding-system/.
2 John Augenblick, *A Comprehensive School Finance Plan for New Hampshire's Public Schools* (Augenblick, Van de Water, and Myers, 1984), 1, gencourt.state.nh.us/statstudcomm/committees/1506/documents/1984%20Augenblick%20Report.pdf.
3 Augenblick, *A Comprehensive School Finance Plan*, 13.
4 Augenblick, *A Comprehensive School Finance Plan*, 18.
5 Augenblick, *A Comprehensive School Finance Plan*, 9.
6 Solomon, "Could ConVal Case Solve."
7 National Education Association, *Rankings of the States 2024 and Estimates of School Statistics: 2025 Rankings and Estimates Report* (National Education Association, 2025), 24, RankingsEstimates.nea.org.
8 Ethan DeWitt, "New Hampshire Public School State Spending Levels Lowest in U.S.," *New Hampshire Bulletin*, April 29, 2025, newhampshirebulletin.com/2025/04/29/report-new-hampshires-public-school-state-spending-levels-lowest-in-u-s/.
9 Drew Atchison, Jessie Levin, Bruce Baker, and Tammy Kolbe, *Equity and Adequacy of New Hampshire School Funding: Key Findings* (American Institutes for Research, 2020), 8–9, carsey.unh.edu/sites/default/files/media/2020/08/20-12540_presentation_of_findings_ed_fmt080520_v2.pdf.
10 138 N.H. at 184 (1993).
11 N.H. Const., Part II, Art. 83. (1784).
12 *Claremont School District et al. v. Governor et al.*, 138 N.H. at 188.
13 *Claremont I*, 138 N.H. at 189.
14 *Claremont I*, 138 N.H. at 192.
15 *Claremont I*, 138 N.H. at 192.
16 *Claremont School District et al. v. Governor et al.*, 142 N.H. 462 (1997).
17 *Claremont II*, 142 N.H. at 465.
18 *Claremont II*, 142 N.H. at 466.
19 N.H. Const., Part II, Art. 5 (1784) empowers legislators to "impose and levy proportional and reasonable assessments, rates, and taxes" upon "inhabitants" and "residents" of New Hampshire.
20 *Claremont School District et al.*, 142 N.H. at 469.
21 *Claremont II*, 142 N.H. at 469.
22 *Claremont II*, 142 N.H. at 470.
23 *Claremont II*, 142 N.H. at 470.

24 *Claremont II*, 142 N.H. at 471.
25 Scott Calvert, "Shaheen Introduces School Plan," *Valley News*, January 16, 1998, A1.
26 Calvert, "Shaheen Introduces School Plan."
27 Editorial, "Shaheen's Plan," *Valley News*, January 17, 1998, A1.
28 New England Public Policy Center, *Discussion Paper 06-2: New Hampshire's Quest for a Constitutionally Adequate Education* (Federal Reserve Bank of Boston, 2007), 4–5. See also *Opinion of the Justices*, 142 N.H. 892 (1998).
29 *Opinion of the Justices*, 142 N.H. at 899–900.
30 *Opinion of the Justices*, 900.
31 This bill was known as the Hager-Below Bill, named for Representative Elizabeth Hager and Senator Clifton Below. See Andru Volinsky, *The Last Bake Sale: The Fight for Fair School Funding* (Peter E. Randall Publisher, 2025), 145–47.
32 New England Public Policy Center, *Discussion Paper 06-2*, 5.
33 New England Public Policy Center, *Discussion Paper 06-2*, 5–6.
34 New England Public Policy Center, *Discussion Paper 06-2*, 4.
35 New England Public Policy Center, *Discussion Paper 06-2*, 7.
36 New England Public Policy Center, *Discussion Paper 06-2*, 10.
37 Solomon, "Could ConVal Case Solve."
38 154 N.H. 153.
39 154 N.H. 162.
40 154 N.H. 163.
41 Joint Legislative Oversight Committee on Costing an Adequate Education, *Final Report and Findings of the Joint Legislative Oversight Committee* (Joint Legislative Oversight Committee, 2008), 3, carsey.unh.edu/school-funding/resources-meetings/resources-analyses.
42 Joint Legislative Oversight Committee, *Final Report*, 24. The adequate education figure, which is currently $4,100 per pupil, appears in N.H.R.S.A. 198:40-a.
43 Committee to Study Education Funding and the Cost of an Opportunity for an Adequate Education, *Final Report* (2018), 3, carsey.unh.edu/school-funding/resources-meetings/resources-analyses.
44 Committee to Study Education Funding, *Final Report*, 5.
45 Committee to Study Education Funding, *Final Report*, 6–8.
46 Committee to Study Education Funding, *Final Report*, 11.
47 Commission to Study School Funding, *Our Schools, Our Kids: Achieving Greater Equity for New Hampshire Students and Taxpayers* (Commission to Study School Funding, 2020), 6, carsey.unh.edu/sites/default/files/media/2020/12/final_report_forcommission_v5_12012020.pdf.
48 Atchison et al., *Equity and Adequacy*, 3–4.
49 Atchison et al., *Equity and Adequacy*, 9.
50 Atchison et al., *Equity and Adequacy*, 38–39.
51 Commission to Study School Funding, *Our Schools, Our Kids*, 77.
52 New Hampshire Fiscal Policy Institute, *Issue Brief: Advancing Equity Through Changes to State Public Education Aid* (New Hampshire Fiscal Policy Institute, 2022), 10, nhfpi.org/assets/2022/06/Advancing-Equity-Through-Changes-to-State-Public-Education-Aid.pdf.
53 New Hampshire Fiscal Policy Institute, *Issue Brief: Advancing Equity*.
54 New Hampshire Fiscal Policy Institute, *Issue Brief: Advancing Equity*, 9.

55 Education Law Center, *Making the Grade: How Fair is Education Funding in Your State?* (Newark, NJ: Education Law Center 2024), 26, edlawcenter.org/research/making-the-grade-2024/.
56 Education Law Center, *Making the Grade.*
57 *Contoocook Valley School District et al. v. The State of New Hampshire et al.*, 174 N.H. 154 (2021).
58 174 N.H. at 156.
59 174 N.H. at 156–57.
60 *Contoocook Valley School District et al. v. The State of New Hampshire et al. Order on the Merits*, Case No. 213-2019-CV-00069 (Rockingham County Superior Court, November 20, 2023), 2, fairfundingnh.org/wp-content/uploads/2023/11/ConVal-Decision-2023.pdf.
61 *Order on the Merits*, 1.
62 *Order on the Merits*, 2, citing *Londonderry School District v. State*, 154 N.H. 153, 155–56 (2006).
63 *Order on the Merits*, 6.
64 *Order on the Merits*, 7.
65 *Order on the Merits*, 52.
66 *Order on the Merits*, 1.
67 *Order on the Merits*, 54.
68 *Order on the Merits*, 54.
69 New Hampshire Department of Education, *Cost Per Pupil By District, 2023–2024* (New Hampshire Department of Education, January 2025), education.nh.gov.
70 *Contoocook Valley School District v. State of New Hampshire*, 347 A.3d 541, 2025 N.H. 29, 2025 WL 1802543, *1, *19.
71 *Rand v. New Hampshire, Order on Cross-Motions for Partial Summary Judgment*, Rockingham County Superior Court, November 20, 2023, 2, fairfundingnh.org/wp-content/uploads/2023/11/Rand-SWEPT-Decision.pdf.
72 *Order on Cross-Motions*, 15–16.
73 *Order on Cross-Motions*, 21.
74 *Rand v. State of New Hampshire*, 343 A.3d 117, 2025 N.H. 27, 2025 WL 1634480, *4.
75 H.B. 550, 2025 Gen. Sess. (N.H. 2025).
76 New Hampshire School Funding Fairness Project, *NHSFFP Testifies in Support of H.B. 550, Increasing Base Adequacy Aid to $7,356* (New Hampshire School Funding Fairness Project, January 2025), https://fairfundingnh.org/testimony-hb550/.
77 H.C.R. 11, 2025 Gen. Sess. (N.H. 2025).
78 Peter Greene, "In New Hampshire, An Attempt to Overturn a Landmark School Funding Decision," *Forbes*, September 10, 2024, https://www.forbes.com/sites/petergreene/2024/09/10/in-new-hampshire-an-attempt-to-overturn-a-landmark-school-funding-decision/.
79 Solomon, "Could ConVal Case Solve."
80 Solomon, "Could ConVal Case Solve."
81 Ethan DeWitt, "With Income Gap Gone, New Hampshire Families Rush to Apply for School Vouchers," *New Hampshire Bulletin*, July 7, 2025, newhampshirebulletin.com.
82 The Vermont Children's Forum and the Public Assets Institute, *A Citizen's Guide to School Funding: Vermont's Act 68* (Public Assets Institute, February 2006), 7, publicassets.org/Act68_2006.pdf.

83 Allen Gilbert, *Equal is Equal, Fair is Fair: Vermont's Quest for Equity in Education Funding, Same-Sex Marriage, and Health Care* (Onion River Press, 2020), 23–24.

84 William J. Mathis, "Vermont" in National Center for Education Statistics, *Public School Finance Programs of the United States and Canada: 1998–99*, (National Center for Education Statistics, March, 2001), 1, nces.ed.gov/edfin/pdf/StFinance/Vermont.pdf.

85 Mathis, "Vermont," 1.

86 The Vermont Children's Forum and the Public Assets Institute, *A Citizen's Guide to School Funding*, 7.

87 New England Public Policy Center, *School Finance in Vermont: Balancing Equal Education and Fair Tax Burdens* (Federal Reserve Bank of Boston, 2007), 3, bostonfed.org.

88 166 Vt. 246 (1997).

89 166 Vt. at 249.

90 166 Vt. at 251.

91 VT Const. Ch. II, § 68 (1786).

92 *Brigham*, 166 Vt. at 254.

93 166 Vt. at 256.

94 VT Const., Ch. I, § 7 (1786).

95 *Brigham*, 166 Vt. at 265.

96 166 Vt. at 268.

97 166 Vt. at 249.

98 Tammy Kolbe, Drew Atchison, Caitlin Kearns, and Jessie Levin, "State Finance Reform Vignettes: Vermont," (American Institutes, 2020), 1, carsey.unh.edu.

99 Kolbe et al., *State Reform Vignettes: Vermont*, 2.

100 Kolbe et al., *State Reform Vignettes: Vermont*, 2.

101 Lawrence D. Picus and Associates, *Final Report: An Evaluation of Vermont's Education Finance System* (Vermont Legislative Joint Fiscal Office, 2012), 12, ljfo.vermont.gov/assets/docs/Education-RFP-Page/518fd42be2/Picus-and-Assoc-VT-Finance-Study-1-18-2012.pdf.

102 Picus, *An Evaluation of Vermont's Education Finance System*, 11.

103 New England Public Policy Center, *School Finance in Vermont*, 5.

104 New England Public Policy Center, *School Finance in Vermont*, 5.

105 Peter Teachout, "No Simple Disposition: The *Brigham* Case and the Future of Local Control Over School Spending in Vermont." *Vermont Law Review* 22 (1997): 24.

106 Teachout, "No Simple Disposition," 23–24.

107 Public Assets Institute, *20 Years Ago, Act 60 Fundamentally Changed the Way Vermont Pays for Public Education* (Public Assets Institute, 2018), legislature.vermont.gov.

108 Mathis, "Vermont," 1–3.

109 Reason Foundation, Commentary: *Vermont's School Funding Model Promotes Equity Across School Districts* (June 24, 2020), reason.org/commentary/vermonts-school-funding-model-promotes-equity-across-school-districts/.

110 Mathis, "Vermont," 2.

111 Reason Foundation, *Commentary: Vermont's School Funding Model Promotes Equity Across School Districts* (The Reason Foundation, June 24, 2020), reason.org/commentary/vermonts-school-funding-model-promotes-equity-across-school-districts/.

112 The Reason Foundation, *Commentary: Vermont's School Funding Model.*
113 The Reason Foundation, *Commentary: Vermont's School Funding Model.*
114 New England Public Policy Center, *School Finance in Vermont*, 9.
115 New England Public Policy Center, *School Finance in Vermont*, 10. In recent years, though, the legislature has suspended the surtax, or "excess spending adjustment," initially because of the coronavirus pandemic (2021) and later because of changes in pupil weights made by Act 127 (2022). The excess spending adjustment remains suspended through FY 2029.
116 Reason Foundation, *Commentary.*
117 New England Public Policy Center, *School Finance in Vermont*, 9.
118 Reason Foundation, *Commentary.*
119 Vermont Legislative Joint Fiscal Office, *2023 Report on Vermont's Education Financing* (Vermont Legislative Joint Fiscal Office, February 17, 2023), 21, 27.
120 Vermont Legislative Joint Fiscal Office, *2023 Report on Vermont's Education Financing*, 21, 27.
121 New England Public Policy Center, *School Finance in Vermont*, 10.
122 Lola Duffort, "Vermont Supreme Court Upholds Act 46 Mandated District Mergers," *VTDigger*, July 10, 2020, https://vtdigger.org/2020/07/10/vermont-supreme-court-upholds-act-46-mandated-district-mergers/.
123 Vermont Legislative Joint Fiscal Office, *2023 Report on Vermont's Education Financing*, 21, 27.
124 Public Assets Institute, *There's More to School Tax Increases Than Spending* (Public Assets Institute, 2024), publicassets.org/wp-content/uploads/2024/09/IB2402.pdf.
125 Erin Petenko, "How Vermont's Education Funding Landscape Has Changed," *VTDigger*, February 22, 2024, https://vtdigger.org/2024/02/22/how-vermonts-education-funding-landscape-has-changed/.
126 Vermont Legislative Joint Fiscal Office, *Introduction to Vermont's Education Finance System* (Vermont Legislative Joint Fiscal Office, 2019), 5, ljfo.vermont_s_Education_Finance_System_-_January.pdf; Vermont Agency of Education, *Vermont's Education Funding System: Explained and Compared to Other States* (Vermont Agency of Education, 2024), 4, education.vermont.gov/sites/aoe/files/documents/edu-vermont-education-funding-system-explained-2024.pdf. The town meeting may follow the traditional format in which votes are taken from the floor during the meeting, or it may consist of an informational meeting one day followed by a vote the next day conducted by Australian Ballot at a designated polling place, much like state and federal elections.
127 Vermont Agency of Education, *Vermont's Education Funding System: Explained and Compared*, 5.
128 Vermont Legislative Joint Fiscal Office, *Introduction to Vermont's Education Finance System*, 5, ljfo.vermont.gov/assets/uploads/954aca7798/Introduction_to_Vermont_s_Education_Finance_System-_January.pdf.
129 Vermont Legislative Joint Fiscal Office, *Introduction to Vermont's Education Finance System*, 5.
130 Vermont Agency of Education, *Vermont's Education Funding System: Explained and Compared*, 5.
131 Vermont Agency of Education, *Vermont's Education Funding System: Explained and Compared*, 5.

132 Public Assets Institute, *Vermont's Tools for Education Funding Equity: Weighting and Categorical Aid* (Public Assets Institute, 2021), 2, publicassets.org/wp-content/uploads/2021/11/Weighting-Explainer.pdf.

133 Public Assets Institute, *Vermont's Tools for Education Funding Equity*, 2.

134 Public Assets Institute, *Vermont's Tools for Education Funding Equity*, 4.

135 Public Assets Institute, *Vermont's Tools for Education Funding Equity*, 4.

136 Vermont Legislative Joint Fiscal Office, *Education Finance in Vermont* (Vermont Legislative Joint Fiscal Office, 2023), 19, https://ljfo.vermont.gov/subjects/education. I am indebted to Jake Feldman of the Vermont Department of Taxes for the updated dollar figures and the explanation of the homestead property tax credit included in this paragraph.

137 For a more complete discussion of the homestead property tax credit, see Vermont Department of Taxes, *Report from Act 183 of 2024: Property Tax Credit Asset Declaration* (Vermont Department of Taxes, 2024), 10–11, legislature.vermont.gov.

138 Vermont Department of Taxes, *Education Tax Rate Calculations: Frequently Asked Questions* (Vermont Department of Taxes), www.tax.vermont.gov/property/education-property-tax-rates/faqs.

139 For a discussion of this calculation, see Public Assets Institute, *The New and 'Improved' CLA* (Public Assets Institute, 2024), https://publicassets.org/research-publications/the-new-and-improved-cla.

140 Vermont Agency of Education, *Vermont's Education Funding System: Explained and Compared*, 11.

141 Vermont Agency of Education, *Vermont's Education Funding System: Explained and Compared*, 15.

142 Public Assets Institute, *A Fairer, Simpler Way to Fund Education* (Public Assets Institute, 2018), public assets.org/research-publications/a-fairer-simpler-way-to-fund-education.

143 Vermont Legislative Joint Fiscal Office, *Report of the Task Force on Pupil Weighting, Prepared in Accordance with Act 59 of the 2021 Legislative Session* (Vermont Legislative Joint Fiscal Office, 2021), 32, lijfo.vermont.gov.

144 Vermont Legislative Joint Fiscal Office, *2023 Report on Vermont's Education Financing*, 20.

145 Erin Petenko, "How Vermont's Education Funding Landscape Has Changed," *VTDigger*, February 22, 2024, https://vtdigger.org/2024/02/22/how-vermonts-education-funding-landscape-has-changed/.

146 Petenko, "How Vermont's Education Funding Landscape Has Changed."

147 Petenko, "How Vermont's Education Funding Landscape Has Changed."

148 Public Assets Institute, *Taking a Beat on Education Funding Reform* (Public Assets Institute, 2024), https://publicassets.org/research-publications/taking-a-beat-on-education-funding-reform.

149 Vermont Agency of Education, *Governor Scott's Education Transformation Proposal: A Plan to Build Stronger Schools, Stronger Students, and Vibrant Communities* (Vermont Agency of Education, 2025), 2, education.vermont.gov/sites/aoe/files/documents/edu-sbe-education-transformation-policy-brief-unabridged.pdf.

150 Alison Novak, "Education Proposal is Latest Attempt to Address Longstanding Challenges," *Seven Days*, February 19, 2025, sevendaysvt.com/news/education-proposal-is-latest-attempt-to-address-long-standing-challenges-42911153/.

151 Vermont Agency of Education, *Stronger Schools, Stronger Students: Governor Scott's Plan to Support Vibrant Communities* (Vermont Agency of Education, 2025), 33–37, ljfo.vermont.gov.
152 Vermont Agency of Education, *Governor Scott's Transformation Proposal: Funding Formula Explained* (Vermont Agency of Education, 2025), 1, ljfo.vermont.gov.
153 Vermont Agency of Education, *Governor Scott's Transformation Proposal*, 1.
154 Vermont Agency of Education, *Governor Scott's Transformation Proposal*, 18.
155 Vermont Agency of Education, *Governor Scott's Transformation Proposal*, 1.
156 Vermont Agency of Education, *Stronger Schools, Stronger Students*, 37.
157 Vermont Agency of Education, *Governor Scott's Education Transformation Proposal*, 13–14.
158 Vermont Agency of Education, *Stronger Schools, Stronger Students*, 40.
159 Vermont Agency of Education, *Governor Scott's Transformation Proposal*, 7.
160 The receiving school may be located inside or outside of Vermont. When students are "tuitioned" at public schools, the sending municipality pays the receiving school district an amount equal to the receiving district's average per-pupil cost. When students are "tuitioned" at private schools for grades K–6, the tuition is usually the lesser of (1) the average announced tuition for Vermont public schools, (2) the average per-pupil tuition the sending district pays for its other students, or (3) the private school's tuition. For grades 7–12, the tuition amount typically equals the lesser of the average announced tuition for Vermont public schools collectively or the private school's tuition. See edchoice.org/school-choice/state/Vermont/.
161 Ethan Weinstein, "Governor Phil Scott's Education Plan Would Create an Optional School Choice Lottery in Every District," *VTDigger*, February 6, 2025, vtdigger.org/2025/02/06/gov-scotts-education-plan-would-create-an-optional-school-choice-lottery-in-every-district/. See also H. 454, 2025–26 Gen. Sess. (VT 2025), §§ 17–19.
162 Lola Duffort, "Vermont Legislature Passes Landmark Education Reform, Despite Fierce Dissent," *Vermont Public*, June 16, 2025, https://www.vermontpublic.org/local-news/2025-06-16/vermont-legislature-passes-landmark-education-reform-despite-fierce-dissent. See also Public Assets Institute, *The Latest: Education Funding Reform*, (Public Assets Institute, August 29, 2025), publicassets.org/research-publications/the-latest-ed-funding-reform.
163 See legislature.vermont.gov/Documents/2026/Docs/ACTS/ACT073/ACT073%20Act%20Summary.pdf.
164 Volinsky, *The Last Bake Sale*, 188; National Education Association, *Ranking of The States 2024 and Estimates of School Statistics 2025* (National Education Association, 2025), 24, RankingsEstimates@nea.org.

Chapter Eight

1 James J. Kiepper, *Styles Bridges: Yankee Senator* (Phoenix Publishing, 2001), 14.
2 Kiepper, *Styles Bridges*, 15, 18–22.
3 Kiepper, *Styles Bridges*, 24–25.
4 Kiepper, *Styles Bridges*, 26.
5 Kiepper, *Styles Bridges*, 29–33.
6 Kiepper, *Styles Bridges*, 38–41.
7 Kiepper, *Styles Bridges*, 37.

8 Kiepper, *Styles Bridges*, 46–47, 50.
9 Kiepper, *Styles Bridges*, 56–64.
10 Kiepper, *Styles Bridges*, 225.
11 Kiepper, *Styles Bridges*, 110.
12 Kiepper, *Styles Bridges*, 79.
13 Kiepper, *Styles Bridges*, 135–36.
14 Kiepper, *Styles Bridges*, 139.
15 Kiepper, *Styles Bridges*, 155.
16 Kiepper, *Styles Bridges*, 204.
17 Kiepper, *Styles Bridges*, 183.
18 Kiepper, *Styles Bridges*, 97, 101.
19 Kiepper, *Styles Bridges*, 89.
20 Kiepper, *Styles Bridges*, 231–32.
21 Michael Sherman, ed., *The Political Legacy of George D. Aiken, Wise Old Owl of the U.S. Senate* (Vermont Historical Society, 1995), 146; Stephen C. Terry, *Say We Won and Get Out: George D. Aiken and the Vietnam War* (White River Press, 2020), 146.
22 George Aiken, Oral History Interviews with Charles T. Morrissey and D. Gregory Sanford, 1981 (Folklore and Oral History Archives, Bailey/Howe Library, University of Vermont): 22.
23 Terry, *Say We Won and Get Out*, 147.
24 Terry, *Say We Won and Get Out*, 151.
25 Aiken, Oral History Interviews, 40–41; Terry, *Say We Won and Get Out*, 152.
26 Aiken, Oral History Interviews, 44.
27 Sherman, ed., *The Political Legacy of George D. Aiken*, 147.
28 Terry, *Say We Won and Get Out*, 155.
29 Sherman, ed. *The Political Legacy of George D. Aiken*, 148; Terry, *Say We Won and Get Out*, 157.
30 Aiken, Oral History Interviews, 48.
31 Terry, *Say We Won and Get Out*, 157–58.
32 Terry, *Say We Won and Get Out*, 161.
33 Samuel B. Hand and Stephen C. Terry, eds., *The Essential Aiken: A Life in Public Service* (Center for Research on Vermont, 2004), 23.
34 Terry, *Say We Won and Get Out*, 160.
35 Terry, *Say We Won and Get Out*, 164.
36 Terry, *Say We Won and Get Out*, 170.
37 D. Gregory Sanford, "You Can't Get There from Here: The Presidential Boomlet for Governor George D. Aiken, 1937–1939," *Vermont History*, 49, no. 4 (1987): 201.
38 Sherman, ed., *The Political Legacy of George D. Aiken*, 150.
39 Terry, *Say We Won and Get Out*, 179.
40 Aiken, Oral History Interviews, 83.
41 Hand and Terry, *The Essential Aiken*, 43.
42 Hand and Terry, *The Essential Aiken*, 24.
43 Terry, *Say We Won and Get Out*, 35–36.
44 Terry, *Say We Won and Get Out*, 21.
45 Hand and Terry, *The Essential Aiken*, 44–45.
46 George D. Aiken, *Aiken: Senate Diary, January 1972–January 1975* (The Stephen Greene Press, 1976), 350.

47 Aiken, *Senate Diary*, 352; Terry, *Say We Won and Get Out*, 175.
48 Aiken, *Senate Diary*, 353.
49 Aiken, *Senate Diary*, 353; Terry, *Say We Won and Get Out*, 176.
50 Sherman, ed., *The Political Legacy of George D. Aiken*, 110.
51 Terry, *Say We Won and Get Out*, 27.
52 Sherman, ed., *The Political Legacy of George D. Aiken*, 115.
53 Aiken, Oral History Interviews, 181–82.
54 Kenneth Johnson and Kristine Bundschuh, *Why People Move to and Stay in New Hampshire* (University of New Hampshire, Carsey School of Public Policy, (2020), 3.
55 Johnson and Bundschuh, *Why People Move to and Stay in New Hampshire*, 3.
56 See vnrc.org/wp-content/uploads/2024/06/DRAFT-H.687-Overview-As-Passed-By-The-Legislature-6-14-24.pdf.
57 Ralph Nading Hill, *Yankee Kingdom: Vermont and New Hampshire* (Countryman Press, 1984), 253.
58 Chuck Wooster, "Vermont—New Hampshire: The Hydropower Difference," *Northern Woodlands Magazine*, April 14, 2002, https://northernwoodlands.org/outside_story/article/vermont-new-hampshire-the-hydropower-difference.
59 Nancy Coffey Heffernan and Ann Page Stecker, *New Hampshire: Crosscurrents in its Development*, 3rd ed., (University Press of New England, 2004), 191–93.
60 Charles T. Morrissey, *Vermont: A History* (W. W. Norton & Company, 1981), 166–67.
61 Michael Sherman, Gene Sessions, and P. Jeffrey Potash, *Freedom and Unity: A History of Vermont* (Vermont Historical Society, 2004), 448.
62 Jason Kaufman and Matthew E. Kaliner, "The Re-Accomplishment of Place in Twentieth Century Vermont and New Hampshire: History Repeats Itself, Until It Doesn't," *Theory and Society* 40, no. 2 (2011): 121–24.
63 Dona Brown, "Vermont as a Way of Life," *Vermont History* 85 (2017): 43.

Afterword

1 Jeremy Margolis, "Governor Signs Law That Responds to Court Ruling on School Funding Without Increasing Aid," *Concord Monitor*, March 27, 2026, https://www.concordmonitor.com/2026/03/27/governor-signs-law-that-responds-to-court-ruling-on-school-funding-without-increasing aid; Annmarie Timmins, "Gov. Ayotte signs bill limiting state's public education obligations," *New Hampshire Public Radio*, March 26, 2026, https://nhpr.org/nh-news/2026-03-26/school-funding-public-education-supreme-court-lawsuit-students-taxes.
2 Ethan Weinstein, "Vermont Legislature Passes Landmark Education Reform Without Forcing Districts to Merge," *VT Digger*, May 29, 2026, https://vtdigger.org/2026/05/29/vermont-passes-landmark-education-reform-without-forcing-districts-to-merge/
3 Carly Berlin, "Partial Repeal of Vermont's Land-Use Law 181 Heads to Gov. Phil Scott' Desk," *VT Digger*, May 27, 2026, https://vtdigger.org/2026/05/27/partial-repeal-of-vermonts-land-use-law-act-181-heads-to-gov-phil-scotts-desk/.

INDEX

BRIAN L. PORTO is a professor emeritus at Vermont Law and Graduate School. He holds a JD from Indiana University Bloomington and a PhD in political science from Miami University (Ohio). He has worked as an attorney in state government and private practice, and has taught political science at Macalester College (MN) and Norwich University (VT). His five previous books cover topics ranging from the American legal system to the governance of college sports to the use of classical rhetoric in US Supreme Court opinions. When not writing, he walks in the woods of New Hampshire and Vermont as much as possible with his wife, Sherrie Greeley, with whom he lives in Windsor, VT.